TRUTH-PROOF

The Truth That Leaves No Proof

by

Paul Sinclair

Best wishes
Paul Sinclair

Truth-Proof : The Truth That Leaves No Proof
by Paul Sinclair

Paperback Edition
Published in Great Britain
by PBC Publishing 2016

© Copyright Paul Sinclair June 2016

Drawings by Paul Sinclair

News clippings courtesy of
and copyright of Johnston Press Plc

Cover created by PBC Publishing

ISBN: 978-0-9575007-8-5

TRUTH-PROOF

*"Paul Sinclair deserves credit for striving to find answers...
whether you are East or North Yorkshire based,
or indeed any part of the world,
and are interested in such investigations...this is the book to read."*

Chris Evers
Editor of *Outer Limits Magazine.*

*"Could not put it down...so much information I was unaware of.
Incredible work...will appeal to anyone who dares pick it up!"*

Steve Mera
Author on the paranormal, lecturer and owner of *Phenomena Magazine.*

*"Great job...there's no substitute for doing the hard work...
A unique and important contribution to the world of paranormal
literature. Your fine book stands on its own merits and always will."*

Peter Robbins
Writer, researcher and international lecturer,
co-author of British bestseller *Left at East Gate*
and leading authority on the Rendlesham Forest incident.

*"Paul is unique in this world...a witness who actually has
verifiable evidence of...some very eerie and disturbing events.
Fasten your seatbelts and prepare for one very,
very memorable journey into some deeply hidden information."*

Whitley Strieber
Bestselling author and writer of the definitive *Communion* books,
renowned lecturer on the subject of alien encounters
and director of the *Unknown Country* website.

PREFACE

'Events of high strangeness' - four words that best describe something that all rational explanations have failed to solve.

I think it is possible to find many more accounts like the ones contained in Truth-Proof, if we just step over the invisible barrier that is within us all. The place where human understanding hits the unknown and stops. These pages attempt to step into the unknown and accept that things outside of our understanding can and do exist.

For Truth-Proof I have concentrated on events within a thirty mile radius of Bempton and Flamborough, in East and North Yorkshire - both on land and out to sea. Here, incidents beyond explanation have been happening from ancient times to the present day.

Early into my research I realised that many of these events seem to be connected to each other. Not only by location, but also by an overwhelming feeling that what has been seen, talked about and experienced, is alien to all that we understand as human beings. With such an abundance of information, this book only touches on a small pool of stories. Some of them run far back in time and I think they could be expanded on to form a much larger account in their own right. I also realised that I could not write a book about the strange events in my area without touching on the mysteries of anomalous lightforms, big cat sightings and the disappearances of many men in Bempton and Flamborough.

I make no claims within these pages that each or any are directly responsible for the other, except that there is an overlap where one event touches the other. This mysterious connection is the missing link. Yet it cuts us short of an answer and the plain truth is, we just do not know. I can only say that the accounts in this book have all happened or are happening in the same area. This fact on its own connects them all. Perhaps we need acceptance before understanding can begin.

ACKNOWLEDGEMENTS

I would like to say thank you to the many people who have helped me during my work on Truth-Proof - especially my wife Mary, who has supported me throughout.

Thanks to my good friend Karl for editing, proof reading and designing the cover of the book. I could not have got to this point without your help.

Thank you to Peter Robbins, your kind words of support have meant more than you will ever know.

I would like to thank Whitley Strieber for encouraging me to talk about my own experiences and my work on his show *Dreamland*, prior to writing Truth-Proof.

Thank you to my friends Debra Jane East and Derek Tiler, your support has been invaluable.

In addition, I would like to thank Johnston Press plc., for allowing me to use material and clippings from their local newspapers, including; The Bridlington Free Press, The Scarborough News and the Filey & Hunmanby Mercury, to name but three.

Thank you to the Royal National Lifeboat Institution for providing me with information about various emergency call-outs over the years, as well as weather conditions and sea states.

Also, special thanks to the staff at Bridlington library for all the help they have given me.

Finally, I would like to thank all the people who came forward to share their stories, images and information with me. Without you, none of this would have been possible and you will always have my gratitude.

INTRODUCTION

I have always had an interest in things that seem to have no logical explanation, because regardless of what a person believes, things do happen from time to time that just don't fit into what we consider as normal.

Truth-Proof is a collection of first-hand accounts and documented evidence of such events. Similar events could even be happening in the area in which you live. It could just be that no one has taken the time to gather all the pieces together.

Some people are collectors of material items from this world, I collect unusual stories and the emotions and life changing events that often accompany them. It was sometime during my fiftieth year that I decided to start writing about some of the strange things I have been told about over the years. I was born in South Yorkshire, England, in November 1962 and as I sit here on this cold March morning of 2016, I am 53 years old. I have been married to my wife Mary for thirty-three years and we have four grown-up girls and five grandchildren, which our daughters have provided to keep us busy in our later years. I have worked for most of my married life as a joiner on building sites all over the UK. I chased money out of a need to provide a better life for my family, but I think before this point, time did not allowed me the opportunity to sit and write of the memories and stories I have been told over the years.

From 2002 until sometime in 2012 I ran a small website dedicated to collecting reports of UFO sightings and information connected to the area of East and North Yorkshire, where I live. So before starting this book, I had already had amassed lots of information on this area - which seems to be a magnet for the strange and unusual. In 2014 The Bridlington Free Press newspaper were kind enough to accept a small article of mine requesting information. I wanted to know what people in the area had seen and experienced, no matter how unusual. I did the same thing in various other newspapers around the area.

From this I made some great contacts which I would not have made otherwise. I would never have been contacted by a ninety-one year old gentleman from Bridlington whose recall of strange events during 1963 was priceless. A retired coastguard shared some information with me relating to the crash of an aircraft in 1998 and a lady named Betty Chadwick contacted me to share her account and photographs of a big cat sighting from 1994, at nearby Rudston.

Locally we have had military aircraft, including Royal Air Force Tornados, which have crashed into the North Sea in strange circumstances, just off the Flamborough and Bempton coast a few miles from my home. I have tape recorded accounts from North Sea trawlermen who found more in their nets than they ever wanted, and they share stories of radioactivity and strange lights seen in the skies. Much has been written about the American exchange pilot, Captain William Schaffner, who crashed his Lightning jet into the North Sea in September 1970, after allegedly pursuing a UFO. My own research unearthed two further unusual events occurring in the same month.

In June 1998 another RAF Tornado crashed off Flamborough Head in an incident which many also believe to be UFO related and I have discovered a log entry that talks of searching for a dark object that was seen descending from the sky. Yet local fishermen have reported seeing UFOs throughout these years and although these sightings cannot directly be connected to the loss of aircraft, they do show events of an high strangeness occurring in the vicinity at the time.

I have been immersed in the subject of UFOs all my life and from the beginning, through no choice of my own, I have had my own strange experiences. Although I never actually thought I would sit down and write about them, since some of the memories have been secret for so long, I suppose I came to a point in my life when I realised that not to tell people about these crazy events, was not being true to myself - even if the truth of what I have seen and experienced is beyond anything we might understand.

As a small boy I recall seeing, what would now be described as alien beings, in my room at night and throughout the 1990s I was plagued by these visitors. I have scars on my arms and back that just appeared overnight and my medical records from that time reveal a path of biopsies and tests, that in the end, give no clues as to why or how they had appeared. I felt even then that I knew the real reason, but dare not say anything, for fear of being labelled crazy or even worse. In the words of Whitley Strieber, *"I do not know of anyone, anywhere in the world, who has as many marks on their body or has been interfered [with] by the visitors as much as Paul Sinclair."*

Perhaps this has always been there, in the background, but the only tools I have to work with are memories, my own and other peoples. It was through my own experiences that I eventually found myself on this path of collecting other people's accounts of the strange. I have now begun to realise that no matter what we believe, be it spiritual, alien related or something else, they are all connected on some unfathomable level.

My research has taken me in many directions and I have found myself looking into mysteries that I never thought I would. For example; on the edge of the North Sea close to Flamborough stands the now derelict RAF Bempton radar station. All around this area ordinary people have vanished without a trace. They have left no clue behind them as to how or why - they simply vanished. Personally, I have wondered whether there could be something within the very Earth and sky themselves, which might open our world to other dimensions.

Then eleven miles inland, just North of Flamborough, lies the village of Flixton where there have been reports of a werewolf. I have collected similar reports only a few miles away from Bempton itself - but I am the only person in the world to have spent years documenting accounts of this creature. I am sure something of truth exists in these stories, but perhaps not in the way people think of a flesh and blood mammal. This creature - whatever it is - I feel to be interdimensional. It is not the only animal sighting either. As mentioned earlier, sightings of big cats have also been reported in the area over the years; including multiple witness accounts from the 1990s of a lioness. Even as I write this, there are ongoing reports of a black panther sighted at Bempton.

In its past, RAF Bempton was a busy radar station, most of which lies below ground and it is common knowledge locally that, after it was closed, the station was being used for occult practices. So was this just a chance location or do strange things actually happen in this area ? And if the right keys are used can we open it's secrets ?

Quite how any of these events fit into one another I do not know, but if we cannot accept that these unknowns are real and happening, we can never begin to understand them. It seems as though we dare not mix the things we cannot believe or understand, with the real world that we can touch and see every day. This is the truth that leaves no proof.

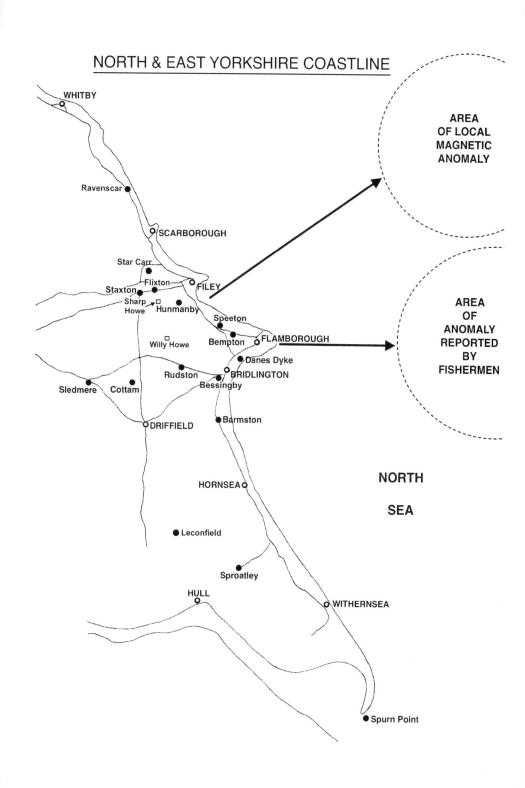

INTELLIGENT LIGHTFORMS

In much of East and North Yorkshire, the areas of land known as the Wolds are as unchanged today as they were in ancient times. The stories attached to this natural and unpopulated landscape are no less amazing than those on the coast and out to sea. Villages to the east like Cottam, Kilham, Langtoft and Thwing are all within fifteen miles of the cliffs of Bempton and Flamborough. The same can be said for Flixton, Folkton and Staxton to the north. Wherever unexplained things have happened on the Wolds, the lightforms are seen in the same area.

In recent years one popular theory to explain unusual sightings is Chinese lanterns, although there are many more. While this may be the correct explanation for some inland sightings over the more populated areas, to use them to explain away sightings over the unpopulated Wolds – and even out to sea - seems ridiculous. There is no reason to believe that unidentified objects seen inland are not the same as those seen off the coast. The speed at which they have been seen to move from point to point, is staggering. Perhaps one way to try and comprehend their speed might be to imagine staring at a destination with the eyes, then blink and you are there. At least this is how I imagine it.

From 2002 to 2014 I ran a website called 'ILF-UFO' (Intelligent Light Forms - Unidentified Flying Objects) solely to collect information on the East Yorkshire Wolds phenomena of intelligent lightforms. The ILF-UFO website was created as a place where people could report their own sightings without the fear of ridicule or judgment. It proved highly successful and gained worldwide respect, due in part to many of my own UFO images and footage that I shared there.

Since the late summer of 2004 I have spent many hours on the Wolds, trying to film the same unusual lights seen over the years by people living in and passing through this remote area. I could see no other way of beginning this study, since there was nothing I could use as a reference that could explain the lightforms. The explanations given by sceptics were, in most instances, highly unlikely. In fact I think scientific minds who come up with certain explanations for unknowns realise that what they say sounds ridiculous, but in the absence of anything more plausible, what else is there ? Yet their kinds of explanation are accepted all too often. It is strange how people readily accept the word of authority without question, even if the explanations do not fit the circumstances.

To admit the lightforms are a real unknown means accepting that we understand nothing. This void of unknowing has not been bridged and never will be, unless we accept them as a real and active phenomenon. Observing and filming them had to be my first step. Yet they were seen long before I took an interest. Local farmers have known about them for years and many who have seen them will not speak openly. They accept that at times, these lights appear and things happen on their land that cannot be explained, but for most, that's where it stops. They have no interest other than mild curiosity and their observations at the time. Reports of orange and yellow globes of light seem to feature in many accounts and have been seen from ancient times to present day, without cause or explanation. On rare occasions blue or white lights have also been seen, although it is interesting to note that I have no reports of the blue lights being witnessed out at sea.

These lightforms are seen in varying locations - from remote areas of land, to miles out at sea - and as our knowledge has grown, the theories put forward by the debunkers has changed. Weather balloons, swamp gas and meteor showers used to be the staple explanation whenever something was seen that defied rational explanation. Today this modern-day myth is usually explained away as Chinese lanterns, along with laser lights and the ever-reliable 'unusual atmospherics.' All of these suggestions are used to explain the unexplainable and in some cases they will be correct - although it is hard to apply them to sightings on the remote Yorkshire Wolds or miles out at sea. I have also noticed that unmanned drones are now being used as the explanation for many UFO sightings. Does this mean that the explanations given in the years 'Before Drones' (BD) were wrong ?

Perhaps a real scientific study is needed, but first there has to be acceptance that this unknown is real. Disbelief and non-action seem to rule when understanding is absent. The concept that everything can be explained by science is a rolling one that serves to smother and suppress first-hand witness accounts.

Mainstream media have a handful of sceptical experts who regularly offer opinion and sarcasm whenever something of an unusual nature is reported. This 'machine' works in perfect harmony with the press who in turn, are worked like puppets by people in power who allegedly want to keep us 'dumbed down'. They are wheeled out like verbal bullshit machines to suppress and silence the witness. This is why people refuse to come forward to share an experience. In the absence of a plausible explanation, the debunker usually coughs up his or her own unproven theories, which are accepted by the media, which are then filtered down to the public. These theories become accepted, however unlikely, because they can be understood by science and they become the only accepted explanation. Acknowledging that a phenomenon is real would mean admitting that we are no closer to understanding it than we were in ancient times.

Over the years I have spent on the East Yorkshire Wolds documenting the lightforms, I have been lucky enough to gain the trust of a few people in the area. They have shared with me a little of what they have seen and experienced. I am now sure that the lightforms seen inland are connected with those lights seen out at sea, off Bempton and Flamborough.

Lights Off Bempton RSPB Nature Reserve
A Personal Experience

Before detailing the accounts of others, I want to relate an experience of
my own from 2009. I had been asked by a locksmith and work colleague,
Michael Marsden, if I could help him with some work at Bempton RSPB
bird sanctuary and nature reserve. They needed a new floor-safe fitting
inside the visitor centre and Michael wanted me on his team. It meant
we had to wait until the centre had closed and we were expected to
work through the night until the job was done, but I agreed and on the
night of Tuesday November 10th, we arrived at the RSPB visitor centre.

It was hard work, which involved taking turns using heavy pneumatic
jack-hammers to chop up the reinforced concrete floor, removing the old
safe and installing the new one. The area we had to work in was
cramped and the job was going to take most of the night. Even though it
was cold outside it was good to step out into the darkness for a few
minutes rest. I remember going outside at about 10.45pm and walking
around the corner of the building. The silence was somehow comforting
after spending thirty minutes using a noisy jack-hammer. From where I
was standing, RAF Bempton was over to my left and the cliffs that
overlook the North Sea were about 500 metres to the right.

I could see the silhouetted outline of the old RAF buildings against the
night sky. I could also see two distinct orange lights high in the sky, that
seemed to be stationary. I suspected them to be the after-burners of a
jet aircraft, so did not give them anymore than a passing thought. I then
noticed a small light on the cliff-top, it was white/yellow in colour and
seemed to be just above the ground and was sort of swaying. In truth I
couldn't quite understand what I was looking at. I estimated the light
would have been about 6 or 9 inches across, but it looked pea-sized from
where I was standing. It seemed to be following the contour of the cliff
path and smoothly dipped and rose with the land. It resembled the light
of someone slowly riding a push bike along the cliff edge.

My eyes briefly switched to the two orange lights I had observed
moments before, then back to the cliff-top. The small light on the cliff-
top was still moving, but I saw it turn slowly then weave its way up
towards the old RAF base. Its journey was uninterrupted, so quite how it

managed to scale the barbed wire fence and work its way up the forty-degree incline is beyond me. It continued up towards the site and then disappeared from view. The orange lights I'd seen a few minutes before had disappeared and now there were five lights hung in a line, out over the sea. They were deep orange, almost red in colour and I was just about to shout to the guys inside the centre to come and look, but as soon as I had processed that thought, then the lights switched off. In different circumstances I would have stood watching the area long into the night, but since I was being paid to do a job, time would not allow it. Although I was puzzled, I didn't speak about what I had just seen from the back of the visitor centre and we continued to work on the safe through the night.

The visitor centre was full of camera equipment, bird spotting scopes and expensive outdoor clothing and the RSPB had placed a member of staff in the centre to stay with us until the work was complete. I suppose they needed to be sure no one touched anything. My sighting began to play on my mind and part of me felt fortunate to see the lightforms, but another part of me felt frustrated at not being able to film them. I turned many things over in my mind; I remember that I hadn't heard any sound from the first set of lights, they did not flash and they remained constant. These were a few points I hadn't considered when I first saw them. I also know that a jet's after-burners would have been loud in any part of the sky over Bempton, due to its isolated position. With all this in mind I asked the RSPB member of staff if any of the bird-spotters had ever reported seeing anything strange in the sky - at least anything that didn't have feathers. He knew right away what I meant and replied saying, *"Yes a few times."*

Then he told me a story about an angler he knew, who used to park his car at the reserve and then go up onto the cliff-tops for fishing. He said that on one particular evening, just before they closed the centre, the angler came in and he was shook up and seemed very frightened. He told them how he had set up his fishing gear and had been sitting on the cliff-top looking out to sea. The sky was full of stars when he suddenly noticed a very bright star that he couldn't recall seeing before. It was just there. He said that he looked hard at the star, but no sooner had he focused upon it, the star was right above him.
He couldn't explain it any other way. He said that for a few seconds the

ground all around him lit up in the most brilliant light. It was so intense that everything around him was white, even the grass shimmered in a silver white brilliance. Then it vanished as quickly as it arrived. The whole experience seemed to last no more than ten seconds and he was sure that some kind of mental connection had also been made - but it terrified him.

I listened to the story of the anglers cliff-top encounter and it was fascinating. Then I thought about what I had observed earlier that night and wondered if there could be any connection. Was the light that the angler had seen able to interact with his thoughts ? He said he felt some kind of connection had been made and the lightform did seem to react to his thought process. I'm unsure whether he'd had a visual connection or simply a mental one, or both, but how else could it be explained ? Considering the distance this object had apparently travelled, in what must have been fractions of a second - one moment it appeared up in the heavens, the next he says it was right above him - how could that happen ? If it did, surely the lightform should have been enormous. I suppose it's rational thinking like this that makes the sceptics giggle. When an account like this is analysed and dissected, they say the events described are just not possible.
I agree that the whole ten-second event sounds irrational and current scientific thinking would probably not accept that a thing like this could have actually happened. Yet I feel that to gather accounts and observations on the ground are essential keys to the early steps of understanding.

First observations seem to show that this light, which puzzled the angler, was able to tap into his thought process in some way that we do not understand. If the light was at point A and the angler was at point B, then the distance it travelled to meet him so quickly should not be possible within the scientific laws that we know and are familiar with. But did the light actually travel ? I do believe the anglers sighting was real, but I wonder if the light was more of a projection, like a torch beam of super-intensity. This might explain its ability to jump so quickly - instantly in fact - and the problem of the distance it needed to travel in such a short amount of time.

Breaking the account down into parts would only explain one small fraction of the ten second experience. Just how point A and point B connected over such a vast distance seems inconceivable. In the end we are only observers and all we can offer is theory and speculation. The lightforms leave nothing behind but a visual memory and unfortunately, we do not have one in a laboratory that we can analyse and study.

Here are two first-hand accounts that I feel fit a pattern of what could be happening. If we consider the possibility that the lightforms are able to respond to mental contact - even though these are giant leaps in the dark, where no proof that we can understand exists - then we must consider what would happen if some form of physical contact with the lightforms were made.

Lightform Encounter In Whitby
1984

The witness first contacted me via my ILF-UFO website about a lightform sighting, but would not go into great detail at first, until I gave an assurance that all personal and contact details would never be revealed. The encounter took place in 1984 in Whitby, North Yorkshire and this first-hand account is in the witness's own words.

"My car broke down on top of a deserted moor road, my girl friend and I had no choice but to leave the car and walk home. We saw a red light, but didn't take much notice at first, assuming that it was a tail light of a motorbike. Our primary concern was to get home - a journey of some seven or eight miles away. We were on foot and there were no vehicles passing us. With nothing else as a distraction, we realised that the red light was still there.
It maintained a constant two to three feet off the undulating surface of the moor. It not only moved so smoothly, as if it was on rails, but was completely silent. Although the distance, parallel to us walking, was about thirty [metres] away, we could hear sheep moving through the undergrowth at twenty [metres]. So if this light did make a noise, it was inaudible to the human ear, or was quieter than the rustle of sheep moving slowly through heather and grass. As the road bent to the right, so the light kept the same distance from us. Eventually, we came to a gradual slope that lead down towards the main Whitby-Guisborough road. The light remained still, it would not follow or keep with us so I went back. I got a strange impression that something was saying, 'I am here and will not harm you. Do not be afraid.'

I started to walk slowly towards it, yet it stayed where it was. My reasoning was that we were vulnerable up there, and if it wanted to, it could have hurt us, but it didn't. So we had nothing to lose and everything to gain from investigating it. My girl friend was frightened at the thought of me going over to the red light and leaving her, and she started to cry, "please don't leave me". I said that she should come with me then, but she became frightened at the thought of that also. I was caught between 'a rock and a hard place' so, I went back to her. The light stayed on top of the moor - I never saw it again. I have visited the same area many times since, hoping I might see it again. The following day when I went back to retrieve the car, I looked for any signs of burn marks, or flattening of grassland over the route it had taken. I could find nothing.

I am a Hypno-Analyst by profession. I am logical and I like to think that there is something 'out there', but I don't believe it without finding the whys and wherefores. I am open to all ideas without being pushed either way. If I had reported this, to whom could I have told ? We weren't assaulted or abducted, and we were not harmed or put under any sort of influence. There is no technology that I am aware of to be so advanced, as to move independently without noise or visible source of power."

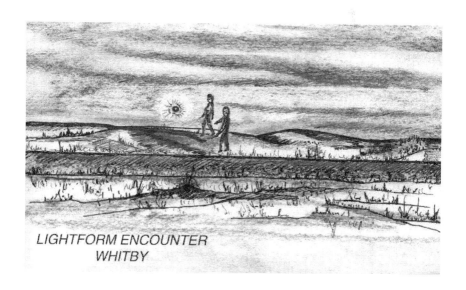

LIGHTFORM ENCOUNTER
WHITBY

Visual Sighting Equals Mental Connection

Below is an anonymous account of a lightform sighting sent to me by email, after I had spoken with the witness by phone earlier the same day.

"Around 7.10pm 6 miles from [location removed by request] I noticed some stars in the sky. As I focused on the highest star, I noticed it was flashing, but the two below it (diagonally) were also flashing simultaneously. I was convinced they must be planes, but continued to watch them. The lowest in the sky continued to move downwards, whereas the second one followed it relatively slowly, before suddenly moving quickly after it. The highest 'star' remained in the same place, and as I watched it, I suddenly felt as though it was watching me. Once I thought this, it began to 'spin' and a pinkish light emanated from it. The other two objects lower in the sky became visible again (behind two houses opposite) and all three objects spun and emanated the same light simultaneously. There was no trail (as in a plane) and no noise. Then all three disappeared very quickly.

I'm not a UFO enthusiast and have never witnessed anything like this before. Around thirty minutes later, I noticed a plane moving from the direction where the objects had disappeared, with a bright red flashing light and a number of white lights all around it. This plane went over my house, and left a trail in the sky. I'm pretty sceptical, although try to maintain a sense of critical open-mindedness. I have never seen anything like this before, and felt compelled to share it with others. It really does make you wonder.

My profession is psychology - I have a PhD in psychology (one of the most sceptical professions ever) and I'm just finishing a doctorate in clinical psychology. I find it amazing that after feeling that the object was 'watching' me, it began spinning immediately afterwards.

This experience has left me feeling quite amazed. I didn't think about the plane that went over at first, but it really does make you think that the military are keeping their eyes open. How much of a coincidence can that be ? Also, planes never go directly over my house, they usually travel in a diagonal direction, which also makes me think. I am going to take this as a sign that I will now be as open-minded as possible, without being subjective."

An Inter-Mind Experience

The above accounts give an insight into the effect the lightforms had on the individuals involved. They were clearly some distance away, yet some kind of 'inter-mind' experience seems to have taken place. In fact, the distance between the stars and the lone man sitting on the cliffs at Bempton is immeasurable, but from his account, the connection was instant. So how could this happen ?

Perhaps eye contact with the lightforms acts as a channel for an experience on a personal level ? It might explain why multiple witnesses see and experience slightly different things when placed in the same set of circumstances. This inter-mind experience could connect us directly to the lightforms, bypassing all the physical ties that would normally restrict such travel in this 'touch and feel' world. This might explain the surreal feelings people talk about when caught within these moments of high strangeness.

When I hear accounts of people having 'out-of-body' experiences, I wonder if what if they are experiencing is just the opposite ? What I mean is, could it all be taking place within the mind ? This is not to say that these experiences aren't real to the experiencer, but could an outside intelligence, with the knowledge to open areas of unknown potential within the human mind, be manipulating the human soul ? Perhaps those who see themselves outside of the body are actually seeing a projection of that 'inner-essence' looking back ?

If we step away from the phenomena of lightforms for a moment to consider the alien abduction experience - which in the end, could be one in the same - witnesses often say that the beings they encounter have the ability to speak directly into their mind. So is this another example of an inter-mind experience that is currently beyond our understanding ? Are all of these examples giving us a glimpse into life beyond the physical ? For the experiencer it is a no-win situation, a mind shock with absolutely no way out and unfortunately, we become the sceptic's dream scenario and a minority that make outlandish claims with no proof other than words. Words which cannot be backed up by anything.

I think these two accounts clearly illustrate that we are dealing with something that defies what we know and appears to have the ability to affect our emotional perception on an individual level. I am not sure if these effects are projected knowingly or not, but I am sure some form of information or 'sense of feeling' - be it good or bad - is passed to the witness. I think it could even depend on the state of a person's mind at the time, as to what the outcome of such an encounter will be.

After my own sighting of the lights from the RSPB visitor centre at Bempton, I decided that I would look deeper into the history of the area. The lights, combined with aircraft crashing into the sea in strange circumstances, were mystery enough, but add to that the reports of phantom big cats and the disappearances of men around Bempton and Flamborough and the strangeness goes off the scale. These events were why I spent years studying in the archives at Bridlington and Scarborough libraries, as well as requesting additional information from archives all over the UK. At the time, I never thought I would unearth as many strange happenings as I did. Did these events connect with each other in some indescribable way ? I had to accept that they had happened in the first place and this became my starting point.

Once I began looking into these mysteries it seemed as though I had fallen into a hollow tree, which had branches firing off in all directions. I needed to look for any crack of light in the available evidence, hoping it would provide an answer, but since nothing about what I was looking into made sense, it was hard to know where to look first. Neither had I any proof that any of this was connected, the only link that glued it all together was the sheer volume of unexplained events, in an area that seemed to be a magnet for tragedy. I seemed to have an impossible task ahead of me, especially when nothing in the verbal or written accounts provided any answers.

Then I thought about the strange lights I had seen from the RSPB visitor centre. All the details were there, but nothing seemed to fit. My head felt like it was a cement mixer full of questions, which kept turning over and over. I began thinking about the reports from local newspapers over the years, of people going missing in the area. These stories always seemed to make the news but quickly faded from memory after a few months had passed. Could they all really have been simply unfortunate accidents ?

I wrestled with the moral rights and wrongs of looking into these sad events, because these disappearances were real and there were real people involved. Should I really write about this for a book ? A book that touched on intelligent lightforms, big cats and even a werewolf ? At this point I didn't feel comfortable with the idea of retelling the circumstances of how these unfortunate men had disappeared, or sharing details of tragic plane crashes from the past. So I just continued quietly, collecting my catalogue of mysterious information, until I had made my decision.

Then, after much deliberation, I finally decided that I wouldn't be doing the book any justice if I omitted the facts of these disappearances from its pages. So I asked myself what it was that they all had in common. The answer was the location.
Then I wondered what was it about the location that attracted such strange events. Was this just a strange place, full stop ?

Something In The Air

The area surrounding Bempton is very remote. The only attraction in the immediate vicinity is the RSPB nature reserve, which only opens during the daytime and the old RAF base which has not been operational since the late 1960s. This underground complex is now sealed off from prying eyes and any secrets it might contain, above or below ground, are well hidden. So how does a place with little interest to the public amass so many unusual stories ?

In 2013 I had several long conversations with the elderly wife of a Flamborough farmer. She invited me to their home to talk about something that happened on the farm back in the 1970s. Whilst there we spoke of many things, including strange lights in the sky, big cat sightings and even stories of a 'satanic' cult, said to have been active around RAF Bempton in the 70s and 80s. None of these things seemed to surprise her, although she was adamant that if a big cat was around, they would have known about it. As for the rumours of a cult, she said there had been talk of witchcraft and supposed Devil worship in the area for many, many years - in fact, long before the RAF base had become associated with such stories.

She added, that the people of Bempton and Flamborough were so close-knit that the proof I wanted would be hard to find, if not impossible. While we talked, I also had the feeling that she already had the answers to some of the things I wanted to know.

She told me that she thought the satanic cult had been exposed in the 1970s, due mainly to the fact that the RAF base was an area of fascination for people outside of Bempton and Flamborough. It could be an exciting place for visitors to explore, but then came the discovery of things of an apparent dark nature taking place inside one of the base's underground bunkers. I was told that in the past, such practices went undetected, since they generally took place in remote areas which held no fascination to anyone.

I asked myself what was it about the area that set it apart ? Studying old maps revealed neolithic burial mounds, ancient standing stones and all manner of historic earthworks - all with interconnecting 'energy lines', so this had clearly been an area of great importance to people in the past. I pondered over these 'ley lines' that were said to connect the ancient sites. It was a connection that showed up again and again in areas of high strangeness all over the UK and around the world. The connection was too prominent to dismiss. On a map these energy lines look like a wiring diagram of the Earth and I think it is more than coincidence that early man built on these locations. It is interesting to note that many military installations are also situated in and around the same areas.

In fact the RAF came to Bempton in the 1940s and played a key role in the United Kingdom's defence network. Prior to 1950 RAF Bempton was used as an experimental radar station, later it was revamped and after the 1950s became part of the Rotor Programme - an upgrade of the war-time radar system. A little later still and Bempton played its part in the little known 'Project Winkle' radar programme and was used as an experimental station during that time.

In some places Bempton's white cliffs are almost three hundred and fifty feet high and in the summer months the loud chatter of nesting gulls fills the air. A glance over the cliffs reveals narrow ledges packed tight with seabirds. In the winter months these cliffs, which look out over the North Sea, are a harsh place to be for even the most hardened walker or bird watcher. I have been to the nearby nature reserve many times during winter and spoken with the visitor centre staff. They say that during some days in winter only two or three people will pass through the centre, since the climate is so harsh. The same can be said of the nearby Yorkshire Wolds, with its bleak landscape, which in places has been untouched by human feet for decades. Yet from these remote areas come stories of unexplained lights in the sky that move with an awareness that implies intelligence.

From land out to sea, fishermen tell of encountering silent balls of light that appear from nowhere which then vanish just as quickly. When these things happen they are so far removed from what is understood that witnesses rarely talk about them afterwards. When we place these accounts from land and sea side by side, they take on a significance that I feel has been overlooked. The lightforms are a phenomena that seem to touch all areas and have been reported for as long as can be remembered. In the end, they may be key to it all.

I have noted that these lightforms seem to be somehow able to tap into human emotions - since at times the observers can either feel extreme fear or extreme excitement. Even the visual experience seems to connect with a person's beliefs or experience - whether it be religious or alien. These sightings seem to fit the mind-set of the observer. Witnesses are also left with a gap where human understanding of the situation should fit. Perhaps in ancient times this bridge of understanding was in place, unless they simply accepted what they saw without actually understanding it. But today, due to what we call progress and superior scientific knowledge, that connection has been lost somewhere in the past.

For these reasons, events of high strangeness can get locked away in the far corners of our minds - for fear of ridicule or fear of just daring to go against public opinion. Opinion smothered by scientific thinking and influence, that in turn is poured into the machine we call mainstream media. A thinking that refuses to accept there are things at work which operate outside the boundaries of our knowledge.

Trying to explain the unexplainable is a stress most people feel is not worth the effort. Early into my research I realised that gathering information from people who had seen and experienced the lightforms was never going to be easy. Then asking questions about missing men was a raw, almost taboo subject, that the public seemed happy to let slip into Bempton's history.

My inquiries into the aircraft crashes off Flamborough Head took on a sinister tone that would have deterred many people and the 'big cat' reports were another story altogether. At times they just did not fit into anything less than paranormal. Even the term 'Alien Big Cat' (meaning alien to the UK) seems to take on a totally different meaning when the reports are given serious study. This research took an even stranger twist that would lead me on the search for the real origins of the 'Flixton Werewolf' - a crazy part of the book that I never imagined would run so deep.

Between Land And Sea

Local anglers who regularly fish off the cliffs up and down the nearby coast have had some of the best observations of the lightforms. Some of these men scale down the cliffs at Bempton on ropes to reach the best fishing places. They say that fresh cod can be caught all year round below these cliffs, since the hazardous waters prevent fishing boats getting in too close. The tales that these anglers have to tell have been previously overlooked, due in part to the anglers themselves, who tend not to care about what is seen in the sky around them. For that reason, it is rarely talked about. A good night's fishing is of more interest to these men, however, if you dig deep enough and ask the right questions they do have an important story to tell. The anglers are stationary observers, with fixed eyes that do nothing but look out to sea for hour after hour. I think if enough of them could come forward with their visual accounts I'm sure a serious case study of the lightforms could begin.

Large Orange Sphere At Speeton Cliffs

In February 2005 I was contacted by a 25 year old man called Jodie Lem from West Street in Bridlington. Jodie was a well-known sea angler in the Bridlington area who spent much of his free time up on the cliffs at Bempton and at nearby Speeton, a mile or two further along the coast. I agreed to meet him and a few days later on Thursday February 10th

Jodie told me what he saw. He started with the usual *"you will never believe this but its true..."*

Statements like this seem to be 'par for the course' when people begin to relate these kinds of stories. Jodie went on to tell me about a bizarre orange sphere that he saw with another angler named John, as they were fishing off Speeton Cliffs just before 11:45pm on February 7th. Jodie explained that the night was very clear, with a light breeze and a calm sea for that time of the year. The two men had set up their rods and been fishing for about one and a half hours. They could see two ships off in the distance, which in Jodie's estimation were about 7 miles out. Suddenly these ships found themselves in the company of a huge glowing orange sphere. Jodie thinks that the sphere was even further away than the ships themselves, but from where the two fishermen were, it looked directly in line with them. In his own words *"it was unbelievable."*

The sphere came from nowhere and just hung in the sky above the two ships. I suggested to Jodie that perhaps it could have been a flare of some sort - maybe something actually launched or projected from one of the ships, but Jodie was having none of this. He insisted that the object was the size of the moon and looked as big as the ships from where he was looking. He says it remained above the two ships for about four minutes, then slowly moved to the left. Moments later it shot up into the heavens at incredible speed and was gone. His description does not make the sphere sound like a flare, lantern or any type of known aircraft.

I contacted Simon Robson who was the helmsman for the Flamborough Lifeboat at the time. He now runs a website dedicated to the lifeboat and its history. Simon's view was that what Jodie and John saw could well have been military, adding that the Americans often 'play' in the same area about ten to twenty miles out.

In March 2005 Jodie contacted me again. He had been fishing off Speeton Cliffs once more and he seen the orange sphere again. This time it was closer to the land and was traveling on a steady course towards Flamborough Head. He explained that without warning the sphere then shot up vertically into the night sky and vanished. No ships were in the vicinity on this occasion, but he was not the only person to have seen the light that night. Jodie told me he spoke with three other men who had also seen it, as they were fishing off the North Beach at Bridlington. A few weeks later I was able to speak with one of these men myself and he confirmed what Jodie had told me, but he was reluctant to give any more details. He did tell me that it was quite low on the horizon when they saw it and that it was coming around the corner of Flamborough Head. He said that it rose at a forty-five degree angle and slowly disappeared from his view. I asked if he thought it might have been an aircraft. He gave me a hard look and said *"I'm not that bloody stupid"* and just walked away.

So we are left with a question. What are the spheres of light seen at sea and inland ? Do we just accept that they are connected to military exercises and that the Ministry of Defence simply forgets to inform the coastguard about their manoeuvres with multi-million pound jets from time to time ? Would they really be so unprofessional ? And if so, do they compensate the coastguard for wasted lifeboat call-outs, of which there must be many ?

Without doubt I feel that the spheres are something else entirely. At times they exhibit incredible speeds and manoeuvrability, whilst at other times they seem able to remain motionless over land and sea, regardless of weather conditions. I have wondered if they could be an, as yet, unidentified life form. I have had conversations with people who claim to have had frightening encounters with these spheres and I do wonder what would happen if a person was to come into close contact with one of them. Perhaps someone already has.

Orange Spheres Over Bridlington

On March 15th 2007 I visited David Hinde at his home in Bempton, to hear his account of a sighting from the 5th, ten days earlier. After a long talk I came away that evening feeling that his experience fitted comfortably into the category of the unexplained. David is a very articulate and level-headed man whose main job involves gathering accurate information which is then passed on to be made into informative books. Before this sighting, he would have been the first to admit to having no interest in unidentified objects. He explained that he'd made a journey from Malton to Bridlington one Sunday in March, which was uneventful until he reached the Dotterel Inn public house, just north of Bridlington. David used this location as a reference point and it was from here that he first saw the lights.

David said that they were quite high in the sky and red/orange in colour. He estimated their size was twice that of a star. He said they were not moving as a plane would, but seemed able to move up and down and sideways. They were so unusual he decided to pull over in a lay-by to watch them. Using the road itself as a guide he noticed that the lights never moved far from the right-hand side of the road. He also estimated that they must be somewhere above the Honeypot Inn, half a mile East of the Dotterel. The Honeypot is quite remote and off the beaten track.

It was now 11.05pm and as interesting as his sighting was, after ten to fifteen minutes of watching, David said he reluctantly got back in his car to drive home. It was at this point something a little unusual happened. 'Spooky' was the word David used. As he started his car engine and turned on his lights, the red/orange lights in the sky went out. They just vanished. At that point David felt a little uneasy. I did ask if it might just be that his car headlights were merely obscuring his view of them, but he shook his head saying that the sky that evening was very clear and bright and that he was, in fact, looking through the open window of the driver's side door. David said that he continued to look for another minute or so, then pulled away to continue his journey home. Then to his surprise the lights suddenly reappeared.

Beside the road where David had parked is an old underground RAF facility, situated just 500 metres to the left of the Dotterel Inn. There is only one house on that road for over a mile in any direction and the facility has a twelve foot steel fence running around its perimeter, with rolled barbed wire all the way along inside. Aerial masts are dotted around the surface area. Not much is known about the base itself except that it is below ground and belongs to the RAF. It is about three miles from RAF Bempton as the crow flies and the two appear to run in a parallel line out to sea.
Some fishermen have told me that when passing an area of sea off Flamborough and Bempton they sometimes encounter a radio 'dead zone' and their electrical equipment acts strangely.

The base and David's sighting may have no connection at all, but I feel it is worth noting if only to give an idea of the lay of the land. During the weeks that followed many people reported seeing the same lights around North and East Yorkshire. They were seen hovering over a field close to the coastal village of Staithes a few nights before David's sighting, by an eighteen year old from the village. The witness, Steven Dye, claims that eight lights remained stationary in the sky as he travelled home. They interested him so much that he went back later that evening with his mother to see if he could see them again.

It would be possible for me to fill this book with accounts of sightings of this type, but this only shows part of the puzzle. Even now, with so many clues laid out before me, nothing makes any sense. Perhaps the closest we can get to an answer is to say that these sightings overlap and then simply dare to suggest that they are somehow connected.

Below is a representation of David's sighting, followed by a news article of similar sightings all within the same month.

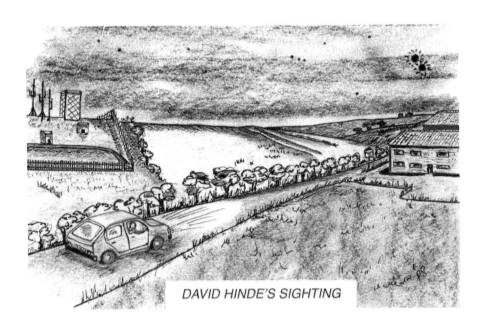

DAVID HINDE'S SIGHTING

More 'UFOs' are spotted

STRANGE lights in the sky seem to be on the increase.

After the Free Press ran the story of David Hinde, of Bempton, who reported seeing slowing spheres of light over the headland, readers have got in touch to give us their experiences.

Donald Rogers, 70, of St Columba Road, Bridlington, believes he saw exactly the same lights from his home at the same time as Mr Hinde on March 1.

"It was around 9.30pm and I saw these brilliant red balls moving quickly in different directions.

"My wife saw them, and more lights, and thought it could be a plane but I don't think they were from the movements they were making," said Mr Rogers, who says he saw similar lights above Sewerby about three years ago.

Connie Shepley, 73, also saw two golden orange points of light hovering over the pumping station off Scarborough Road on March 1.

"They were just still in the sky. I got my binoculars and watched them for about four minutes but they didn't move. I used to live close to Manchester Airport and they were nothing like aeroplane lights," said Mrs Shepley, who saw them around 6pm.

William Lester, 61, of Woodcock Road, in Flamborough, was looking for the laser beam from The Eye On The Bay site while visiting his daughter in Tudor Close, Bridlington, at around 8.30pm on March 1.

He, his brother-in-law and a friend all saw a set of about six orange and red balls which seemed to be quite low and moving independently of each other in a line.

"They didn't look like any kind of aircraft," he said.

Carol Scholes, 31, and her fiance Stephen Pemberton, 40, were at home in Scarborough Crescent, Bridlington, at about 8.30pm last Wednesday when they saw lights in the sky over Grindale.

"There were a couple of red lights, then three and then five and they were moving in all directions.

"I don't believe in UFOs but it was really strange," said Carol.

Abigail McKenzie and Shauna Marshall also saw something strange the night after, at around 7.30pm in the Easton Road area.

They said: "It had blue and red flashing lights and it was circular. It went over Old Town and back. We saw it fly across the sky twice."

And Dave Johnson can back it up. He said: "My friends and I were driving towards Danes Dyke when we spotted a bright reddish orange light in the sky fitting the description of the lights Mr Hinde saw.

"As a joke I said to my friends 'look a UFO' then another appeared.

"Following the appearance of the second light, the first disappeared. Then another light appeared and the second one disappeared, shortly followed by the third.

"Then the most interesting thing happened; we saw all three, close to each other, shining very brightly, then they faded.

"More than anything I would like to know what they are."

Celia Mitchell, of Bempton, saw similar orange and red lights moving up and down and sideways to the left of the Dotterel pub in December.

She watched them for quite a while and her neighbours said they had also seen them.

Terry Edwards, of Jubilee Walk, Bridlington, said his whole family saw the lights in the sky.

Mr Edwards said: "We were looking for the search light on the seafront and then we saw the lights.

"There were two red lights and one more off-white. They were not moving in a normal manner and were not flashing like a plane."

If you have seen strange lights, send a text starting BFPEDITOR followed by a space, the details, your name and address, to 84070 (texts cost 25p plus your standard network charge) or e-mail letters@bridlingtonfreepress.co.uk

The Poachers Sighting

Back in 2007 our youngest daughter used to go to a karate class for an
hour each Tuesday and Thursday evening. I would drop her off there and
then take my car up to Woldgate for forty-five minutes or so, until I
needed to collect her again. It was pointless driving all the way home to
just to drive back again a short while later and from the top of Woldgate,
which is a minor road, I had great views of Bridlington Bay and the
sweeping arc of Hull off in the distance.
It was November and a cold clear night. My phone rang and I answered,
instantly recognising the voice of a friend named Dave. He spoke in a
half-whispering tone.
*"Paul, Paul, you have to get up to Bempton now. I am up here on the
cliff-top shooting rabbits. You have come and see this."*
I tried to explain that I could not come as I had to collect my daughter
from her class. *"But there's a row of six orange lights out at sea,"* he
said. *"They are just hanging there..."*
I asked him where exactly. *"Just off Bempton, up past the old RAF base.
No wait...they have gone out."*
There was a pause on the phone then he returned and was even more
animated. *"They're closer now. They've come back on now, closer to the
cliff-tops."*

I was naturally frustrated that I could not join him to see what he was
describing. Although chances are, they would have been long gone
before I arrived. These had to be the orange lights I had been told about
many times in the past. *"They have gone, they have gone."* Dave said.
Before I had a chance to reply, Dave said the lights had again
reappeared, miles down the coast towards Hull. To my amazement I
could see for myself that he was right. From my clear vantage point on
Woldgate, far into the distance I could see a row of orange lights.
Unfortunately they were so far away that I found it impossible to
distinguish anything more than a band of amber light. I only saw it for a
few seconds and then it was gone.

I wondered if the lights Dave saw from the cliff-tops were actually in a
row. If he had seen them in a line of six, over the sea to the left of my
position, then a short time later we *both* saw them for a fleeting
moment, some ten miles to the right. Yet how was it possible for Dave to

see them as a row of lights ? We were both more or less looking straight out to sea, Dave from the cliff-tops and me from Woldgate, so we were about five miles apart. When Dave saw them for the final time, in theory he should only have seen a single point of orange light. Even though they were now down the coast to the right of me, even I saw a *band* of light. So with this in mind, could we assume that the object had sides with lights all around it ?

I have since spoken with people who have offered explanations for these sea lights and lots anglers who claim to have seen them. Many have said that the lights are the RAF on training exercises out at sea, an explanation that appears to be brought out every time they are seen - and for the vast majority that explanation seems to work. After all it is not uncommon for the RAF to conduct training exercises off the coast. They apparently drop missile deflector flares and use them for practice. Of course this is a plausible explanation, but no aircraft were heard or seen when these lights appeared. And could they hover motionless, blink out and then reappear close to the cliff edge - then seconds later perform the same reappearing trick miles down the coast ?

I am told that the coastguard are unhappy with this because the RAF are supposed to inform them of what they are doing. Apparently sometimes they don't and the public phone in to report strange lights out at sea. Perhaps the RAF do not always inform the local coastguard because they are not always responsible for the lights. The Bridlington coastguard have told me that these lights had been reported for many years and each time they seem to amount to nothing. Yet the sheer volume of visual accounts indicate that they are more than just nothing.

Orange Lights Off North Pier

Darren Yoginson from Bridlington contacted me in 2008 to tell me of his own sighting. He said that whilst he had been fishing with another angler at Bridlington harbour off the North Pier, he had seen a strange sequence of lights. Darren said they had no explanation for what they had seen, adding that they remained in view for quite a while. He explained the lights had gone on and off in a strange rectangular fashion and were going up and down and up and down, as if across a board. *"At one point"* he said, *"they went out and we phoned the coastguard to tell them what we had seen. As I was on the phone they reappeared. The coastguard officer acknowledged that they could also see them."*

Darren told me how they then watched the Bridlington lifeboat head out to investigate, closely followed by a Sea King helicopter.

"We were on the phone to the coastguard as we were looking at them, all of this was going off and they just went out. It was surreal. The seas were rough and it was very windy but these things weren't moving. The coastguard officer said they would send out a patrol car to talk with us. They wanted to be sure I was a genuine caller."

Darren thought that was an odd thing to say, due the fact that the Sea King helicopter and the lifeboat had already been sent out to investigate. They called Darren later that night and asked if the lights had been seen again. They informed him that no boats had been reported being in distress, no planes were in the area and no oil rigs were anywhere close to where they observed the lights. So by their own admission the coastguard had ruled out all of the most likely explanations for the lights. Darren assured me that no aircraft would have been in the same area as the lights since the weather was so bad that night.

The mundane explanations which are usually put forward to explain this local phenomenon now seem so ingrained into our thinking, that whenever the lightforms are seen no one ever really seems to consider that any military exercises over the North Sea *have* to involve aircraft.

In 2008 another angler contacted me from Hornsea, just 16 miles south of Bempton. He said after fishing around this coast for many years he had quite often seen strange things in the sky, but had never bothered to contact the coastguard as he felt it was a waste of time. He knew of other people who had done so in the past who were told that it was nothing to worry about. Other anglers have told me that they used to see them regularly over the sea off Flamborough Head and Bempton and they usually consisted of a horizontal line of three or four red/orange lights, well above the horizon. They would be there for a few minutes then just disappear.

With every report of this type that I receive, I make a point of asking if any aircraft are seen at the time or if any sound can be heard - and every reply I receive back confirms that no sound is ever heard.

Occasionally aircraft are observed, but they are usually between ten to fifteen minutes after the lights have disappeared. Does this sound like RAF training exercises ? Of course military jets *are* seen on training manoeuvres out over the sea, however they do not usually lead to multiple calls to the coastguard, since witnesses usually recognise a military exercise is taking place.

Variations In Colour

The red/orange spheres seen off the Bempton coast are without doubt real and I wonder if variations in their colour and intensity mean anything. People have said that the deeper red ones can give off a feeling of anger. It is interesting to note that when they are observed out on the Wolds they usually appear singly, sometimes in pairs and are usually a bright and vibrant gold colour. Although one account I have from a witness who lives close to RAF Staxton Wold, involves one sphere separating to become three separate lights. Out at sea however, three to six lights seem to be the norm.

One young woman, from nearby Weaverthorpe village, contacted me to report that in 2006 she had witnessed a blue sphere over a field near Langtoft, adding that it gave her an emotional high or feeling of elation. I also have reports of the darker red/orange spheres bringing about feelings of fear in some, but if they do have the ability to change colour, are the colours actually able to affect the emotions of the witnesses ? Or do our moods dictate their colour and reaction. I cannot help thinking that something more than a visual connection is taking place.

Gold Light Off North Landing Beach

In 2008 I spoke at length to a Bridlington fisherman who prefers his anonymity. He told me that whilst out collecting his crab and lobster pots with two other men, close to an area known locally as Crab Rocks, they saw a yellow coloured object off Flamborough Head. His words to me were, *"It was like nothing we had ever seen before Paul. It was a gold glowing thing the size of a Sea King helicopter. It was moving slowly and silently about fifty feet above the surface of the sea."*

The two other men in the boat were watching the object with him, but none of them had any idea what it could have been. I held back from saying that Sea King helicopters were bright yellow in colour. I knew what he was talking about was not a helicopter, but in my mind I can already hear the sceptics reading this and belittling this genuine man's description of what he and the other crewmen had seen.

"We had no idea what to make of it. Nothing seemed right. It couldn't have been a helicopter because we would have heard it. But the thing I don't understand and never will, was how it was able to be so low over the sea without disturbing the surface of the water. It just did not make any sense."

These men work on the ocean for a living, they are familiar with most aerial activity out at sea, yet they still contacted the coastguard. They were told that the Sea King was not in the area and they should ignore it. The fisherman explained to me that the object they saw was all 'lit up' and seemed to glow a bright yellow to gold colour, in shimmering waves of light. I made a point of asking how it made him feel at the time and he told me that he felt shock and disbelief, but he assured me that they did not feel threatened.

He went on to say, *"It seemed to be searching for something, or that's the way its movements appeared to us. Everything was wrong about what we were seeing, even when it moved away. It seemed that one moment it was there, large and bold, and the next moment it sort of shrunk away to nothing but a dot of light. We could not tell if it had moved away at speed or it did just shrink to nothing. We talked about nothing else that night, but now I don't even think about it, unless someone mentions seeing something strange."*

Considering this account and many similar accounts, I have wondered if the silence and lack of disturbance to the surrounding area, be it land or sea, can actually affect our ability to understand what we are looking at. We know what we *should* be seeing and hearing and we instinctively know how water reacts to objects, either living or mechanical. We also know that a large body of light should, in theory, be connected to something mechanical and therefore make some sort of sound. Then there is the emotional impact on witnesses, which follows many of these experiences. Trying to come to terms with something that does not fit with logical thinking is like facing a wall that we cannot break down.

At this moment in time, I believe that first we have to accept the concept of what is being reported is real, then accept that not understanding it is the only thing we can be sure of. This may seem like madness, but I can see no other way to move forward in this study of the unknown. For witnesses, I think that combined with the absence of what is expected in the form of sound, the visual experience which cannot be understood and the mental state that these sightings seem to evoke, just create a system overload.

Another interesting point is that in some instances, multiple witness accounts show that individual witnesses do not always have the same shared experience. They share the sighting, but they don't always agree on what is seen and experienced. Personally, I suspect that the lightforms are somehow able to work with human emotion. Whether this is intentional or not I do not know, but I do think the mood and emotional state of the witness affects the experience they have. I believe that some sort of inter-mind connection is taking place that makes multi-witness sightings an individual experience.

Below The Surface

The anonymous fisherman told me of another sighting he had with his colleagues. He described the surface of the sea being lit in a brilliant white light, which seemed to be coming from something above them. At first they presumed it was the moonlight reflecting on the water, but quickly realised when they looked to the right, that the moon was already casting its light in a different part of the sea. They saw no light above them and there were no shafts of light coming down. Nothing. Yet they described an area of the sea which was lit in a circle of white light. The fisherman said that it was not until a few days later that he wondered if the light could have been coming from beneath the surface.

In the past I have looked into the phenomena of 'marine bioluminescence' as a possible explanation for some of the lights seen out at sea. Most accounts say that the lights are well above the water, so this theory can be ruled out. Yet in this case, the theory is worth mentioning. I have spoken with other seasoned Flamborough fishermen, who tell me they are familiar with this phenomena and at certain times the sea can sparkle with purples and greens. The fisherman told me that the white light he saw formed a solid circle, about ten feet in diameter, but when I suggested marine bioluminescence he said that he had seen the waters off Flamborough sparkle in this way, but did not think this light was the same.

It seems that the bulk of these sightings can be seen just around or 'off the corner', which is local terminology for something off Flamborough Head. This places them in a similar position to where many military jets have crashed over the years - exactly where many other strange and silent lights have been sighted. All are just above sea level and off the coast of Bridlington and Flamborough Head. This report is not connected to the Jodie Lem sighting, discussed earlier, although it is possible the witnesses may have all seen the same objects.

A Coastguard's View

An officer at Bridlington Lifeboat Station who I asked about the lights seen off the coast told me that many people, from fishermen to members of the public, have all reported seeing them over the years. On reflection he said that he did think they were unusual and he said that they never questioned witness accounts. They did just what they were meant to do - which is to search for boats, missing aircraft or people in distress.

He told me that usually after investigation, nothing more came of the sightings and they were soon forgotten about. He suggested that if the weather conditions were suitable, some of the sightings could be nothing more mysterious than gas platforms burning off shore. He also said that witnesses may have been seeing the RAF conducting exercises out at sea or even a meteor shower. I told him that the earliest report I have is from 1937. I interviewed a local lady of eighty-one years old who, back then when she was a little girl, remembered seeing the lights whilst walking with her mother at Flamborough's North Landing beach.

I have also spoken at length with a retired coastguard officer from nearby Hornsea, who told me that sometimes they felt frustrated when contacting the MOD. If they needed to enquire whether any exercises were taking place out at sea, he said that on occasion they could not get a straight answer. Since the retired officer also used to work at a station further down the coast, I asked if he had any memories of an aircraft that had crashed off Flamborough Head in 1998. He paused and stressed that what he was able to tell me was limited, but he did remember the incident. At times I am sure these explanations are the reality behind many of the sightings of unusual lights seen off-shore, yet should it not be a matter of protocol for the military to inform the coastguard of any aerial activity out at sea ?

I think that stationary lights which blink out and then reappear miles away in another position, rule out military flares. These lights are seen to move vertically, something we do not generally associate with flares. Yet I never hear any reference to the trails of smoke that usually accompany flares, as they slowly descend. Also, when military exercises are taking place there has to be aircraft in the sky, although they seem to be absent whenever these lights are seen. Gas platforms out at sea are also an unlikely explanation for the rows of lights, which are usually seen well above the horizon. Some witnesses have noted that a short time after observing them, usually ten to fifteen minutes, jet aircraft are then seen in the area. Bridlington Lifeboat Station told me that the bulk of the lights reported are seen to the south of Flamborough Head and down towards Hornsea. This further confirms my suggestion that cliff anglers do not bother to report lights seen off the Bempton coast.

It is a pity that I seem to be the only person investing serious time and effort in reviewing accounts of these strange phenomena. If official explanations do not fit with what is actually seen, then perhaps it is time for some serious investigation and observation to be done.

The Withernsea Close Encounter
1994

In March 2006 I was contacted by a freelance reporter from Bridlington named Judith Broadbent. She asked if I would interview an older lady and her daughter about a terrifying encounter they both experienced when they lived on a farm in Sproatley near Withernsea, just east of Hull. I agreed and phoned them the following day. The lady who answered was seventy-two-year-old Muriel Rowbottom, who began to tell me the incredible story of what they had seen and experienced in 1994. Over the next few months I spoke with Muriel many times and a mutual trust was formed. In May 2006 I agreed to meet her and her fifty-year-old daughter Sandra Walton, at their home in Knaresborough.

She told me they had things they wanted to say to my face and had photographs to show me to prove they were not lying.

I drove to Knaresborough the following weekend with my friend and fellow researcher Steven Ashbridge. Steve had accompanied me many times in the past on investigations and after a two hour drive, we pulled up outside of a red-brick semi-detached house. From the car we could see three people standing in the back of the living room, observing our arrival. It became apparent soon after we entered their home that all was not well. The front door was opened as we walked up the path and we were led into the dining room. Seated at a table was a large heavily built man in his late thirties who nodded as we entered. Muriel explained that this was her son, who was there because in the past, people had visited them to hear their story and things had not gone well.

During one of our previous phone conversations I had been asked if I knew of a particular investigator from the North East Yorkshire coast. I never realised at the time that my response would dictate whether or not we would be able to meet the ladies. It turned out that this other man had visited them previously and attempted to steal the photographs they had taken during their experience.

After a few hard looks and a warning to be respectful, Muriel's son left the room. My ears traced his heavy feet going up the stairs and finally settling in the bedroom above us. Muriel's daughter Sandra then placed an article from the Hull Daily Mail on the table in front of us. It was dated Wednesday 21st December 1994 and entitled "Mystery Face At The Window." I glanced at the paper but really wanted to hear their first-hand account.

The ladies told us how, back then, they were living in a bungalow on a small farm in Sproatley, East Yorkshire. Sandra explained that the back of the property looked onto open fields and woodland and had no light pollution. At the time of the incident Sandra had been in the kitchen doing the tea-time washing up, when through the kitchen window she noticed unusual reddish orange lights high in the sky. She leaned closer to the window to get a better look and realised they looked like orange balls of light, that were just hanging there.
"Mum ! Mum come and have a look at this." Sandra called out to her

mother. Muriel wondered what the fuss was about but knew from her daughter's tone she had better come and look. She made her way from the lounge to the kitchen as quickly as she could. By this time Sandra had dried her hands and was already unlocking the kitchen door to go outside.

The night sky was filled with stars and now amongst them were these bright balls of reddish/orange light, that just hung there in eerie silence. They both stood in the open doorway trying to make sense of these six lights, the size of car headlights in a row. They turned and looked at each other but said nothing. Their expression's said it all. Sandra then turned and ran into the house to find her camera which was in her bedroom. Minutes later she was back with her Mum, gazing at the balls of light which were still hovering motionless in the sky. Without warning the lights blinked out and they were gone. The ladies both stepped out from the kitchen doorway into the garden and scanned the sky. Suddenly the lights reappeared, but now they were much lower in the sky. Both ladies agreed that they appeared to be about half a mile away and seemed to be hovering in the direction of a small wood, just beyond the adjacent fields. The number of lights seemed to be changing constantly and they could not be certain, but they both thought they saw at least six spheres of light at one time.

It was hard to comprehend how six lights could be anything more or less than what they were seeing - a perfect example of phenomena outside of human understanding producing effects that our brains are unable to comprehend, even though our eyes are receiving the information.

Sandra fumbled around in the darkness trying to get her camera ready to take a photo. She held the camera out at arm's length in the direction of the orange spheres and pressed the shutter release. The flash went off in an explosion of light and then without warning, the spheres silently zoomed over the fields towards them. Now they were hovering low in the sky and were only about twenty metres away. Then even closer than the orange spheres, both Muriel and Sandra noticed an enormous white ball of light, which had some kind of shutter attached to it. It is not clear if the shutter was either a door or just an attachment of some kind, but in the excitement Sandra continued to take her photos until her Mum, who had become frightened, urged her to stop.

They told me that the air felt like it was buzzing with static electricity and their skin felt prickly. Overriding all this was a fear that told them both it was time to move. The situation was way out of their hands, but the spheres of light just hovered as if observing them and what had started out as something unusual, had turned into full blown fear. The ladies turned and ran back into the kitchen, banging the door shut and turning the key to the locked position.They retreated to the furthest corner of the room and cowered in the darkness. The spheres still seemed to be hovering above the nearby field and the ladies said that through the window they could see that the sky had now taken on an orange glow. They were both in shock, neither of them had ever seen or experienced anything like it before.

Muriel said that at that moment they actually felt captive in the house and feared for their lives. As they sat in the darkness Sandra whispered to her Mum that she thought she could hear something moving outside. Their eyes and ears were now fixed on the window. Ignoring the pleas from her mother to remain still, Sandra slowly shuffled along the kitchen floor on all fours until she was just beneath the window sill. With a shaking hand she raised the camera and took a picture, then another and another. In the minutes that followed they told me that the silence and the air itself felt very different to anything they had ever experienced before, adding that it was almost like being in a dream state. They waited a good while until no more sounds from outside could be heard, then Sandra raised her head above the windowsill and looked into the darkness.
"I think they've gone" she said. She sighed and slumped back against the wall, relieved and exhausted. Muriel was still in shock and not that keen to move from the back of the room where she had been the whole time. Sandra stood up and reached for the door handle, turning the key as she did so and with a loud snap, the sound broke the silence.

Outside the sky was very dark and they both remarked that it still had some kind of redness to it. Muriel stood beside her daughter in the doorway and whispered, *"Have they gone ?"*
They assumed that they had, so now they could begin to try to work out what had just happened. They continued to study the sky whilst talking about the strange encounter, then they noticed stars. The stars slowly

began to reappear and they could clearly see a huge, dark circular mass above them which seemed to be rising. As this happened, the night sky and all the stars gradually came back into view. Later they discovered huge dents in the grass outside the property, where they think the white sphere could have landed. On reflection they both thought the white sphere was where the 'beings' came from.

Other things had happened on the night the spheres showed up, which only registered days after. They remember hearing a loud noise and house alarms starting to ring, they also remember hearing dogs barking although they could not say whether these sounds were heard before, during or after the event.

A few days after their encounter Sandra came home with the much anticipated photographs. The ladies desperately wanted answers to an encounter which had turned their lives upside down and frightened them. They didn't know what to expect from the photos and opened them up with a kind of nervous excitement. Sandra could hardly believe her eyes. She said that the very first photograph showed something standing outside the window - and as she looked at it, she shivered. A part of her knew that whatever they had experienced was nothing they could understand. Yet another part of her wanted it explaining, so they could settle the deep unrest it had caused them both.
It was true to say Muriel and Sandra's lives changed forever after they saw those orange lights outside their home. They moved house several times afterwards but always felt a connection had been made which would never leave them. Steve and I studied the photographs that lay on the table before us and we tried to be as objective as possible. I could not say with all certainty that we were looking at images of aliens photographed through a kitchen window, but the pictures did show something unexplained.

A montage of Sandra's photos is shown over the page.

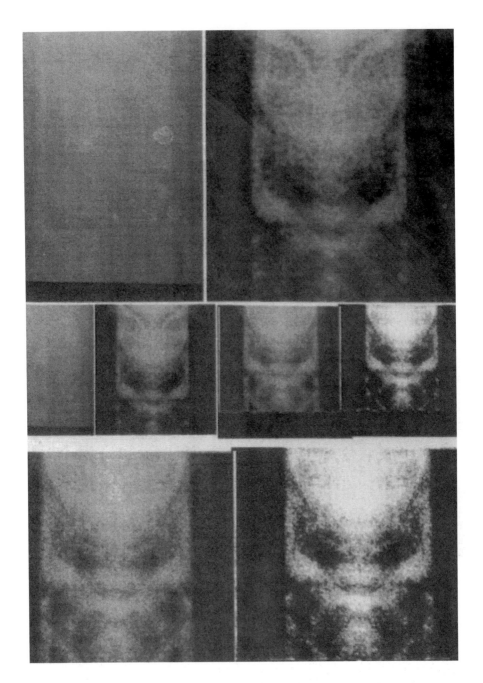

A Pilot's Encounter

Here is a first-hand account from 1996 that gives a little insight into just how difficult it is to understand what we are dealing with. I was first told about this in 2008 by the pilot and witness himself. It is his own account and I have not added anything or changed a word. On reading it, we have to consider why anyone would even create such a story.

"It was one of those bright, still sunny days that you sometimes get in winter, and it was mid-November in 1996 when I decided to take a flight up the east coast from a small airfield in East Yorkshire to Whitby. I was late setting off as I had problems with the electrical system blowing the fuses of my radio system. In trying to trace the problem I 'borrowed' the fuse from the aircraft navigation lights, but also managed to blow this into the bargain. Not wanting to miss out on the good flying conditions, I set off on my flight up the east coast without a radio or navigation lights - neither of which were a legal requirement. It is not a legal requirement to have a radio in an aircraft, and given that the aircraft was of 1946 vintage, one was not installed at the factory and my radio consisted of a plumbed-in hand-held unit. I was not concerned regarding the lack of navigational lights as I knew that I would be back before dark, and in any case, the airfield was not equipped with landing lights, nor did I have a night rating, so I couldn't legally fly in the dark anyway.

The flight up the coast was uneventful, and I did a couple of circuits over Whitby before flying inland a little to a point over the North Yorkshire Moors not far from RAF Fylingdales, where I headed due south back towards my home airfield. On the way back I realised that I had cut it a bit fine, and the sun was setting quite quickly. Because it was a vintage aircraft I used to keep the engine revs relatively low to be gentle on the 50 year old engine, but on this occasion I opened the throttle to 2400rpm, but by the time I had arrived at my turning point, not far from Weaverthorpe, the sun shining over in the west through the starboard window was very bright and low in the sky.

As I looked to the east in preparation for my turn I was mystified by the apparent bright sun in the east as well. Looking through the port window was like looking directly into the sun. At first I thought that perhaps it was a reflection of some kind, but it was obvious that this was not the case. The view ahead was clear although it was beginning to get dark and I scanned my instruments and all were indicating normally. I was still puzzling about the bright light from the east and I was just about to commence my turn to the east when suddenly the aircraft seemed to bump into an invisible brick wall in the sky. There was no sharp jolt, but there was a sudden feeling of deceleration rather like the brakes being rapidly applied on a car. It was if I and the aircraft suddenly had become stationary in the sky.

I again scanned the instruments. The airspeed indicator was indicating that I was still flying at 80 mph but clearly I was not. The engine note did not change and all the other instruments were indicating that I was flying straight and level. The rate of climb indicator was on zero, indicating that I was not descending or climbing.

From this point I can remember absolutely nothing, and the next thing I can remember was that I was flying in exactly the same place in the sky but it was dark...Very dark ! And the lights of Driffield could be clearly seen ahead. The cockpit was in total darkness and I could not see any of the instruments. The cockpit was equipped with a light, but this was not working as I had blown the fuse earlier while trying to fix the radio. In addition it was not possible to turn on any navigation lights as the fuse for these was also blown. It took quite some time to come to terms with my situation and I honestly began to think it was some kind of dream, but the truth of the matter was that I was piloting an aircraft in the dark and had no idea how this had happened.

I continued to fly towards Driffield thinking about what to do next. I could not call anyone on the radio as it was not working. I then considered flying to Humberside Airport as the lights of the Humber Bridge towers were clearly visible, and I knew that I could probably find the airport from there. But given that I didn't have a radio or navigational lights, I didn't think it would be a good idea to just turn up and land, not to mention the fact that there could be other aircraft in that area. Given that I knew where I was, I thought that the best option was to fly back to my home base. Even if I had to crash into the ground I could fly the aircraft slow enough to probably walk away from it. I therefore turned towards the coast and Flamborough Lighthouse could be clearly seen ahead. Fortunately, I knew the area well and I was able to work out where the airfield was as it was close to a small village which was easily identified from the air, even in the dark. Although some distance away, there was a road that ran parallel to the runway and with another stroke of luck the farmer was ploughing the field (or spreading slurry) that ran between the road and the runway, and the headlights of his tractor could be clearly seen.

I circled around for some time to pick up on other clues as the where the runway was and commenced on the approach. My main fear being that fact that I knew that 33kv power cables ran across the final approach to the runway. Descending into the blackness was scary and not being able to see the instruments to judge my airspeed or height above the ground made the situation very scary indeed, but fortunately I made an almost perfect landing.

I shut the aircraft down and just sat for several minutes trying to get my head around what had just happened. I checked my watch and reckon about an hour and a half had elapsed of which I have absolutely no recollection. From the point of apparently stopping in mid air to finding myself flying in the dark is to me totally unexplainable. The next day I checked the fuel quantity in the aircraft and this also indicated that the aircraft cannot have been flying for the missing hour or so. Again I have no explanation for this.

Officially I should have reported this incident to the CAA, but given the circumstances I decided against this. I have never told anyone this story before, not even my closest friends, but a chance meeting with Paul has encouraged me to write this account."

Willy Howe - A Window To The Unknown

The pilot's encounter with the lightform is just one of the many amazing stories coming from this area. Very close to where it took place is the neolithic burial mound known as Willy Howe, a place I mention in Truth-Proof many times because of the many mysterious happenings surrounding it. Historic texts that span hundreds of years tell of fairies and goblins frequenting the mound and surrounding lands. The accounts of William of Newburgh, the 12th-century historian and priest from Bridlington, tell of his encounters with little beings seen in chambers of light within the mound. Perhaps today we might interpret such encounters as being alien related. I do not want to venture too far into tales of folklore within these pages, but I do wonder if the pilot's encounter over Willy Howe will one day be considered a tale of folklore. We already have enough modern-day mysteries to work with which all need documenting. Some of these stories show that the pattern of events have never really changed. It is only our interpretation of them throughout time that has. These locations are felt to hold as much power and significance today as they did centuries ago and although we may have made huge scientific and technological advances since then, our understanding of this great unknown is no more advanced than it was when the stories were first documented. It could be that mankind's belief in his own superior knowledge has actually restricted or closed down our ability to accept that these things are real and happening, even though we do not understand why.

In 2015 on June 12th my wife and I spent most of the day at Willy Howe burial mound. Our last visit two years earlier had been with a small group of people and I remember some of the group used dowsing rods to good effect, which is a first for me to be honest. Since then we have used them ourselves many times and I cannot deny that it appears that some energy force is at work when using them. We wanted to see if we could mark out the exact location of any ley lines, so we went all over and around the huge burial mound with our dowsing rods. We each covered the same area several times to be sure of what was happening and each time the rods closed in the same places for us both.

Interestingly, we discovered two ley lines running through Willy Howe and we estimated that they crossed in the centre of the mound. So if the theories of ley lines are true, how could ancient man have known this ? We now believe that a concentrated point of energy appears to converge at Willy Howe and I am unaware of anyone who has documented this before.
I am of the opinion that other points of energy are yet to be discovered in other locations where unexplained events take place. I should have taken a compass to get an accurate reading of the directions of these lines, but I may do that on our next visit. I am quite certain that one line may stretch as far as the giant monolith within All Saints Church grounds at nearby Rudston village. We also saw a series of large 'fairy rings' in the adjacent field, about a hundred yards from the burial mound itself. Anyone familiar with folklore will know that these rings

are associated with fairies and little beings. Although I am not saying I believe this to be the case, it was simply an interesting addition to our visit to one of the most mysterious burial mounds in England.

Conclusions

It would be wrong to say that the strange lights seen in the sky are the reason for people vanishing or for military aircraft plunging into the sea. I have no physical proof to support this idea, but the truth is, these things have been happening in the same area over a long period of time. When viewing the diverse accounts associated with this area, I found myself drawing comparisons to the events surrounding the Skinwalker Ranch in Northern Utah - said by some to be the strangest place on Earth. I think locations of high strangeness are present in every part of the world and the remoteness of these areas and lack of any real evidence run the mysteries into a brick wall, long before any investigation can take place. There are few who would dare to consider the impossible, so these things remain unexplained.

I think, as a species we are simply passengers in a shell and we have developed just enough awareness to become separate from the breathing and eating machines that we inhabit. Perhaps the lightforms left their physical shells behind, long before we even developed an awareness ?

ALL ABOUT THE BASE

The RAF Bempton Connection

It seems that the ley line connection is never very far away, since just a short walk from an area of land depicted on old maps as 'The Leys' is RAF Bempton. I find it interesting that many areas associated with unusual activity seem to be or have been, areas which have seen military activity. RAF Bempton is one such place.

The RAF's Chain Home Low (CHL) Radar Station was established in East Yorkshire in early in 1940. It was positioned just a few hundred feet away from the lighthouse at Flamborough's South Landing beach. The station was originally known as RAF Flamborough Head, however, soon after becoming established it became evident that the location was unsuitable. Since being at an elevation of around a hundred and thirty feet it could not achieve the desired results, so months later a new site was found, four miles up the coast at Bempton. With its rugged, white chalk cliffs rising three hundred and fifty feet from the sea, this location was deemed much more suitable. In July 1940 the new site was opened and renamed RAF Bempton.

In its early years the base was used as a Ground Controlled Interception (GCI) Station, but until November 1945 it was also used as an Air Ministry Experimental Station (AMES) Type 31. After that it was handed over to the Northern Signal Regiment (90 Group) who became responsible for its maintenance. On June 1st 1949 the base once again became fully operational and in February 1950 it was transferred to Fighter Command. In November 1951 it became home to the 146 Signals Unit, but by December 1961 they had disbanded and the station became known as RAF Bempton once more. In early April 1964 the base became a domestic satellite station, but by April 1972 RAF Bempton's gates finally closed forever, after becoming entirely redundant. The site was finally sold off towards the end of 1980.

However, after reading an old Bridlington Free Press newspaper article from 1967, I learned that RAF Bempton was not in use, in any official capacity, at that time. The report states that three men from nearby Hull had been found hiding in the disused base - note the word 'disused'. It appears that they entered the building to steal copper cable and other valuable metals. The article goes on to say that the men were found at the end of a three hundred metre underground passage. They were crouched inside a cable duct only four feet square in size. If this article is correct then the underground passage was over nine hundred feet in length. This is certainly something to consider before dismissing claims made by some that, even today, there is more hidden below the surface of Bempton than can be seen above ground.

After closure the base was targeted by the unwanted attention of thieves, urban explorers and people hell bent on nothing more than vandalism. Below ground its walls are said to be made from ten feet thick concrete, reinforced with tungsten rods and its roof is two feet thicker than the walls that support it. It is believed to have originally been constructed for protection against huge Soviet free-fall bombs weighing over a one thousand pounds and was thought to be strong enough to withstand a near-miss nuclear blast. In early 2015 the visitor centre for the RSPB nature reserve at Bempton underwent a major rebuild to transform their dated old building.

By chance I knew some of the contractors working there and they told me that three different concrete breaking machines, all of increasing size, had to be brought in to break away sections of the floor. I was told that they had never come across concrete as strong before. I remember myself how difficult it was when I helped to fit the visitor centre's floor-safe back in November 2009. We only had to chip away at a small section of floor back then, but it took us all night. One of the contractors told me that this was because the centre was built above part of the underground section of the old RAF base. I had heard before that there was much more below ground than could seen, yet the visitor centre is over five hundred metres away from the base.

During building work at the RSPB visitor centre, comments were made by security guards who were based there overnight during the work. They were also employed by a major house builder in the area and the site agent, who I know very well, informed me that the guards had told him the old RAF base was not as inactive as people think. They refused to tell him more when asked, but it was evident that they did not want to work at the visitor centre due to its close proximity to the old base.

In October 2015 I spent a few evenings observing the skies from a high point on a lane which overlooks both the RSPB reserve and RAF Bempton. On one occasion I was with my friend Steve Ashbridge. The weather conditions were perfect for a sky watch and we were the only people mad enough to be there at such a late hour. At about 10.45pm we heard a thunderous thudding sound of something very, very heavy. We agreed that it seemed to be coming from the base, but we also thought it sounded like it was coming from below ground. We both became very alert and we strained our ears to see if we could pick up anything more. Steve noticed how everything seemed to have had gone very still and was even more silent than before. Then without warning we heard the sound again. It was a series of loud, dead bangs that seemed to be coming from below ground somewhere around the old base. It could in fact have been nothing more mysterious than something collapsing below ground, but when I think about the effort needed to break up the surface concrete I am not so sure.

Talk Of A Cult

In recent years local newspapers have made reference to RAF Bempton once being used for 'satanic' practises. However I can find no reports from the 1970s or 80s that back up these claims. Many people from the surrounding areas do however support the notion that it was once used in this way. I spoke with one man who told me that his father was one of the only people in the immediate area to hold an explosives licence. He was one of the most experienced and respected people qualified to be given the job of safely removing items from below ground. In the 1980s he once assisted his father in the removal of steel and heavy machinery from below the base and he was adamant that some kind of cult had been using the underground bunker. He confirmed this when he said that he recalled hearing that alleged cult members were forcibly removed by military police in the 1970s.

One reason that I could find no information on this in the local press, is perhaps because the MOD did not want it to become public knowledge. Other clues that point to the possibility of alleged cult-like activities taking place within the bunker are the satanic-style paintings seen to cover the walls beneath its subterranean surface. Yet I have also spoken with people who live very close to the base, who say that talk of satanic practises and 'witchcraft' are totally unfounded. Although it was certainly widely talked about during the 1970s and 80s and even now the base is remembered for such things.

On October 1st 2015 I was in Flamborough and Bempton once again, as a local farmer wanted to speak with me about a nearby sighting of a huge black cat. His description was vague but it more than fitted with similar sightings I was investigating at the time. After our meeting I stayed in the area for while to take a few photographs. It was then that I spoke with a local game keeper named Vic who was out in the fields at the time. I initially wanted to ask him if he had any information on the big cat sighting and Vic said he had heard of this rumour. Out of the blue he said that strange things seem to happen all the time around this area, then he asked me if I had heard of the satanic cult and witchcraft in Bempton, from back in the 1960s. I asked if he was mistaken and could it have been in the 1970s ? His reply was that he knew for sure it was happening in the 1960s and it was probably still happening today.

The people of Bempton and Flamborough are known for being very guarded about sharing local information with outsiders, so finding someone in the immediate area who is prepared to step forward with hard evidence is unlikely to happen. Yet I do not want to mislead readers into imagining groups of 'cult worshippers' were below ground in robes - as depicted in old horror movies. I think it is far more likely that the reports amount to just a few people practicing some kind of magic, in an area that is already charged with strange energies.

During May 2015 I was given a report of similar activities happening just fifteen miles away at Irton Moor, on the outskirts of Scarborough. Irton Moor military station is currently an active and important military installation known as CSOS, short for Composite Signals Organisation Station. Its primary role is intelligence gathering through the interception of signals. I do not think the report about Irton Moor is in any way connected to the accounts of dark practices at RAF Bempton, but it is nevertheless interesting and something that may feature in future research. I often wonder however, whether we can blame pure chance for military installations being situated around areas of high strangeness.

Tales Of The Occult At Bempton

Perhaps when looking at RAF Bempton and the stories attached to it, we should also consider the surrounding villages.
Stories of witchcraft and the occult have been documented throughout the whole area for hundreds of years. The inhabitants of the villages were and still are very distrusting of outsiders. In the not so distant past Flamborough and Bempton were once considered dangerous places to visit for outsiders. Sorting people out 'the Bempton way' is still talked about today. I have one credible report from a farmer who lives in the coastal village of Hunmanby. He talks of people being actively involved in witchcraft around Irton Moor on the outskirts of Scarborough, a location associated with military installations and only fifteen miles away from Bempton and Flamborough.

When looking for evidence to back up stories connecting RAF Bempton to the occult, I looked at the area as a whole to see if there was a history of dark practices. I then began to look into the whether these locations were actually accessible - would people of different age groups be capable of accessing the underground base during the night ? I have visited the area many times over the years, so I know the roads and paths that lead onto the cliff-tops very well. With that in mind I decided that the only way to find out was to do the journey myself at night. I first assumed that the people involved would be of various ages, so ease of access would have been a deciding factor. If a person were to leave their car at Flamborough's North Landing, then walk along the cliffs to the base, they would have a four mile walk ahead of them.

Assuming these alleged activities took place in the night, walking on uneven ground during darkness would not be recommended and seems highly unlikely that anyone would do that. Another reason it would have been unlikely was that Flamborough's lifeboat station at that time was still situated at North Landing. Although it was not staffed at night, if there was an emergency lifeboat call-out and there were cars in the cliff-top car park, I am sure concerns would have been raised and the police would have been informed.

Another route to the RAF base can be found by parking close to the pond at Buckton village and walking up Hoddy Cows Lane to the cliff-top. Bearing right to walk along the coastal path, the base is about two miles away. The walk would be quite difficult during the night, but it would be possible. I tried this route in darkness myself and have to say I never want to repeat the experience. So unless the people taking part lived close by, I would rule it out. If any of these routes were used, it is safe to say that no elderly people could have made the journey. This leaves just two possible locations to gain entry to the base, but even these would be difficult during the night.

The RSPB nature reserve is less than five hundred metres away from the base. It is as remote a location as all of the others, this was even more so during the 1970s and 80s. Nothing much has changed on the land in all those years. Concrete posts are evidence that an eight foot fence once surrounded the perimeter and in front of that is a low, three-strand barbed wire fence, which is still used as a deterrent. The fence has been repaired and patched many times during its life.

In 2015 I spoke with the farmer and land owner, who told me he was tired of repairing the fence, because of the number of people climbing over it to gain access to the base. If there is any truth in the stories of a satanic cult connected to RAF Bempton, I think this would be the only way to reach it undetected. The route is not ideal, but it is possible to walk there in less than ten minutes. The only other way would be to take the small single track road which runs directly to the base entrance. This would have been the main entrance during its operational years. I think anyone wishing to visit the base for such secretive reasons would be unlikely to take this path, as it means passing the only occupied property on the road - and that belongs to the farmer who owns the land where the base is situated.
It is worth pointing out that from the farmhouse it is not possible to see the base, because there is an ancient earthwork known as Standard Hill situated between the two, so any unusual activity would have gone unnoticed.

It is self-evident that the base's underground bunker was used for occult practices sometime in during 1970s and 80s, so unless some of the people involved lived very close, the land around the nature reserve had to be used to gain access. Below ground the bunker walls are painted with images of pentagrams, devils and animals engaged in explicit sexual acts, which give a feeling of foreboding.

This does not prove that the bunker was ever used for ritual magic. It may only show that a person or persons with unnatural thoughts did spend time inside the bunker. It does however, place the location on the edge of a mystery. What kind of people would take the time to create such artwork ? I have spoken to local men and women living in Flamborough and Bempton, who would have been teenagers during the 1990s. Some of them told me there was truth in what I was looking into. Yet the artwork is too explicit and too well executed to be the work of adolescent teenagers running around in the darkness with torches. As an artist myself, I am sure that it could not have been achieved without large areas of the bunker being lit up.

One man, now in his fifties, told me that his father was actually employed by the MOD to remove scrap items from the bunker during the late 1970s. He said that he spent many hours working with his father inside the bunker and is certain that people had been actively using it at night when they were not present. He told me that in the 1980s, military police once forcibly removed a satanic cult from below ground in bunker. I was told that I wouldn't find any local newspaper report on the story because the MOD did not want it to be known. He was right, because when I searched the local newspaper archives I found no account of the incident - if it was true at all.

I spoke at length with another Flamborough man named Paul. He has lived in Flamborough all his life and is now in his forties. He told me about a time he went to the bunker as a teenager to explore it with friends. He said they went below ground with torches to look at the artwork on the walls and to just experience the thrill of being there. It was something that many of Flamborough's youth did. I first visited the bunker myself in 1998 and have to say that I have never felt an atmosphere quite like it.

Paul told me that on one particular day they found something more shocking than they ever expected. He said they were quite deep into the bunker when they came across a large wooden crucifix leaning against a wall. Hanging from the centre of the cross was a spaniel dog, with a steel spike nailed through its head. He told me that the cross was not just a couple of old planks nailed together, it was well made and looked heavy, as though it had been taken there for a reason. He said the dog had clearly been there for some time as it had started to decompose. Stories like this suggest something unnatural was taking place at the location - and locations are the key.

I then began to think the unthinkable. I have long believed that the strange lightforms seen by many, are able to interact with human emotions. The visual connection and interaction experienced by witnesses on the Wolds certainly suggests this. What if there is energy within an area or place, which combines with the emotional state of the witness, which then allows these things to manifest ?
Could location *and* human emotion be the key ? If this theory is correct, could concentrated human emotion unlock some of these local mysteries, perhaps even creating 'flashpoints' where it may be possible to study the phenomena ?

In January 2014 I visited Grange Farm, landowners of the base - so I know first-hand how difficult it would have been to pass through the main gates undetected. It was with reluctance that the farmer spoke to me and I would say that it was not without good reason. I genuinely felt for them, as they were constantly on alert to the unwanted attention that the RAF base still receives. Anyone who might consider visiting the base today should be aware that it would be a pointless journey. The underground complex is now completely sealed off by huge concrete slabs that could not be moved without the aid of heavy lifting equipment.
When I arrived, it had been raining and the ground was water-logged. I had to park close to the farmhouse and walk the rest of the way to the cliff-tops. In my opinion, access to the base via the farm entrance is a no-go. I told the farmer and his wife about the book I was writing and some of the reports I was looking into. He spoke fondly about their memories of the base and gave me the number of a man who served there in the 1960s. The farmer said the man might be able to tell me about the UFOs that were seen and tracked there at the time. As he continued to tell me stories of the base and surrounding land, the farmers wife abruptly told him to stop, saying, *"We don't want to tell him all our secrets."*

This changed the whole tone of our conversation. I could not help feeling that they knew much more than I was being told, but I had to respect their wishes. These were good people who had been plagued by the attention the disused base had received over the years.

I had previously been told by the man who worked on the base with his father, that there was more below ground than the eye could see. Walking to the base that day, I wondered if that might be true. Small outcrops of squares in red brickwork could be seen in random places, far from where the bunker should have ended. Then when I looked northwest towards Scarborough, I could clearly see another base three miles away across the open fields.

Very little is known about RAF Speeton which sits between RAF Bempton and RAF Staxton Wold. It is still operational and has a twelve foot steel fence around its perimeter, with rolled barbed wire all around the inside. Two large radio masts can be seen sticking out of the ground and there are other smaller masts of varying shapes, dotted around the interior. Raised grassed areas, that look like upturned dishes covered in turf, are the only evidence that there is more below ground. The main gates have notices warning people to stay clear, with references to The Official Secrets Act and another notice refers to RAF Staxton Wold eleven miles away. I have wondered if the bases were connected at one time. By plotting a line through a local Ordnance Survey map, I noticed that the three bases run in a line. I also noted that the line runs directly through the burial mound known as Sharp Howe, an unusual place which is discussed later in the book.

I also considered the possible connections between the radio 'dead zone' mentioned to me on occasions by local trawlermen and reports of magnetic anomalies off Bempton and Flamborough, but without more research it is impossible to say what effect - if any - the three bases have had on anything connected with the accounts recorded here.

MISSING MEN

Of all the strange incidents in this part of North-East Yorkshire, the most tragic involve men who have disappeared. No one really seems to know what happened to them. They just vanished.

I wish to make it clear however, that I can make no connection between these multiple disappearances and the strange events reported within Truth-Proof. If patterns seem to emerge between the dates and times of these events and reports of strange happenings, they are out of my control. I am only the messenger who is simply gathering a collection of reports which are concentrated from within a small area.

Personally, I think the area itself acts as some kind of conduit for strange events and it is impossible to say which elements are or are not responsible for one another. I think it would take a major shift in our understanding of the phenomenon to accept this reality. Perhaps if that were to happen, then it might be possible to conduct a genuine study. Yet I am convinced that an unknown energy or life force exists in this area and I think whatever it is has been present, here and at other locations, long before mankind evolved the awareness to even notice. As early settlers evolved they knew and accepted these places were different, and over time they left their own monuments. Giant stones and ancient earthworks remain, like signals from the past, telling modern man that something more than bones and memory rest within the land.

In April 2010 I began to ask questions about eleven men who had seemingly vanished from the area of Bempton and Flamborough Head between 2004 to 2014. There were many things I wanted to know, questions that in the past I had kept to myself - primarily out of respect for the families that are still without their missing loved ones. In spite of this, I feel that the subject needs to be addressed. It cannot be denied that people *are* going missing in and around Bempton and Flamborough Head and it appears that no satisfactory answer has been found for any of the disappearances.

Bempton's three-hundred and fifty foot cliffs are well-known for suicides and in some recent newspaper reports, the area has been described as a 'known suicide spot'. With this in mind I began a thorough search of the archive at Bridlington library. I decided my starting point should be 1930, because if suicide was the main contributing factor in these disappearances, then going this far back into the archives might reveal some kind of pattern. I began my research by focussing only on key-words, but even working in this way I realised that studying over eighty years worth of newspapers would consume years of my time. Yet I was not deterred and in total my research took me over three years. I knew there had to be reasons why this small area of the country, within a thirty mile radius, was affected by so many disappearances. I began to realise that if, after looking at rational explanations and finding nothing, then the irrational had to be considered. Just because something is outside of our understanding, does not mean it is not happening.

I realised that before I started my research it would not only be about looking for accounts of missing people. Over the years this area has been associated with many strange events, so it was only right that I should study more than one specific group. Some might accuse me of mixing fact with fiction and indeed, it is true to say that some reports do seem to be other-worldly. Yet the people who have actually stepped forward to tell their strange stories are ordinary men and women, with nothing to gain but public ridicule.

My archive research revealed many strange and interesting things over the eighty year time period I was studying. I discovered that Bempton RAF radar station seemed to feature quite often in many reports of the missing. Indeed, it is a location where many unexplained lights have been seen and in its operational years, unidentified objects were tracked on its radar - even though many of these lights were so close in proximity to the base, radar would have been of no use. I found unexplained deaths at Flamborough, Bempton and at nearby Danes Dyke, as well as suspected suicides in and around the Bridlington area.

However, when suicide is not suspected and there are no suspicious circumstances, then it is not unreasonable to presume that something else has to be happening. Yet even after gathering together so many pieces of the puzzle, it seems that no pattern of suicide emerges. I say 'pattern' because in the past, when people have chosen to end their life at Bempton, their deaths are usually determined, without doubt, to be due to the person's history or state of mind shortly before they died. I also think the term 'known suicide spot' can be ruled out for the years before and after this cluster of eleven men who disappeared.

It is true that many suicides have been reported at Bempton and Flamborough and this will no doubt continue to be the case, but no more than any other location along the coast or inland. I think these areas gain notoriety when a person goes missing due to all the professional bodies that become engaged in the search - it therefore becomes bigger news. Looking through the years of old newspaper reports did not reveal that Bempton was a 'known suicide spot'. It is no different to other locations inland and rarely do the coastguard, lifeboat and Sea King helicopters get involved in the search for missing people outside of this area. It is my belief that there may be an unconscious attempt by some, to pin a rational explanation onto some of these deaths, simply because no other explanation can be found.

Statements such as, *"he must have fallen due to a lapse in concentration"* or *"he may have gotten into difficulties whilst walking"* are used for no other reason than that the authorities have no real clue. In the absence of any other, it seems that the only given theories are those which fit within our understanding. Perhaps this is due to man's mind-set, which seems fixed not to look beyond what is considered possible.

However, events outside of our understanding *are* taking place within this area. The multiple accounts of lightforms prove this. Now I do not claim that the missing men are connected in any way to these events, but to deny that the lightforms are real and that they do appear in the skies around this area, would be madness. Clusters of events *do* occur - and more than one would expect. This includes Bempton's missing men, whose disappearances fall into the mix of so many events of high strangeness that occur locally.

It could be pure coincidence that all the missing men chose to visit Bempton and Flamborough, before leaving this world without reason or trace. In which case, there is no mystery and we should just allow the disappearances to slip away into the history of the area. Yet there is a marked difference between the disappearances of the missing men detailed in this chapter and others who have tragically died or gone missing along the coast. For comparison, below are four examples which are no less important, but in these cases the facts were established very quickly and nothing unusual was said to have taken place.

53

On March 31st 2008, The Hull Daily Mail reported that local police were investigating two deaths within 12 hours of each other. At 5.30pm the Bempton coastguard were called after a report of a woman who had disappeared off the cliffs. Fishermen who were on the cliff-tops at the time say they saw a figure climb over the fence and disappear from view, adding that a loud noise was heard a few minutes later. A Sea King helicopter later pulled a woman from the sea who was pronounced dead on arrival at Scarborough Hospital. The police said that the woman's death was not being treated as suspicious. She was later identified as a sixty-four year old from Bridlington.

At 4.10am the following morning, police were called by a man reporting the death of an elderly man on Stone Pit Lane at Bempton. The caller was later arrested on suspicion of murder. A coastguard spokesperson said: *"There have been two deaths within a quarter of a mile of each other in twelve hours."* Police said at the time that the deaths were not believed to be connected and their investigations soon established that the woman's death was suicide and the elderly man had been murdered.

On June 15th 2009 Flamborough Lifeboat Station submitted the following news release to the RNLI.org website, as written by RNLI Press Officer Jane Heaton:

"Flamborough RNLI lifeboat crew respond to two calls for help in the Bempton area in one evening. Flamborough RNLI lifeboat launched for the first time at 4.08pm on Monday June 15th 2009 in response to a call that a man in his 60s with Alzheimer's disease had gone missing in the Bempton area. The lifeboat carried out a search for the missing man along the coastline, working from the Thornwick Bay area towards Bempton. The search was carried out in conjunction with the coastguard, RAF rescue helicopter and the police. Thankfully, the man was found safe and well, walking along Hoddy Crows Lane in Bempton by a local PCSO. [Police Community Support Officer.]

The second launch took place later the same evening at 6.17pm, with reports that a thirty-two year old woman was threatening to commit suicide over Bempton Cliffs. Despite having just left the boathouse following the earlier incident, the lifeboat crew were again quick on the scene. As they were on their way to assist in the rescue of the potential suicide, a message came through at 6.35pm that the Police had

managed to get the situation under control, so the RNLI [lifeboat]
'Elizabeth Jane Palmer', returned to base, hopefully for the last time that
evening."

The time frames in which these reports occurred are interesting, with nothing of any significance happening for long periods of time either before or after. However they cannot be classed as mysterious. They were pretty clear cut and the facts were established quickly, with no one in any doubt about what had happened. Yet the disappearances of Bempton's missing men offer no clues as to how or why they vanished.

The Missing Men Of Bempton 2004 To 2014

Although it is possible to find earlier reports of strange deaths and disappearances, I am concentrating on eleven that occurred between 2004 to 2014.

There is no real explanation as to why they all vanished, so can it be assumed that somehow they all 'got into difficulties' on the cliff-tops ? This is a sweeping statement which covers all but tells us nothing. Difficulties on the cliff-tops ? Did anyone stop to ask where they went afterwards ? How could so many people have got into difficulties then simply vanished ? Another suggestion put forward is that whilst in a day-dream they climbed the four foot high fence which runs along Bempton's cliff-tops and simply fell to their deaths. The fact is no one has a clue, but as far as the media are concerned, it is as though pre-prepared explanations are used and used again. Suicide being one of them.

John Deakin
Disappeared November 4th 2004

"How did my husband vanish off the face of the Earth ?" These words were spoken by John Deakin's wife. His disappearance was the first that caught my attention. Nothing about it seemed right.
John was fifty-three and from Sheffield and his strange disappearance has baffled everyone involved ever since he went missing. The mystery is no closer to being solved today than it was all those years before.

John had gone walking for the day around Flamborough Head and Bempton. He was an experienced walker who knew the area very well.

The police were able to trace his movements using signals from his cell phone and when the area was searched, his blue Renault Laguna car was found at North Landing car park in Flamborough Head, just four miles from Bempton. Along with the police, a helicopter and two lifeboats from Flamborough and Bridlington were also used in the search. Anyone familiar with Flamborough would agree, that this would have been a difficult enough task, but in November it is a bleak and lonely place to be. Yet this extensive search for John revealed no trace of him.

An appeal was made in the local press for information and one couple did come forward. They told the police that John had spoken to them on the day he disappeared. They said he asked them if he needed to pay to use the car park out of season. Another man came forward to say he had seen John leaning on an information board, just a short time before setting off along the cliff path. From that point nothing more is known about his movements.

John was described as white, average build and around five feet six tall. He had black thinning hair, brown eyes and wore glasses. He was a keen walker who had never gone missing in the past and he had no history of depression. Yet his walking boots, walking stick and uneaten sandwiches were still inside his car. The cliff-tops would have been a keen walker's first choice destination after parking at North Landing car park. But why did he leave his most important items for the walk inside the car ? Was he distracted ? And if so, by what ? And why would a person who may have been intending to take his own life concern himself with the price of a parking ticket ?

John's wife was adamant that her husband would not have done anything to harm himself. She added that their daughter was expecting a baby and he had everything to live for. None of the circumstances surrounding John's disappearance make any sense. Nothing seems to fit. He took everything he needed for a day's walking, but left them in the car. He was seen studying a nearby information board, but knew the area well. What could he have been looking for - or waiting for ?

Quite a period of time passed before the next report was made of a man missing in strange circumstances.

Coastal search for missing man

POLICE from three forces joined three coastguards units and a lifeboat crew to search for a man who has been missing for a week.

Officers are increasingly anxious to trace John Deakin after his car, containing his walking stick, boots and uneaten sandwiches was found at Flamborough Head.

A search involving officers from Humberside Police and South Yorkshire Police and a police helicopter was launched over the week-end.

Coastguard units from Speeton, Flamborough and Bridlington also took part a n d Flamborough Lifeboat launched for 40 minutes last Saturday afternoon.

On Monday, North Yorkshire Police joined in as the search was extended towards Reighton, follow-

Missing – John Deakin.

ing reports Mr Deakin may have been in the village last Thursday, the day he went missing from his home in Stannington, Sheffield.

His blue Renault Laguna was later found at Flamborough Head, but at the time the Free Press went to print, there had

been no sightings of Mr Deakin.

The 53-year-old is said to be a keen walker who has never gone missing before. he is 5ft 6ins tall, of medium build, with brown eyes and black hair which is thinning on top.

He wears glasses and was last seen dressed in a navy jumper, grey fleece top and dark trousers.

Anyone who may have seen Mr Deakin should contact South Yorkshire Police on 0114 296 4304.

<u>Six years and three months later...</u>

Russell Bohling
Disappeared March 2nd 2010

Russell Bohling was only eighteen years of age when he went missing.
In many ways his disappearance caused more of a mystery, due in part
to the relentless insistence of his parents that the search had to
continue - and rightly so. Newspaper reports at the time suggested that
Russell had disappeared in mysterious circumstances and while I believe
this to be true, it is no more mysterious than the others contained within
these pages.
Russell was a regular student at Bishop Burton College near Beverley
and had a full driving licence. He was said to be very happy with his
studies and life in general - attributes generally associated with a well-
adjusted young adult. He was, however, described as 'vulnerable' due to
a speech disorder. The word 'vulnerable' can be used to mean more than
one thing when describing a person. Obviously his parents knew him
better than anyone else, but anyone with children will know that they
can take on a completely different persona when outside of the family
environment. I may be wrong, but personally I do not think that having a
speech disorder somehow makes a person vulnerable.

His family's blue Renault Clio car was found at the RSPB nature reserve
at Bempton, after Russell had driven it there and paid for a days
parking. Like John Deakin before him, this simple action suggests to me
that Russell may not have taken his own life. Whatever he had in mind
required time and if my own intention was to commit suicide, the last
thing on my mind would be to pay a days parking fee. From this point
trail ends and apart from the parking ticket and the car, no trace of
Russell has been found since. A massive search involving police, the
coastguard, and an underwater search unit failed to find any evidence of
Russell. Reports stated that nothing could be found to indicate Russell
had suicidal tendencies and police said that if he had fallen from
Bempton Cliffs, they would have expected to have found a body.

Many theories arose in an attempt to explain how or why Russell had
disappeared. His parents feared that he may have been killed. They
spoke of an inheritance of over £300,000 which he was due to receive

and it was suggested that this may have, in some way, been connected to his disappearance. Humberside Police even called in outside help to assess whether or not to treat Russell's disappearance as murder. Another suggestion was that Russell simply wanted to run away. Although if that was the case, then surely it would have made more sense for him to have waited until he received his inheritance ? It is so difficult to second guess someone's actions when the details make no sense.

Russell was said to have shown an interest in the alleged 'satanic' paintings that adorn the walls of RAF Bempton's derelict underground bunker. It is true that its subterranean walls are covered in sexually explicit paintings of naked women with horns and are accompanied by images of pentagrams and suggestive writing. Now the paintings cannot be denied, since they are a fact. So at some time in Bempton's past, something dark and secretive appears to have taken place below ground. Soon after this, stories of witchcraft and activities of an occult nature grew, so it has become difficult to separate fact from fiction. But I wonder, would a secretive satanic cult leave such a calling card in the form of paintings ?

It is known that at 7.30am on March 2nd, Russell had been online and viewed a website about RAF Bempton. This was just thirty minutes before he left home and was never seen again. His parents had said that Russell had a USB memory stick containing images of the underground bunker, although the memory stick has never been found.

Early into the search for Russell, his parents were convinced that his body lay somewhere within the bunker. They thought he could have been lured there and killed, although no evidence was found to support this. At the time, Russell's mother questioned why the police were conducting a 1.5km radius search. Together with mounted police, the search continued for a number of days, covering the RSPB nature reserve car park, nearby ditches and buildings - yet they did not search the bunker. Those involved in the search were informed that, before he disappeared, Russell had been looking at online plans of RAF Bempton, so searching the bunker should have surely been a priority ?

Five days after his disappearance a search of the complex was finally carried out, although some sections were flooded and could not be accessed. Heat-sensitive cameras were used initially, but they would have been ineffective in the flooded areas. It is also thought that the first search was held back to an extent, due to the presence of asbestos within the bunker. However, fire and rescue services would have had access to protective clothing and breathing equipment to deal with toxic environments. We will never know why an extensive search of RAF Bempton was not carried out in the earliest stages of Russell's disappearance.

Three years later, on Wednesday February 27th 2013, it was reported that Humberside Fire and Rescue Service had carried out an extensive search of the RAF Bempton site. It was done in the form of a training exercise and all areas were searched. The sealed bunker was reopened by the existing land owner, at a cost of approximately £1000. This new search was partly due to the continued pressure of Russell's parents, who paid for this out of their own pockets. They wanted to know once and for all if their son's body was in the bunker. The fire service allowed Russell's parents to sit with the operations manager throughout the search, which was conducted over a three hour period. This time the search included all of the flooded areas which had been missed in the first searches. Sadly, no sign of their son was found.

On January 16th 2015, I called Humberside Fire and Rescue Service to ask for dates of when the searches were actually carried out. I received a call back on the same day and was told that two searches were made; one on March 7th 2010 and another on September 15th 2010. No mention of the bunker being reopened and searched in February 2013 was made. Russell's family believed his interest in the abandoned bunker was the key to his disappearance. The missing memory stick that contained information about the bunkers dark past suggests a link. A simple search online can bring up lots of information about RAF Bempton. I wonder if Russell's memory stick could have contained additional information about the bunker which was unknown outside of a select few. His family believe he was murdered, although the police treated his disappearance as a missing person's case. There the trail ends in the search for Russell Bohling. His disappearance is now just another mystery added to Bempton's past.

Appeal for news of missing man

Bridlington Free Press - March 11th 2010

POLICE are appealing for information on the whereabouts of an East Yorkshire teenager who went missing at Bempton Cliffs last week.

Russell Bohling, 18, from West Ella, is being treated as missing after last being seen by his family on Tuesday, March 2.

His car was discovered at the RSPB car park at Bempton Cliffs and police are appealing for help in finding him.

Russell is described as white, around 5ft 8ins tall and with a medium build. He has short, straight, brown hair.

He was last seen wearing a black Ben Sherman jacket, blue jeans and black leather trainers. He suffers from communication difficulties.

His father, Roger Bohling, said: "He is an 18-year-old boy who has got no interest in bird sanctuaries.

"He bought a pay and display ticket and I think he has intended to come home and something has then happened.

"We can't help but think some sort of foul play has happened to him, otherwise we can't understand why he hasn't contacted us.

"He went to meet somebody there because it's not a place he would go.

"He has a speech and language disorder he has had since birth and he doesn't always fully understand what people are saying to him.

"He can say 'Yes, all right', without really understanding the impact of what somebody is saying to him, so that makes him vulnerable because he could go along with something not really understanding what was happening."

The search along the coast is continuing and involves mounted police, underwater search units, the coastguard and a search and rescue helicopter from RAF Leconfield.

Flamborough Lifeboat was launched on Wednesday, March 3 at 8.38am after receiving a call to assist police in the search.

In freezing cold conditions and a Northerly swell, the volunteer crew scoured the area at the bottom of Bempton cliffs.

However after just over an hour they were stood down by the coastguard and returned to base at 10am.

Officers are continuing to search the area in order to try and locate him.

Missing Person Officer PC Steve Norfolk, of Humberside Police, said: "We are continuing to grow increasingly concerned at this time as this is totally out of character for Russell, who has been missing for a week now.

"Again, we are asking for Russell or anyone who may have seen him to contact us in order for us to locate him as soon as possible."

Police are appealing for Russell or anyone who knows his current whereabouts to contact Humberside Police on 0845 6060222 quoting log 55 03/03/10.

David Binns
Disappeared September 9th 2010

When the East Yorkshire newspapers reported that 'tunnels were being searched' for a missing man, I knew what they were referring to even before I read the next line.

It was reported that Humberside Police were searching for a missing fifty-nine year old named David Binns. They were hoping to find him in the underground bunker at the former RAF Bempton. Why they chose to search the bunker so quickly is not known. In the case of Russell Bohling, it took five days before a search of the bunker was made. David was described as white, about five feet seven to five feet eight tall and of small build. He had grey hair, was balding and wore glasses. At the time he disappeared, he was wearing a brown fleece jacket, jeans and brown suede shoes. He was last seen at his home in Otley, West Yorkshire, around 6am on Thursday September 9th. His grey Renault Clio car was found abandoned at North Landing car park, Flamborough, at about 7.45pm on Saturday September 11th. Information regarding David's disappearance is limited, so I cannot find any information that states the location of his car between those dates. It may have been there for the entire three days.

The car park is four miles away from RAF Bempton, yet for some reason the base was one of the first places the authorities chose to search. Along with helicopters and the local coastguard, the Humberside Police searched the area but found no trace of the missing man. It was as though David Binns had vanished off the face of the Earth.

Seven months and five days later...

Two Bodies Found

At around 6.48pm on Thursday April 14th 2011 police, paramedics, the RLNI coastguard team from Flamborough and an RAF Sea King search and rescue helicopter rushed to Flamborough's North Landing. A week later it was reported in the Bridlington Free Press that the search had been for a seventy-nine year old man from Scarborough, who had fallen down the cliffs at North Landing.

The report does not state whether anyone saw the man fall, but he *was* found. Unfortunately, attempts to revive him were unsuccessful and he was declared dead on arrival at Hull Royal Infirmary. The following week, on April 28th, the same newspaper reported that the man was thought to have fallen down the cliffs. For me, the use of the word 'thought' suggests that no one really knew how he came to be at the bottom of those cliffs.

Eleven days later...

On Monday April 25th two kayakers, who were in an area of sea called Breil Nook, close to North Landing, discovered a body floating in the water. The alarm was raised and a coastguard search and rescue team from Bridlington, along with the police and ambulance service, were called. The body of a man was recovered from the sea and brought ashore by the Flamborough lifeboat team. He was sixty years old and thought to be from West Yorkshire.

A police spokesperson said at the time that the man's death was not thought to be suspicious, yet in the space of eleven days the bodies of two men had been found, with no real clues as to how they had died.

UNEXPLAINED OBJECT: What the CCTV camera saw ... the ball of light meanders down the street ... it crosses over to the Rose and Crown pub and pauses outside the first floor living room window ... and then slips silently through it. The footage has been a hit with locals and villagers wanting a look.

Strange object is caught on camera

By Alan Brook

alan.brook@yrnltd.co.uk

THERE is a spooky new attraction at a village pub - and everyone wants to see it.

Regulars and local residents at the Rose and Crown in High Street, Flamborough, have almost been queuing up to take a look.

The star attraction is what the pub's CCTV cameras caught in the early hours of last Sunday morning.

In a jaw-dropping couple of seconds, a mysterious ball of white light can be seen travelling across the deserted street at about first floor height, before pausing outside the pub's upstairs living room window - and then disappearing through it!

The unexplained object was captured on camera at exactly 1.16am by one of the pub's security cameras on the corner of High Street and Greenside Road, which points toward North End.

Gerry Ellis, landlord at the Rose and Crown, has been left puzzled.

He said: "We have no idea what it is. My wife Janice and I were asleep at the time and our two sons were staying with friends."

He said there was nothing unusual in their living room when they got up and he is completely in the dark about his weird visitation.

The CCTV footage has now become an attraction in the village.

Mr Ellis said: "I have had people bringing their children to see it.

"It only takes a few seconds, but it's the look on their faces, they are puzzled and amazed at the same time."

Having seen several examples of supposed unexplained happenings, UFOs, ghostly figures, and faces of the famous appearing on slices of toast, I was not phased by tales of the phantom ball of light at the Rose and Crown - until I saw it.

After several replays of the footage, I ruled out someone shining a torch in the street.

Could it be a searchlight from a police or rescue helicopter, I asked?

"No it isn't," said Gerry, "Because it then comes back out of the window and disappears up the street just after 2am!"

With a quick fast forward of the recording, at exactly 2am the glowing ball of light does just that!

I was stumped, so is Gerry and so are most of his regulars. Does he believe in things that go bump in the night, alien forces and ghostly happenings?

"Well, half and half, but I can't explain this at all," he said.

So far, no-one has come up with an explanation of what it could actually be - or is it really a ghost, a UFO, or something never to be explained?

WHAT DO YOU THINK?

● Do you know what the mystery object is? Did you see it anywhere else in the village? What do you think it is?

Send us your comments by email at: newsdesk@bridlingtonfreepress, or call our newsdesk on 677338.

Landlord Gerry Ellis points to the upstairs pub window that the object appears to float into.

Mysterious Light Recorded

On April 28th 2011 the Bridlington Free Press newspaper also reported that a mysterious light had been captured on security cameras in Flamborough town centre. Their front page displays a still from the footage, which had first been recorded at 1.16am by CCTV cameras on Sunday April 24th. The camera belonged to the Rose and Crown public house and was mounted outdoors to record the exterior of the pub and part of the high street.

The remarkable footage clearly depicts a slow moving ball of glowing white light, which moves slowly across the empty street. At first it appears to pause for a moment outside the upper floor window of the pub. It can then be seen to change direction and literally move through the closed window and into the landlords upstairs living room. The footage clearly shows the ball of light pass through the closed window and into the property. Anyone viewing the recording can clearly see this independent ball of light enter the premises, but what perhaps is not considered is *how* it is able to pass through the glass. If we were to shine a torch at a piece of glass, the light would naturally pass through it to light up the room inside. This footage shows that the ball of light does exactly the same thing.

After the landlord of the pub Gerry Ellis, had viewed this segment of film, he forwarded the recording to around the 2am mark. The glowing ball of light is then seen to reappear from inside the upper room, where it passes though the glass of the closed window and outdoors once more. Then it slowly makes its way up the street and off into the distance. I spoke with Mr Ellis a few days after the report had appeared in the newspaper. Neither he nor his family had reported anything out of the ordinary on the night before the light appeared.

It would be easy to say that at 2am the sphere re-emerged from out of the pub, then turned right and disappeared up the street. However these spheres of light seem able to travel in any direction without giving any indication that they have turned either one way or the other. I am not sure that they even have to turn at all. We tend to think of things as having a front, a back and sides, but these spheres of light seem to exhibit an intelligence and offer no clue how they seem to be able to travel in any direction, without giving any indication that they have turned either one way or the other. Mr Ellis told me that many people had come into the pub asking to see the CCTV footage, but so far nobody had been able to offer him any explanation of what it could have been. Although no connection can be made between the recording of this unusual lightform and the recovery of the two deceased men mentioned earlier, it is nevertheless an interesting story of an event that occurred between their deaths in April 2011.

Two years and six months later...

Brian Torbett
Disappeared October 22nd 2013

The car of fifty-nine year old Brian Torbett was found at Bempton Cliffs on October 22nd 2013. He was thought to have gone missing from his home in Bridlington sometime on the previous day. Sixteen days later on November 7th a human leg was found on the nearby beach of Reighton Sands, Filey. DNA testing confirmed that the leg belonged to Mr Torbett.

Earlier that week on Sunday November 3rd, fisherman Andrew Colling spotted what he thought was a seal in the water. On closer inspection however, he realised that it was not a seal, but in fact a partially decomposed human body. Mr Colling attempted to pull the remains to a safer place on the beach and for a short time was able to hold onto it. Unfortunately a large wave washed over the body and pulled it from his grasp. It was then washed back out to sea and lost. The leg was found four days later along the same stretch of beach.
At a hearing in 2014 Coroner Michael Oakley stated,
"To reach a conclusion that [Brian Torbett] *took his own life, not withstanding the history, I have to be satisfied beyond reasonable doubt and I cannot be so satisfied. Equally, I cannot be so satisfied to reach the conclusion that this was an accident and that he entered the water and drowned. We have no evidence to fully disclose the means by which he came to his death, so I am going to reach an open conclusion."*

We have to accept that there is no evidence to show how Mr Torbett died, therefore his death remains a mystery.

Simon Hodgson
Disappeared December 20th 2013

Simon Hodgson, also known as Simon Greaves, was aged forty-eight when his family last saw him at their home in Riccall, North Yorkshire. He was last seen at the RSPB nature reserve car park in Bempton on the December 20th 2013, shortly before his disappearance. His Citroën C15 camper van was found a day later on December 21st.

Simon was described as white, about six feet tall and of slim build. He had sandy coloured hair, a greying beard and moustache, blue eyes and wore spectacles. A North Yorkshire Police spokesperson said he was known to dress very smartly and often wore a tweed jacket with a shirt and scarf. At the time the police said that Simon was known to take frequent camping trips and liked to go walking, but said they were concerned for his safety and were exploring the possibility that he may have got into difficulties while out walking. Simon was yet another regular walker who had simply vanished without a trace.

Police team up with charity in search for missing man

Bridlington Free Press - January 9th 2014

BY MIKE BROWN
mike.brown@jpress.co.uk
Twitter: @MBrownFreePress

Police have renewed their appeal to find Simon Hodgson-Greaves who was reported missing on December 21.

Officers have teamed up with the Missing People charity to help boost their appeal, and released a new picture of Mr Hodgson-Greaves.

Concern for the 48-year-old, from Riccall, near Selby, was raised when his camper van was found unoccupied at the RSPB visitor centre car park on Bempton Cliffs near Bridlington. He was last seen with the van the day before, Friday December 20, at the same location.

PC Scott Gatman of Selby Safer Neighbourhood Team, said: "Simon's family are worried sick about him and just want him home. I am appealing to any members of the public, including motorists, public transport workers, passengers and walkers who believe they have seen Simon or given him a lift since Friday 20 December to contact the police as a matter of urgency.

"Better still, if Simon sees or hears this appeal, please get in touch with friends, family, the police or the Missing People charity and let us know that you are safe and well.

"The Missing People charity can be contacted in confidence if you do not want to contact the police."

Simon was last seen by a member of his family on Sunday 15 December. He is known to go on frequent camping trips and likes to go walking. He also has an interest in the RSPB and had visited the area in the past. It is now known that Simon had been staying in his van on and off for a number of weeks.

Although it is not unusual for Simon be away for days at a time, police are growing increasingly for his safety due to his lack of contact with his family and his lack of shelter.

Officers are exploring the possibility that Simon had gone walking in the area and may have got into difficulties. Or that he may have left the area on foot, perhaps using public transport or has been given a lift by a member of the public.

Humberside Police have searched the Bempton Cliffs area on foot and using air support, but there was no sign of Simon.

Simon is described as white, around 6ft tall and of slim build.

He has sandy coloured hair, a greying beard and moustache, blue eyes and wears spectacles. It is not known what he will be wearing, however, he is known to dress smartly and often wears tweed jackets, shirts and scarves.

Anyone with any information is asked to contact North Yorkshire Police on 101, select option 1 and pass information to the Force Control Room.

The Missing People charity can be contacted on 116 000, the line is open 24 hours a day and information can be passed confidentially.

Approximately two weeks earlier...

Encounter With A Stranger
A Personal Experience

Of all the disappearances detailed so far, Simon Hodgson's is the most interesting for me personally. My investigations into the unexplained have unearthed many strange stories and it is true to say that people began to take an interest in what I was researching. People began contacting me to report their own 'big cat' sightings from around the area and others wanted to tell me about the strange things they had seen in the sky. Yet despite making it known in local newspapers that I was researching events of high strangeness, no one came forward with any information about the alleged satanic cult at RAF Bempton and no one mentioned anything to me about the missing men. I was beginning to think that I was the only person in the world who thought the disappearances of these men were odd. Then again, perhaps most of us lead such hectic lives, that news items become irrelevant to us after a few weeks.

I want to relate an incident that I experienced personally, during late November 2013, while I was with my wife.

It was one of those bright but very cold days, just before the real onset of winter. At around one fifteen in the afternoon we had to go to a local computer shop, which was about a ten minute walk or so from our home. As we walked along the street I noticed a man on the opposite side, who was sitting on a wall. He caught my attention immediately as I could see that he was not wearing a shirt and although the day was bright and sunny, it was cold. So it just did not seem right.

Leaning beside him was an old green bicycle with a worn, brown leather bag on the back. The bike had rusty wheels and looked like it belonged in a museum. It seemed so out of place. My wife noticed that it didn't even have any brakes.
He was sitting there casually reading a newspaper, but what caught my attention was his body. I remember thinking to myself, *"wow, he looks like he would be a handful if he was crossed."*
He looked to be about six feet tall, pale skinned with a bald head and was very lean and muscular. Even from across the street I could see

thick blue veins in his upper arms. He had a clean sharp appearance about him that, like the bike beside him, just seemed out of place. I should point out that in my younger years I was known for my own strength and fitness, so I knew that I was looking at a body that was quite distinct.

He looked over to me and shouted. *"You have brought down the light."*
I smiled without really registering what he had said and replied,
"Yes enjoy it. We will not have many more days like this."
At that point I thought he was referring to bright weather and sunshine. Even then it seemed a strange thing to do - the road is very wide at that point, almost seventy-five feet at its widest point and yet here was this total stranger shouting over to us. He shouted again,
"You know what you are doing, you have brought down the light."
I looked at my wife with a raised eyebrow.
"Yes," I shouted back. *"Enjoy and have a good day !"*

Yet again he called over to us about the problems I was causing by 'bringing down the light', but I chose not to look or listen this time. We rounded the corner and were now out of sight, but for some reason I felt very unsettled by this strange looking man. I could not get the image of him out of my head. I even considered walking back a different way on our return and entering the street from the other end, just so we would not have to pass him on the way back - which was crazy as I had no way of knowing if he would even be there when we returned.
I told myself I was being stupid. He was just a man, nothing more. We finished off at the computer shop and within minutes we were heading back home. I doubt that more than twenty minutes had passed, but as we rounded the corner on our return, there he was again. Now he was sitting on the wall on the other side of the street. The side we were walking on. I said to my wife, *"Oh God it's that strange man. He's on our side of the road now."*

Even though we were over two hundred metres away I knew it was him. He was now wearing a tight-fitting dark brown pullover and wore black wraparound sunglasses, but he was still unmistakable. I cannot explain why, but I really felt as though he was waiting for us.
He had his back to us as we approached the corner, then he turned and spoke. How he knew it was us I will never know, but once again he spoke about the light. I don't know why we stopped, but we did and he began to talk. He seemed so clever with his words and even now it's

70

difficult to comprehend what they meant, since everything he said had a double meaning. He explained to me that I was 'causing lots of trouble' and that I was 'bringing down the light'. He said I knew what I was doing and had to stop. He kept on warning me that I had to stop bringing down the light. Every time he spoke and I answered, he replied with the opposite of what he had originally asked, turning my reply into some kind of insult. It was almost as though my answer had upset him, but the questions he asked me in the first place, required the answers I gave. If this sounds confusing, believe me, it was.

He spoke of politics and religion and implied one view, then when I answered him he somehow turned what he had said into the complete opposite. I just could not untangle his words, yet for some crazy reason we stood and listened. It was as though his presence had us captured. I have never been a man to shy away from confrontation, but I felt very uneasy standing before this strange man. We could definitely feel danger and warnings in his tone and overall presence. At one point he reached out and placed his right hand on my wife's right shoulder. Then he looked at me and there was a spell of silence - just for a moment, like a frozen second.

I could not see his eyes behind the dark glasses but I felt he was gauging my reaction. I instantly knew that if I tried to remove his hand we would have been in conflict. I just knew it. It was a test of something inside me and I think he knew what I was thinking and what my reaction was going to be. He was not threatening towards my wife in a physical sense, he just did this and then looked at me saying,
"I'm not talking to her, it's you. You are causing lots of trouble. You are bringing down the light. You have to know what you are doing. You have to stop bringing down the light."
Afterwards I asked myself why I didn't question him about the light he was talking about. It's the kind of thing I would have expected someone else to do. I suppose it shows that in such strange circumstances rational thinking can be none existent.
By now I knew that we had to move on. The situation did not feel good and was beginning to feel threatening. I remember glancing over at his beat-up old bicycle, which was still propped up on the other side of the road, then I looked back at him. His black wraparound sunglasses gave no hint of the person behind them. At this point I think it's worth mentioning that I could tell now that he was not over six feet tall, as I

had first thought. He was about five feet eight, so only a little taller than me at five feet six and if I had to guess his age, I would have said about thirty-five, although I couldn't be sure. I remember looking at his face to try and figure him out, but I couldn't. He seemed wrinkle-free, but devoid of any expression and he had a pale pink tinge to his skin that could have been make-up. *"Where are you from"* I asked.

"Riccall." He replied. I had to ask again, because the word made no sense to me. *"I'm from Riccall"* he said, but his words meant absolutely nothing to me. I'm not even sure what my reply was, but I had heard enough and knew it was time we left. As we began to walk away he remained at the bottom of the road, still shouting about the light and how I was causing big trouble. *"You know what you are doing. You have to stop calling down the light,"* he called out to us.

We could still hear him as we walked into our home. Once we were inside my wife said the strangest thing. She looked right at me and said in a calm voice, *"That man frightened me. I think he was an alien."* I have to say that she does not share my interest in the unexplained, so for her to say something like that is strange in itself. I walked into the living room and immediately switched on the TV. I quickly scrolled down the on-screen options and pressed the keypad. I wanted to see what he was up to via our CCTV, but he had already gone. Chances are that he had immediately walked across the road, then got on his bike and left.

A few days later a friend from the local barbers shop at the bottom of the street spoke to me. He asked about the man we had been talking to and told us that he had been observing him for a while before we arrived. At the time our friend thought that the man was waiting for someone. He commented on how unusual he looked and remembers seeing him talking to us, but then didn't really pay any further attention, because he presumed it was us he had been waiting for. This strange encounter affected me so much that at the time I wrote down as much detail of the encounter as I could remember. I know his interaction with us was some kind of warning and I am not usually intimidated by anyone, but this man had me on edge. I also recall trying to remember where he had said he was from, because at the time I just could not remember the name of the place. Then a few weeks later I read in the newspaper of Simon Hodgson's disappearance. The report stated that he came from Riccall and I instantly remembered that this was where the strange man had said he was from.

Yet Riccall is almost fifty miles away from my home and the stranger had a rusty old bike without brakes. I am not suggesting there is any connection between the stranger we met and Simon Hodgson's disappearance. How could I ? I have no evidence in the slightest, but I am telling the truth about our experience on that cold day in November 2013. Perhaps it was simply a strange coincidence ? I'm not sure.

A few months later I had a conversation with my friend Brenda Butler. Brenda co-authored a book called Sky Crash, which documented the strange events in Rendlesham Forest in December 1980. I told Brenda about the unusual man that my wife and I had encountered and she listened with interest. Brenda's own experiences at Rendlesham Forest have taught her that nothing is impossible. She then told me of something similar happening at Rendlesham. Apparently a man was reported to have told people that 'they had brought down the light'. Brenda then told me of her own encounter with a strange man named David Daniels. He just appeared one day at her home and ended up staying with Brenda for a few weeks. Her description of David Daniels is nothing like the man we encountered, but she was convinced that he was no normal human being.

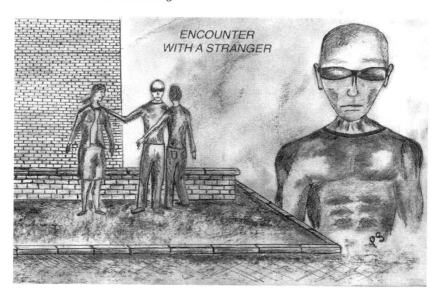

Thirty-four days after Simon Hodgson's disappearance...

Edward Machin
Disappeared January 23rd 2014

On Thursday January 23rd 2014 thirty-nine year old Edward Machin had left his home in York. He was last seen in Bempton, then he simply vanished leaving no clues as to how or why.

It is known that Edward had purchased a return train ticket to Bempton. Then because of problems with the train service he had to leave the train in Scarborough. From there he completed his journey to Bempton travelling by taxi, which would have taken around thirty minutes. He was last seen that afternoon leaving the taxi outside the White Horse pub in Bempton at about 12.30pm. It is worth pointing out that the public house is on the corner of a single track road called Cliff Lane, which leads to the RSPB nature reserve and RAF Bempton. Aside from the pub, the only other main focal point in the village is the local church. Edward is then thought to have made his way on foot towards the nature reserve. CCTV footage from Town Criers Cottage on the High Street, close to the pub, certainly suggests this is what happened.

Edward was described as five feet four in height and of slim build with short brown hair and blue eyes. He was wearing a dark coloured jacket, T-shirt and jeans. The police conducted house-to-house enquiries in the village, along with cliff-top searches with rescue officers and volunteers. Edward's family said at the time that everything that happened was completely out of character. Extensive searches of the surrounding area continued over a period of weeks, but nothing was ever found. Edward Machin had just vanished without trace.

Seven days later...

Nigel Savage
Reported Missing January 30th 2014

Although the disappearance of Nigel Savage cannot be connected to the areas of Bempton and Flamborough, the circumstances in which he vanished are very similar to other disappearances. I include the account here simply due to the location and the timeframe in which it happened. Forty-nine year old Nigel Savage was from Beverley in East Yorkshire. He was described as six feet tall and of medium build. He was bald, had green eyes and a little facial stubble. He was driving to the coast that day for a fishing trip and took his two Springer Spaniel dogs with him in the car. He drove to a place called Burniston, just nineteen miles north of Bempton Cliffs and was never seen again.

At around 4pm that afternoon a woman reported seeing the two dogs and a rucksack and fishing gear on the cliff-tops, but she saw no sign of Mr Savage at all. Some newspapers later reported that when the two dogs were found, one of them was on a ledge below the cliff-edge. This suggests that Nigel might have fallen as he attempted to rescue the dog. However, the fact that *both* of the dogs had been seen together earlier suggests otherwise. Just before 3.30am the next morning Nigel's green Peugeot 206 car was found in a lay-by at Crook Ness, Field Lane, Burniston.

A massive search was launched involving a rescue helicopter from RAF Boulmer in Northumberland, coastguard lifeboat teams from Scarborough, Burniston and Ravenscar and many volunteers. The search was later moved inland along the cliff-top paths and towards Burniston village. By the early morning, the lifeboat crews had stood down after their extensive search had found nothing.

It is impossible to say what happened to Nigel Savage, as with many of these unfortunate men, each disappearance was so unexpected and final. Any evidence that could offer clues to the truth is none existent and all we have are suggestion and assumption. In the absence of a plausible explanation, the authorities have to offer an opinion on what they believe happened, which has to fit within what is considered normal. No one would ever accept an implausible theory which suggests that an unknown phenomena may be at work. To accept that such a possible truth is responsible for people going missing is unthinkable.

Police looking for missing man after huge search

Scarborough News - February 2nd 2014

Nigel Savage has not been seen since Thursday

BY CARL GAVAGHAN
carl.gavaghan@jpress.co.uk
Twitter: @carlgavaghan

A massive air and sea search was launched near Burniston after an angler failed to return home after a fishing trip.

Scarborough's inshore and all-weather lifeboats were launched on Friday to join in the search with an RAF Sea King helicopter.

Nigel Savage, 49, from Beverley, was reported missing to Humberside Police just after 1am on Friday after he failed to return home following a fishing trip with his two springer spaniel dogs to Burniston the previous day.

Mr Savage's green coloured Peugeot 206 car was located later in the day in a lay-by at Crook Ness, Field Lane, Burniston, and the two springer spaniel dogs were found at the cliffs near by.

His rucksack and some fishing tackle have been located on the cliffs but there was no sign of Mr Savage.

Humber Coastguard co-ordinated the search and rescue operation.

A search and rescue helicopter from RAF Boulmer, and Scarborough RNLI, along with Coastguard rescue teams from Scarborough, Burniston and Ravenscar, went to the scene but they could not find Mr Savage.

Mike Green, Humber Coastguard watch manager, said: "It was quite a complex operation. The local coastline has very steep, craggy cliffs."

Public urged to be on look-out

SIGHTINGS SOUGHT
Nigel Savage is described as white, 6ft tall with a medium build. He is bald with facial stubble and has green eyes. He is believed to be wearing dark coloured Craghopper trousers and a dark coloured outdoor jacket.

Police would like to speak to anyone who saw Nigel Savage in the area of Burniston and the cliff location or anybody that has had any contact with him since 8am on Thursday.

Anyone who can provide police with information about his whereabouts is asked to call Humberside Police on 101 quoting log 14 of 31 January 2014.

<u>Three months and twenty-six days later...</u>

Mark Haddenham
Found May 25th 2014

On May 29th the Bridlington Free Press reported that the body of a man
had been found in an area of water known locally as Crab Rocks, below
Bempton Cliffs.

The man was named Granville Mark Haddenham who lived in the nearby
village of Buckton with his wife Jacqueline and their family. He was a
special effects expert in the movie industry and had worked on many big
film projects during his career. At the time of his death he was working
in Watford near London, on the new movie 'Dracula Untold'. He had
returned home from work the night before to spend the weekend with
his wife and family. Jacqueline had said that Mark was not depressed or
in a stressed state, but did say that his job was very demanding. She
explained that it would not have been unusual for him to spend a little
quiet time alone to 'think things through' and that he had left home on
the morning of Sunday 25th to 'clear his head.'

It is believed that after leaving home at 8am Mr Haddenham drove the
ten minutes distance from his home in Buckton, to the RSPB nature
reserve car park. After that nothing more is known about his
movements. Later in the year on October 7th, the Hull Daily Mail
reported that a member of the public had seen a body in the water at
8.50am on that Sunday morning in May. The report stated that the body
was about 150 metres out from Bempton Cliffs and floating face down in
the water.

Mr Haddenham's body was recovered by the local lifeboat rescue team
and taken to South Landing in Flamborough. A post-mortem
examination found that he had died from multiple injuries, as would be
expected from a fall from a three-hundred foot sheer drop. Police and
members of Bridlington coastguard carried out an extensive search of
the area, where they found a patch of flattened grass on Bempton cliff-
tops. There were also a number of heart-shaped stickers, some red
beads and some red carnation petals stuck to the top of a nearby fence-
post. This fence is approximately a metre high and runs along the top of
Bempton Cliffs. Beyond the fence is a 'track' which leads to the cliff-

edge. In a report by The Yorkshire Post, police officer Andrew Redshaw said they had found nothing suspicious. There is a waist-high fence around the perimeter of the area which is "easily accessible."

No suicide note was found and at an inquest, to try and establish the circumstances of Mark's death, his wife said she did not think her husband intended to end his life. She said: *"It was a particular job he was worrying about, but that is why he went off to drive somewhere quiet. It was no more problematic than most things at work. He was a very creative thinker and I think, if anything, he would have been distracted while walking."*
She added that it was unlikely the flower petals were her husbands, since he did not like carnations. Recording an open conclusion, the coroner for Hull and East Riding, Rosemary Baxter, said, *"I can find no evidence* [that suicide] *was what the deceased intended. He did not appear to be depressed, he had a lot to live for and he had no financial worries."*

The following comment from the Yorkshire Post newspaper shared an interesting quote by the coastguard, *'Watch manager at Humber Coastguard Mike Green said, "instances of people falling over the cliffs were very unusual."'* I find the coastguard's use of the word 'unusual' fits perfectly into this set of circumstances, especially where it is said that a man with no real life problems, apart from challenging pressures of work, is found dead in tragic circumstances.

I have visited Bempton's cliff-tops and the nearby nature reserve many times, to try and make sense of what could have happened to Mark Haddenham. I have stood at the metre high fence on the cliff-top and looked out to sea. This fence is not right out on the edge of the cliffs, it is set back. In some places it lies between fifteen and thirty feet from the edge. If someone was to slide under or climb over it, it would be impossible to simply fall over the edge of the cliff without walking on a little further. It seems logical to me that someone who is so deep into a train of thought would need to take a break from their concentration, before choosing to climb over this fence and proceed to the cliff edge. In my opinion that such a person would almost have to be in some kind of 'hypnotic trance' to do so unintentionally. There is no evidence to suggest that this is what happened in this case at all, but nothing happens without reason.

In an attempt to work out what could have happened to Mark, on January 4th 2015 I retraced his final known movements. I took the same route he had and drove my car at a reasonable speed from Buckton village High Street to the RSPB nature reserve. The journey took me approximately eight minutes. From there I took a steady walk down towards the cliffs, which took another eighteen to twenty minutes in total. Even then it was impossible to know just how his body could have ended up a hundred and fifty metres out to sea, in under the thirty minutes or so that followed. Later, I checked tide times for the morning of May 25th and discovered that there had been a high tide that morning, so it *is* possible that the waves could have carried his body out to sea - although I am told that even then, the water does not reach the bottom of the cliffs in many places around Crab Rocks where he may have fallen. Many of the rocks are clearly visible, even at high tide. So what really happened to Mark Haddenham may forever remain a mystery.

Wise old fishermen may tell us that 'the sea always gives up its dead', but for Bempton this does not always hold true. The deaths and disappearances of all these men are no closer to being solved now, than they were when they first happened. If those men who had disappeared did get into difficulties whilst out walking, where are they now ? What set of circumstances leads a man to vanish without trace or reason ? I suppose if we consider the impossible, the possibilities become endless.

Mark Haddenham's untimely death may well have been nothing more than a tragic accident and some may feel that including the account and the reports of some others in this book, is wrong. Yet I do not think it is wrong to question something that, from many angles, just does not seem right. No one will ever know the facts that led to Mark Haddenham's death. In fact all of these disappearances and deaths are a mystery and any conclusions we draw can only be based on assumption.

'Steven'

Midway into my research for Truth-Proof I was contacted by a young man who I'll name 'Alan'. He had been a friend of the family since his childhood and now he wanted to tell me of something he thought might be connected to my investigations into 'incidents of high strangeness'.

He asked if I could recall him talking about two local UFO investigators, who I'll name 'Nathan' and 'Steven'. They used to run a UFO group which held meetings from time to time and although I never met them personally, I knew of their activities.
I had actually been keeping my distance from them, because I understood they had been showing some of my film footage at their meetings, without my permission. The footage itself was of the lightforms, which I had been documenting since 2004 from the East Yorkshire Wolds area. Over the years this film has been used in TV news reports and documentaries on the unexplained, as well as websites throughout the world. At the time I was unhappy with Nathan and Steven, since they hadn't even asked me if they could show the footage at their meetings, yet to ask was all that was needed. It had taken me years to gain the trust of the Wolds farmers to gather that footage and I had been worried that Nathan and Steven's actions might have undone some of that trust.

However, our friend Alan then began to tell me the story and to be honest, I thought it sounded like something straight out of the X-Files. Although I have to say, I have not changed the story or sensationalised it in any way. It is written here exactly as it was told to me.

It turned out that Nathan had known Alan and his family for many years and he was considered a close friend of the family. Over a period of two to three weeks Nathan began to tell Alan that he and his colleague Steven had been investigating something connected to RAF Bempton - and that it was alien related. Alan admitted to me that when he first heard Nathan's story he did not believe it, but as the days and weeks passed, it became apparent that whatever they had been looking into was becoming serious. He said the secrecy surrounding what they had found slowly dripped out and the more he was told, the darker it became.

Alan had always been a reliable and level-headed young man and I could think of no reason why he would make up such a story. Yet for me to accept it as truth at this stage would have been be wrong, although to dismiss it out of hand would have been equally wrong. So I remained open-minded and listened to what he was telling me. One afternoon in September 2008 Alan received a phone call from Nathan, who was apparently crying down the phone and asking for help.

Alan learned that Nathan and Steven had information about where to find something extraordinary around RAF Bempton, although whether this was on the base or within the surrounding area is unknown. Whatever it was they *had* discovered was clearly causing Nathan great distress. Nathan told Alan that he and Steven had gathered information over a period of many months and at first they began making regular trips to Bempton. Then as their investigations progressed Nathan felt they were getting in too deep and it was actually becoming frightening.

They began to notice black cars, which would just appear and then sit at a distance, as if observing them. The same cars even showed up in different places when they were away from Bempton. Nathan felt this was more than coincidence. Then they began receiving silent phone calls at all hours of the day and night and they both felt that their calls were being listened to.

Fear now overtook their excitement and in the end, Nathan wanted nothing more to do with their research. He began to distance himself from Steven and anything connected to RAF Bempton. He felt that it was all just too frightening. Nathan advised Steven to let it go too, but he wouldn't and Steven continued their investigations alone. Then weeks later Nathan got a call from Steven who said that he wanted to meet him at Bempton. He told Nathan that he had found something that would change things forever. Nathan wondered if Steven had found a crucial bit of information - perhaps some proof they had been looking for, so he reluctantly agreed to meet Steven and headed out to Bempton.

When he arrived, he found his friend's car abandoned with the door open and there was no sign of Steven.

I asked Alan why Nathan never contacted the police after finding his friend's car abandoned and Steven apparently missing. He said that Nathan was convinced that once the police became involved, other authorities would step in and he was just too frightened. It seems that they had become entangled in something intense and complicated, which in the beginning seemed exciting, but then it started to become frightening. The black cars following them and the silent phone calls all had an effect. The 'fear tactics' had worked on Nathan and he took the warnings and backed off. If only his friend had done the same.

Alan said that Nathan would sometimes arrive at his house shaking and really messed up. He would turn up at all times of the day and night and he seemed genuinely terrified that the government or some agency was after him. Nathan was convinced that Steven had been 'taken' because of what he had discovered.

When Alan first told me this story I did not know what to think. He seemed very reluctant to tell me everything anyway, as though he was genuinely scared about what had happened to his friend Nathan. He did not know all the details of Nathan's story, but he believed what he had been told. Perhaps he thought it might be better not knowing too much, because Alan felt that even talking with me about it might somehow have an effect on us too. What Alan did know though, was that Steven had been able to uncover something really serious, that in the end, had a massive impact on both Nathan and himself. Nathan said that the day he got the call from Steven to arrange a meeting at Bempton was the last time they spoke, even though Nathan said he tried to ring him back several times, but got no reply. The only evidence was his friend's abandoned car. Steven had vanished and Nathan has never seen or heard from him since.

When I look at this story as it stands, it sounds quite sensational. After all, this is Bempton and not Roswell, New Mexico. But then considering the other accounts in Truth-Proof perhaps anything is possible.

I must point out that Alan told me this story over a period of weeks, it was not just some random conversation that took place over a drink in a busy bar. This was a serious conversation and the information did not come easy. In fact I don't think he would have even said anything to me, if I wasn't already looking into events of high strangeness around Bempton. Alan was only the messenger and not directly involved with what ultimately happened, although he was well placed to relate the story. If this was true, someone had genuinely gone missing while investigating a mystery at RAF Bempton - and no one has even noticed.

The Final Revelation

When Alan finally told me what the pair claimed to have discovered, I was quite taken aback. I thought it would be some strange UFO account they had been told by a friend of a friend, but this was different. *"Paul I can only tell you what I was told. I'm not even comfortable talking about this. Nathan has now left the area and I don't think he'll be coming back and Steven is still missing. It is serious stuff they got involved in."* Alan paused. The words were there but he was reluctant to let them loose. I asked him if he knew what it was that Steven had found, that was so dark and sensitive and led to his disappearance.

"He got too deep. Nathan only told me parts. He was scared that I would get drawn into it as well. But Paul, I saw what Steven had found, they had pictures. Steven found the remains of something. It definitely looked like the remains of some unidentified life-form. I think some agency must have known about the area for a long time. That's why all these things you are looking into keep happening. It's frightening Paul, they basically erased his existence. After Steven vanished Nathan would come to my house in tears and he only had me to speak to about it. He was frightened for his own life. That's why, in the end, he moved away."

Alan told me that for a short time, Nathan took refuge at his home before moving away from the area entirely. Whatever it was that the two had found, resulted in one going missing and the other leaving for good. He then told me about one of the pictures Nathan showed him, of the strange remains Steven had found at Bempton. It showed a small round skull, which was different to anything he had ever seen before. It is unknown who gave them the information or told them where to look in the first place, but I suspect it may have been someone at one of the UFO meetings.

Finding Steven's abandoned car was the final warning for Nathan, from that moment on, he switched off from the world. He did not know who he could trust. Together with threatening phone calls, he says a large black car was following him and monitoring his every move. That was when he contacted Alan asking him for help and a place to hide. In the end Alan even said that he no longer wanted to talk about it. Our conversations reached a point where I knew he even regretted telling me Nathan's story. Then I decided to do a little digging myself, to see if I could find any truth to back up what the two men had told him. Without doubt, we know that Nathan and Steven were real and that they were actively investigating the subject of UFOs. We know that Nathan moved away from the area and cut all ties with Alan and his family. An online search for missing people certainly suggested that a forty-seven year old man from the Bridlington area with Steven's real name, had been listed as missing. The website now seems to have disappeared, but there were two messages from a woman asking Steven to let her know that he was safe. One message read that she had waited for him at the airport, another stated that she felt sad and was so worried. However, messages on a missing person's website are not proof that this story is real, but they do suggest that something happened.

* * *

Accounts such as this will never sit right with rational thinkers as they offer no explanation that we can understand, but then most of what has been written in these pages has no explanation. Parts of Alan's story sound crazy, but no less crazy than tales of men who simply vanish without a trace. When unexplained events and disappearances are broken down and studied in detail, sometimes even the final conclusions do not give a definitive answer for what is happening around Bempton.

My research highlights activity that clashes with everything that is considered normal. I don't think anyone even dares to consider that in some instances, other forces are at work. Both Nathan and Steven were actively looking into something connected to Bempton and my work on the lightforms seems to have been part of what they were looking into. I suspect that somewhere within it all, the lightforms may have been connected all along.

Similarities between some of the cases of missing men are also quite interesting, once all the dots are connected. Ten missing between 2004 and 2014. I haven't included Steven in this number since I have no actual dates for his disappearance, although the missing persons website place him missing sometime before February 2011. All of them were male, six of them had vanished without trace. Five disappeared on a Thursday, two on a Tuesday, one on a Monday, one on a Friday and the last on a Sunday. The actual times they were all last seen are somewhat vague, apart from the Mark Haddenham tragedy, where it seems pretty certain what time he left home.

I even noticed similarities in phases of the moon when the men disappeared, although this was just something that showed up when I was researching information on the tides. It is the sheer number of unknowns in these cases that make it impossible to rule out anything in this area. During my research I have spoken to police officers, fire crew and the coastguard and none of them seem to have given any consideration to the short periods of time between all of these disappearances. They invest their time in trying to find an answer to the question of *why* these men disappeared on an individual basis, but none have looked at them as a collective.

Yet the missing men of North-East Yorkshire are not limited to the years 2004-2014. There have been both men and women disappear in the area over many years before and they continue to do so. Perhaps the answer lies so far out of the box, no one dare look that far. The first step is to accept that something unusual is happening, but we must remain open-minded enough to accept that answers to some of these mysteries might lie in something beyond our understanding.

CRATERS

The Hood Farm Crater

One farm associated with a strange occurrence from the 1960s belonged to F.R. Hood. The family worked their land around South Landing in Flamborough and are still doing so today. I found the unusual story in an archive edition of The Bridlington Free Press and Chronicle, which reported that on Friday July 19th 1963, a ten foot wide shallow crater had been discovered on local farmland.

The account, from July 1963, went on to say that a mystery crater had appeared at the Hood Farm at Flamborough Head and was thought to have been caused by a lightning strike on the nearby cliff-tops. At first it was thought that an explosion of some kind had taken place, so the MOD bought in bomb disposal experts who used mine detectors to examine the area. The newspaper explained that the crater had been created by a pocket of gas beneath the surface which had been ignited by lightning. This 'official' and quite ridiculous explanation was one that the locals did not accept - including Colin Hood, who first discovered the crater on his father's farm.

Official reports stated that the land could have been disturbed by some kind of explosive object, because of this and the crater's sudden appearance, the police and coastguard were informed. The Flamborough Head coastguard has a lookout station about three hundred metres away from where the crater appeared, which is staffed twenty-four hours a day. At the time, the coastguard said that they noticed "*no out-of-the-ordinary happenings*" and no explosions had been heard either. They added however, that the disturbed land was situated at the back of the lookout, so would not have been seen from inside the building.

I discovered that also in the same month, more mystery craters had appeared in different locations around the UK. Could they have all been nothing more than coincidence ? At the time they caused a bit of a stir in the various locations they appeared. Back then however, news did not travel so quickly and a connection between these different craters was not established until much later. This fact was evident when I interviewed Colin Hood, fifty years after the crater had originally appeared on his father's farm. Until I told them, his family knew nothing about the mystery craters in other parts of the country. The only people in the loop were the MOD, who clearly took the craters seriously but seemed to act as though none of them were of any importance.

Interestingly, the newspaper also states that the lightning theory *"exploded the fanciful suggestion"* of those who thought the crater had been caused by something from *"outer space"*. So if the question was already being asked, maybe this was an attempt to quickly suppress theories of anything UFO-related. But do the media really think the public are so dumb that they believe all these craters, which appeared in different parts of the country, were formed when random lightning strikes happened to ignite pockets of flammable gas - all in the same month ? There were also reports of unexplained lights made around the same time, yet no one in an official capacity announced the possibility that they may have been connected with the Flamborough crater.

Colin Hood was seventy-two when I interviewed him. He told me that it was during his early twenties that he first came across the crater, while he had been cutting hay on his father's farm. According to the newspaper report at the time, Colin had said that the crater was not there when the hay had last been cut, but it wasn't until he returned home that day that he first told his father about his discovery.

This vintage account intrigued me enough to look a little deeper, so I decided to contact the Hood Farm to see if anyone there could remember the story. I was not sure what to expect, since fifty years had passed since the crater's discovery and I was not even sure if Colin Hood would still be around - but I found the number and called the farm. A man answered the phone, so I asked if I could speak to Mr Colin Hood. *"I am Colin Hood"* replied the man in a soft tone.
This surprised me. Even though I had asked the question, I was not expecting Colin Hood to answer. It would be even better if he was willing to talk about an event that happened over fifty years before.

I explained to Colin that I had been looking into strange stories connected to the area and that I had found the report on his mystery crater from 1963. I asked him if he remembered.
"Yes I remember it, I was twenty-two years old at the time and for the life of me, I still cannot explain it. It was just a large shallow hole, when

I first came across it. I thought it was pigs or badgers that had been scratching at the earth to get at roots. But on closer inspection I realised it was too neat. It was round and sort of rounded at the sides, even though earth had been disturbed and thrown around. Something about the shape was just too neat"

Colin told me that he and other members of his family had no idea what could have caused it. I asked him if he recalled hearing any loud noise before the crater was found. He said he heard nothing. I also asked if he remembered seeing any evidence of an explosion, because if that were the case, I would have expected hay and earth to have been scattered all around. Colin said that he did not recall seeing anything like that and that everything looked normal around the outside of the crater. He said there were no signs of burnt earth or heat, but he did recall how neat the round shape of the crater was. Colin said it was as though that section of earth had been removed. Although lightning was the suggested explanation as the cause of the crater, he did not recall any freak weather in the weeks and days before the hay was cut. Out of interest I later checked weather data for the month of July 1963, from the UK Met Office, and found that it had been wet and dull that day. There was no mention of a lightning storm.

I later spoke with Colin's brother who told me much the same story. Later they kindly gave me copies of a photograph that was taken of themselves with the bomb disposal men, as they all stood around the crater in 1963. Both men thought the lightning explanation was ridiculous, saying that some people had been talking of UFOs, which had been seen in the area at the time.

As unusual as the Hood Farm crater may sound, it ties in with the others which appeared all over the country in the space of a few weeks. Fifty years ago I think the suppression of information must have been so easy, yet the crater was not the only strange occurrence to be reported in July 1963. The account of the Hood Farm crater and the following account, of the Flamborough coastguard UFO, occurred so close together in both distance and time, but have remained unconnected for over fifty years - until I began my research and found a link.

The following photograph was taken on the day of the crater's discovery.

Bridlington Free Press July 22nd 1963

Mystery crater caused by lightning

AFTER examining a 10-ft.-wide shallow crater on the cliffs at Flamborough on Monday, bomb disposal experts, using mine dectors, suggested it had been caused by lightning striking a pocket of natural gas.

The bomb disposal squad had been called after 22-year-old Mr. Colin Hood came across the hole on Friday of last week while cutting hay.

When Mr. Hood returned home that day he told his father, Mr. F. R. Hood, of the North Moor Farm, Flamborough, about the appearance of the hole, which had not been there when the grass had last been cut. Because it was thought the land might have been disturbed by an explosive object, the police and coastguards were informed.

Coastguards who man a look-out station 24 hours a day about 300 yards from the scene, had noticed no out-of-the-ordinary happenings and had not heard any explosions.

Station-Officer Charles said: "The disturbed land, however, is behind the look-out, and could not be seen from inside the building."

The theory of the bomb disposal experts exploded the fanciful suggestion of those who thought the disturbance had been caused by "something from outer space".

There also had been theories that the hole had been made by either lightning striking a piece of metal, or by land subsidence

Eight days later...

Flamborough Coastguard Sighting

This report is of great interest due to the length of time the object was observed and that it was taken very seriously at the time. Plus the fact that it just happens to have been reported around the same location as the Hood Farm crater - so we seem to have a double mystery.

For this account we need to jump forward eight days after the crater discovery, to Saturday July 27th 1963. The Bridlington Free Press and Chronicle announced; "*Coastguard See Mystery Object In Sky*" and they go on to tell the story of the Flamborough coastguards, who were monitoring an unidentified object in the sky throughout that Saturday morning in July. The coastguards first saw the object from their lookout station at around 5.20am. At that time it was to the east of the station, from there it moved overhead and could not be seen for a time. They estimated the object was at an altitude of around 40,000ft and that a short time before noon, it could be seen north-west of their lookout station, shining bright white in the sky over the coastal town of Filey. They last saw the object at 12.30pm that afternoon, north-west of Flamborough.

The newspaper's own reporter stated that he also saw the object. He said that it was easy to pick out in the sky without the aid of a telescope and that to the naked eye, it resembled a bright star, but when viewed through a telescope it seemed to change shape as it moved. He said that at one moment, it appeared to look like a triangle with a deep white line running along one side and then at another moment, it resembled something like a shortened bullet. It is interesting to note that the reporter was describing defined shapes in his account.

The coastguard commented that a considerable number of military aircraft were taking part in an exercise that morning, which they observed to be at an altitude of about 30,000ft. They noted that the object looked well above them and that it moved against the wind direction at ground level. That morning they contacted both RAF Leconfield and RAF Preston and were told that they might have been seeing a meteorological balloon, which could have expanded until it reached a diameter of a quarter of a mile, then burst into fragments. Personally, I would like to see a balloon that resembles a huge triangle one moment and then morphs into the shape of a bullet the next. The newspaper report ended with a quote from RAF Leconfield, whose spokesperson said that the aircraft exercise that morning "was not connected" to the sighting at Flamborough Head.

It is interesting that yet again, such a large military exercise was taking place around Flamborough and Bempton and none of the local authorities had been notified - yet it just happened to be on the same day the object appeared. Of course, wind speed and direction at ground level, as mentioned by the coastguards, will not always be the same as conditions at an altitude of 40,000ft, but regardless of this, we have to consider that the object was first seen at 5.20am and last seen at 12.30pm. Although it could have been there much longer, would a weather balloon really hang in the sky for a total of seven hours and ten minutes ?

I think that if the public are expected to believe such ridiculous explanations to describe the unexplainable, then it is perfectly reasonable to state that only something controlled could remain in the sky for such a long period of time. We can also rule out that the object was tethered, since Flamborough's coastguard station is approximately ten miles away from Filey - and the object was first seen to the east of the station, in virtually the opposite direction. On the front page of the Scarborough Evening News on the same Saturday in July 1963 was the headline; *'Thing In The Sky.'** The newspaper is for the town of Scarborough, which is twenty miles north of Flamborough, yet they were clearly reporting on the same object seen by the Flamborough coastguard.

A point just worth mentioning, although not directly related, is the use of the word 'Thing' in the Scarborough Evening News headline. In 1965 witnesses in the town of Warminster in Wiltshire reported lots of unusual UFO activity of their own. The phenomenon is now referred to as 'The Warminster Thing'. Use of the word 'thing' in The Scarborough Evening News headline predates Warminster by over a year.

THING IN THE FILEY SKY

THROUGHOUT this morning coastguards at Flamborough kept track on an unidentified object in the sky at about 40,000 ft. Shortly before noon the object was north-west of the look-out station at Flamborough and appeared to be over Filey.

An Evening News reporter also watched it. Once spotted, the object could be easily picked out in the sky without the aid of a telescope. To the eye it looked like a white star. When looked at through a telescope the object seemed to change its shape as it moved. At one time it looked like a white triangle, with a deep white line running along one side. At another time it looked something like a shortened bullet.

The object was first seen at Flamborough coastguard look-out station at 5.55. It was then to the east of the station. It then moved overhead and was lost for a time. Later it was seen to the north-west over Filey, shining white in the sky.

A coastguard said : " There were a considerable number of aircraft taking part in an exercise in this area this morning. They seemed to be at about 30,000 ft, and the object was well above them. It must have been about 40,000 ft. The object moved against the wind at direction of the wind at ground level."

When the object was first sighted by the coastguards they informed R.A.F. Leconfield and R.A.F. Preston. They were told that it might be a large meteorological balloon which would expand until it had a diameter of a quarter of a mile and then burst into fragments.

An R.A.F. spokesman at Leconfield said : " The exercise this morning was not connected with the report on the sighting at Flamborough."

Early this afternoon Scarborough coastguards had not received any reports of unidentified objects in the sky.

COASTGUARD
SIGHTING
1963

COASTGUARDS SEE MYSTERY OBJECT IN THE SKY

THROUGHOUT Saturday morning coastguards at Flamborough kept track on an unidentified object in the sky at about 40,000 ft. Shortly before noon the object was north-west of the look-out station at Flamborough and appeared to be over Filey.

A Free Press reporter also watched it. Once spotted, the object could be easily picked out in the sky without the aid of a telescope. To the eye it looked like a white star. When looked at through a telescope the object seemed to change its shape as it moved. At one time it looked like a white triangle, with a deep white line running along one side. At another time it looked something like a shortened bullet.

The object was first seen at Flamborough coastguard look-out station at 5.20 a.m. It was then to the east of the station. It then moved overhead and was lost for a time. Later it was seen to the north-west over Filey, shining white in the sky. The object was last seen by the Flamborough coastguards at 12.30 p.m., north-west of Flamborough.

A coastguard said : " There were a considerable number of aircraft taking part in an exercise in this area this morning. They seemed to be at about 30,000 ft., and the object was well above them. It must have been about 40,000 ft. The object moved against the direction of the wind at ground level."

When the object was first sighted by the coastguards they informed R.A.F. Leconfield and R.A.F. Preston. They were told that it might be a large meteorological balloon which would expand until it had a diameter of a quarter of a mile and then burst into fragments.

An R.A.F. spokesman at Leconfield said : " The exercise this morning was not connected with the report on the sighting at Flamborough."

The 1963 Scarborough report said that their local coastguard had not received any reports of unidentified objects in the sky, although it had been reported over Filey. When I spoke to Colin Hood about the crater on his family's farm, I also asked if he recalled hearing anything about an object seen in the sky by coastguards at the time. He could not remember anything about it, but I suppose a twenty-two year old man returning home after working all day, would not look for anything connected to the mystery crater that he found. Sometimes it is only when looking back at these events that comparisons and connections can be made.

Colin and his family were surprised when I told them about the coastguard sighting and the craters that appeared in other parts of the country. Through the local archives I was able to uncover interesting details of some of these other craters. They were very similar to the Hood Farm crater and had appeared in the same month.

An article from The Yorkshire Post from August 1st 1963 reported that a mystery crater, eight feet round, had been found in field in Wiltshire in the South of England. The report also stated that a cow in a nearby field had been found with its skin "peeling in scales", as if it had been scorched. This crater was first reported on July 20th 1963 by farmer Roy Blanchard, of Manor Farm, Charlton village, Wiltshire, who found the crater on his land. It was reported that a blast or explosion was heard close to the farm on the same day and police constable Anthony Penny was reported to have observed an orange object in the sky. The officer said that it vanished from the area where the crater was discovered.

Roy Blanchard said that whatever came down in his field crushed stone and rock to powder, yet he said that whatever it was came down gently. There was apparently no trace of the potato or barley either, which had been growing there before the crater appeared. I have wondered if it could in fact have been extreme heat that reduced the stones and rock to powder - this would also tie in with the condition that the cow that was found to be in.

In the adjoining fields of wheat, observers also found oval-shaped depressions in the crops. This was something that did not get overlooked by the astronomer Patrick Moore, later Sir Patrick, who visited the site soon after the crater was found. He wrote about what he observed in an open letter to the New Scientist magazine in August 1963. It is fair to say that Moore's observations of the crater and the crop formations would have been accurate. He described defined circular and oval areas in the wheat with evidence of spiral flattening. It is interesting to note that crop circles had also been reported on the same farm back in 1952, so I wonder what it was about the location that attracted this activity ?

Again in July 1963, two craters were discovered on a farm owned by Mr James Brown, twenty miles south of Dunbar in East Lothian, Scotland. They were said to be twelve feet apart, fifteen feet in diameter and up to three feet deep - which is deeper than the Flamborough crater. They were described as having 'channels' that looked like the spokes of a wheel, radiating from the centre of each crater. Over forty feet away were found large lumps of earth, also with channels, radiating out for up to forty-four feet in distance. Close to the craters were square holes in the ground, measuring one foot wide and two feet deep. The fact that these depressions were square must certainly rule out them being created by atmospherics or freak weather conditions. The police investigated and bomb disposal experts were called, but they were all just baffled by what they found.

Three people also reported seeing a 'flying saucer' over the Lothians and Edinburgh on July 26th, 1963. It was described as silvery-grey in colour and was travelling high overhead. They said it had no wings and looked like an 'upturned cup on a saucer'.

Mystery craters were also found on Dufton Fell, Westmorland, Cumbria, in the centre of Northern England. These were much larger than the Scottish craters by comparison, at a hundred and eleven feet across and two feet deep. One of the local farmers who discovered them, wondered if there was a connection to the disappearance of forty sheep in the area around the same time.

The Bempton Crater

In April 2013 I was contacted by an elderly man from Bridlington who said he had an unusual story to share with me. He asked that his real name should not be used, since he valued his position in the local community. I have renamed him 'John' for this report.

John used to work in Flamborough and the surrounding area for many years and I found him to be very knowledgeable with many unusual stories to share - despite his public image, which portrayed him as a man who usually believed in nothing but stone-cold facts. He told me, *"It is hard to change the way you grow up and view the world. Even when things happen that contradict everything you have been told cannot be real. For some people, saying nothing is the safest option."*

John and I spoke on the phone several times before he finally trusted me enough to meet. He was over eighty years old the time and he had memories from the past that could help with my research. I listened in fascination to his sharp recall of events from the distant years of his long and interesting life. We have spoken of many things since that day, including the Hood Farm crater - which he informed me was not the only one to appear locally that month.
"I know of another crater that came out of the blue." He said. *"I know, because I found it in July of 1963."*

John explained how he had discovered a forty-foot wide circular depression in the ground in Bempton all those years ago, just like the Hood Farm crater in Flamborough. He explained that a large circular scoop of earth had just suddenly disappeared. John had an in-depth knowledge of the land as a result of his job at the time, which involved the removal and transportation of aggregates from around east and North Yorkshire. As part of his work he visited many farms and businesses, including some locations that the public would not normally be allowed access.

"I can't imagine where all that earth went to. It was a good ten feet deep in the middle. Whatever took it must have been big, because I estimated that about sixty tons of soil and rock had gone. I suppose I cannot say it went overnight, but it did go in July of that year. I know that because I remember all the fuss made about that hole that

99

appeared on the cliff-tops at Flamborough - and all the talk at the time about people seeing things in the sky. Some schoolboys even reported seeing a UFO at Danes Dyke.

I laughed about it at the time and even poked fun about that crater on the cliffs at Flamborough. That's why I never said anything when I found the one at Bempton. I couldn't understand it, but I didn't want people laughing at me, so I said nothing. And I valued my job. In those days hardly anyone would be around that area. Security was quite tight due to its closeness of RAF Bempton and knowing Flamborough and Bempton folk like I do, they would have kept tight-lipped. It was just the way we were in those days. I even found Roman remains, skeletons and all, on that land and never said a word. So the sudden appearance of a strange crater in 1963 was no different."

After listening to John, I wondered what type of machine could extract so much earth at once and go undetected. There are no roads within miles of the crater and nothing has changed on the land, at least in the fifty years since John last worked in the area.

The Bempton Crater is still there, about half a mile away from the RAF base, going towards Speeton cliffs. In May 2016 I visited the site to find that the landowner had begun to dump farm waste there, although I was still able to take some measurements. The crater actually measures sixty-two feet in diameter and has a depth of six feet. On an earlier visit, before the farmer had begun to fill the site, I noted the depth was closer to ten feet. It also appeared that little vegetation was growing within the depression itself.

RAF Bempton would have been a fully operational base back in 1963, so it is hard to imagine that a series of events, so unusual, could have gone undetected within sight of the base. This was three strange incidents, all within a very close time frame, under the noses of one of Britain's key defence installations and no one seems to have a clue how or why they happened.

Could all these craters from July 1963 really be put down to sheer coincidence ? I wonder how such a thing would be viewed today ? Yet so many years have passed since their discovery, that any answers they may have revealed have long since been lost. In 1963 the Hood Farm crater was just one piece of a much larger puzzle, which is no closer to being solved now than it was all those years ago. Perhaps it might take another fifty years before more pieces of the puzzle are found, leading us to an answer that connects them all.

However, I think that reviving these reports shows strong evidence that there was probably more to the creation of the Hood Farm crater and perhaps some of the others, than just lightning strikes hitting pockets of underground gas.

The photograph below of the Bempton Crater was taken in January 2016, with myself standing in its centre.

The Bempton Crater

1966 - A YEAR OF UNUSUAL ACTIVITY

The Trawlermen's Close Encounter

I was now becoming quite familiar with the trawlermen who worked out of the harbours around our coast, particularly Bridlington. They are a very close knit group who are wary of strangers asking questions, but due to my friendship with a few of them, whom I got to know outside of the fishing environment, they tolerated my presence. Some even seemed to have an interest in the unusual information that I was unearthing, after all, some of it related to themselves in the past and present.

I was told about a daylight sighting of an unusual round object, seen just off Flamborough Head in early 1966. An elderly man from Bridlington old town told me how he remembered the subject of UFOs being regularly talked about by fishermen during the 1960s. One daylight sighting in particular had apparently caused quite a stir at the time. The gentleman gave me the names of a few men from the past, who he thought might have known about this sighting or may have even been witness to it.

A few days later I took my information to Bridlington Harbour and asked two of the trawlermen, brothers named David and Tom Quinn, if they recognised any of the names I had been given. They told me that one of them was a retired fishermen who still visited the harbour. They said that on warm days I would find him sitting in his motorised scooter near the harbour cabins, reminiscing with the men about the past.

I finally caught up with him on April 24th 2015 and it was a difficult conversation to say the least. He was an ageing man, who probably did not talk to many people outside of his own community and here was I, a complete stranger standing in front of him, asking questions about a bizarre incident from fifty-three years earlier. I tried my best to explain what I was doing and that the Quinn brothers had told me where to find him. At first he was very reluctant to talk and said that it was too long ago to remember, but I realised that this might be my only chance to speak with him, so I was not about to give up. My questions were one liners which received replies in the familiar broad Yorkshire dialect that belongs to Flamborough. The man's name was Dennis Jewitt.

He remembered that in 1966 he was hauling up crab pots off Flamborough Head with two other fishermen in their small motorised fishing boat named 'The Imperialist'. He told me that they were in close under the cliffs when it happened. He said,

"Suddenly we all ducked, sort of instinctively. We somehow knew this thing was above us. I think we might have caught its reflection in the water, but we must have seen or felt something, because we all ducked at same time.

We looked up and just above our heads we could see a perfectly round object. It was hovering right over our heads and made no sound. It was low, well below the cliffs and it just appeared from nowhere. It gave us all a fright and vanished as quickly as it came."

Dennis told me that the object was a whitish-brown in colour, adding that it might have had some yellow in it. I asked if it was glowing or luminous and he said that even though it was daytime, the visibility was quite poor, but he did not think that it was glowing. I asked him if he could give an estimate of its size. *"Fertbal size"* were his words, in his broad Yorkshire dialect. I deciphered from that he meant 'football size'. He told me that a few reporters came to talk to him and the other two men, about what they had seen. He said that everyone was talking about 'them things' - meaning the UFOs that had been seen by lots of people around that time. I asked Dennis if he had seen anything else unusual and he did admit to having seen other strange lights out at sea, but said no more about it.

The sighting was clearly of sufficient interest to be reported in the Bridlington Free Press and Chronicle, but it is not known which other newspapers covered the story. Dennis remembered that more than one person came to speak with him and the men and added, that they were not the ones who contacted the press. Quite what he meant by that, I do not know. However, I got the impression that the three fisherman did not welcome the attention at the time. On my next visit to the Bridlington library I decided to take another look at the newspaper archive for 1966. True to his word, I found Dennis's story in a newspaper dated Friday June 24th 1966 with the headline: *"Fishermen See Mystery Object in Sky."*

If Dennis Jewitt's account from over fifty years ago is correct - and I have no reason to think otherwise - then what type of man-made aircraft did we have back then, that could do the incredible things the three fishermen described ? The whole event may have only lasted seconds, but they saw a circular object the size of a football, that could hover silently and move so fast they did not even see it go. Either that or it had the ability to render itself invisible. This brief, but incredible sighting from over fifty years ago stands as proof that we understand very little about such phenomena. Even with the huge scientific advances that we have made, if it were reported today I think we would still have nothing to compare it to. Of course in recent years we know that military drones are one of the new explanations for unexplained sky objects. It's just a shame that Dennis Jewitt's sighting happened in 1966 and not 2016.

Other fishermen told me that many other strange lights were seen throughout 1966 and I wonder if the coastguard or MOD would have misinterpreted those as flares, meteors, gas platforms or weather balloons. Yet the 'fertbal-sized' ufo witnessed by the crew of The Imperialist trawler stands apart from any rational explanation that I can think of.

FISHERMEN SEE MYSTERY OBJECT IN SKY

A mystery object was seen at Flamborough on Monday by three fishermen — Mr. D. Jewitt, Mr. T. Stephenson, and Mr. J. Stephenson. They were hauling crab pots off Flamborough Head in the motor fishing-boat Imperialist when they noticed a round object hovering directly overhead.

The fishermen instinctively ducked, and then the object vanished.

Mr. T. Stephenson said: "It came from nowhere and it went as quickly as it came."

The object was described as being whitish brown. Visibility was poor at the time, and the fishermen could not see it well enough to give details.

Bridlington Free Press
June 24th 1966

THE TRAWLERMEN'S ENCOUNTER
1966

Disc On The Horizon

On April 20th 2015 I interviewed a sixty-five year old Bridlington man named David Mooney. David is a well-respected man in the town who was President of The Lords Feoffees historic charitable trust. He is also a prolific writer and historian. David wanted to tell me about an object that was seen by many people in the Summer of 1966.

David explained that as a young boy of sixteen he worked on the Bridlington sea front at Joyland Amusements, Britain's largest amusement arcade. His job was to supervise rides like the ghost-train or dodgems and generally do whatever was asked of him. He told me that on some days he had lots of free time to just sit and do very little, except observe the beach and pretty girls in their costumes.

David recalled that on one particular sunny morning, he saw a small group of people gathered on the seafront. They were all looking at what appeared to be a large round disc on the horizon. David saw the object himself and said it looked as big as the moon. He said it remained there in exactly the same place out at sea for a number of days and was one of the most peculiar things he had ever seen. He told me that at times it looked almost transparent and at other times it looked more solid. No one knew what it was and many who worked at the arcade observed it. Some said it was a weather balloon and that explanation seemed to satisfy most people.

For many it was a just curiosity that was there and nothing more, but David had always known that this was not the case. Even today, he is adamant that it was no weather balloon. He said he could not deny what he saw with his own eyes as he watched it that summer's afternoon fifty years before.

"For a start, this thing was low in the sky - I would say only three to four hundred feet." David told me. Then he said, *"And I saw it go. It suddenly shot vertically up into the sky and was gone. Balloons don't do that."*

Could what David Mooney and the others have seen and described leaving Bridlington bay that day, really have been a weather balloon ?

One Year Later

On July 14th 1967 The Bridlington Free Press newspaper reported that a large mystery object had been seen over a wide area, on the previous Saturday. The official explanation was that people had seen a 'meteorological balloon' with the sun shining on it. This in itself is interesting since some witnesses report seeing it at night. The newspaper said that the police and coastguard received many reports about the object, although they only make reference to it being seen on Saturday 7th - which is incorrect. From other witness accounts I know that it was seen over a number of days. Back in the 1960s weather balloons seemed to be the staple explanation for unusual things seen in the skies.

I remember once myself as a small boy in 1967, I was sitting in my bedroom with my father and through the window we were both watching a moving ball of luminous white light in the sky. It looked to my eyes to be as big as the moon and appeared to be travelling across the roof-tops of the town of Mexborough, just a mile or so away from where we lived at the time. My father told me that it was a weather balloon. Yet in my mind's eye I can still recall it now, moving slowly from right to left across the sky. I still don't think it was a weather balloon, but today I suppose the explanation would be something like drones.

A Nine Hour Search

On Sunday December 4th 1966 the coastguard and lifeboats were called to search the sea off Flamborough Head, after what were described as green and yellow rockets or flares, seen ten miles off the headland.

The first reports came into Radio Humber from the coaster trade-ship Achilles. The radio station contacted the coastguard after three other reports of the mysterious flares came in; one from a lightship, one from a game warden thirty-nine miles south at Spurn Point and the third from Withernsea police officers, twenty-five miles south of Flamborough.

Bridlington and Humber lifeboats were both launched and began an intensive search. They arrived back at 7.30am on the following Monday having found nothing. They had been assisted by two Naval patrol vessels who, like the lifeboat crews, could not explain the lights either. The Bridlington Free Press suggested that the lights could have been flares, but no one could explain them. Flares of that colour are usually associated with aircraft and yet no planes were reported missing or in distress at the time. Many other ships in the area also reported seeing the lights but they too were unable to explain them.

Another theory put forward was that the flares were just meteorites re-entering the atmosphere. However, those who reported seeing them did not think this was the case. A meteor will act very differently to a flare. Meteors are objects from space that flash through the sky at incredible speeds. Flares burn brightly and slowly descend on the wind. I would expect the coastguard and lifeboat crews to have established whether these lights were flares, through experience and by assessing the weather conditions and wind direction at the time. The fact that so many trained men and women could not explain what they were seeing gives us a hint that this was a highly unusual sighting. It must have been quite a display to have been taken so seriously.

Both the Bridlington and Humber lifeboats spent nine hours searching over a thirty mile area of sea - and they found nothing. It is interesting that those who witnessed these lights could not say with any certainty what they were. If in fact it was a meteor display, I am sure the lifeboat crews would have returned home much sooner. So were they flares or meteorites and would so many independent professional observers really confuse the two ?

I shared my findings with some of the local retired trawlermen and they brought back memories for a few of them. I was told that strange lights were seen on the coast and out at sea throughout 1966. One fisherman recalled seeing a large white light that was moving along the cliff face at Danes Dyke, as he was fishing off the coast. The cliffs at Danes Dyke are a hundred and fifty foot sheer drop and they cannot be climbed without the aid of ropes. I suggested to the fisherman that he may have been seeing someone climbing with a powerful torch. I was told in no uncertain terms that the light he saw was not a flat round light, nor a beam, but a ball of light, which moved slowly around the cliff-face as though it were searching for something.

Riddle Of The Empty Campsite

One mystery that came out of the area was first reported in the Bridlington Free Press and Chronicle on April 29th 1966. The newspaper tells of a tragedy that unfolded during that Easter weekend, when three young men simply disappeared. The three were from Halifax and on a camping trip at Danes Dyke in Flamborough. The alarm was raised when they never returned home for work on Wednesday April 13th.

The young men's concerned parents travelled to Flamborough where the police were notified. A short time later their tent was found in the woods, just twenty metres back from the cliff edge. It contained all their bedding, a hurricane lamp and other equipment and three heavily laden haversacks, which had not been used for several days. Helicopters searched the cliffs and coastline and police with dogs searched the surrounding area. On Monday April 18th, five days after he should have been home, the body of one of the missing three, nineteen year old Rupert Barrett, was found by a man walking the beach at Primrose Valley - eight miles away from Danes Dyke.

There was no clue how Barrett's body had ended up on the beach so far away from Dane's Dyke. It was presumed at the time that it was just a tragic accident. The report says the young men may have been returning back along the beach to their camp and were cut off by the tide. It went on to say that when found, Barrett's body had no obvious sign of injury. Dr. G. A. Dibb who examined the body was of the opinion that death was due to drowning, adding that the body had clearly been in the water for some hours. Yet by then, he had been missing for five days or one hundred and twenty hours, so for the doctor to say 'some hours' seems somewhat inaccurate. It has to be presumed the three went missing sometime before the April 13th, but however much time had passed, missing for days is not the same as missing for some hours.

Ten days later on Thursday April 28th, the bodies of Rupert Barrett's friends; Eric Reynolds and Stuart Greaves, were found in the water near Selwicks Bay beach off Flamborough Head. Their bodies were located in a deep water gully by two members of the British Sub-Aqua Club. At the inquest into the young men's deaths the coroner said there was no doubt that all three had drowned and that the bodies had no evidence of injuries that could have been caused by a fall and there was no suggestion that they had been trying to climb up the cliffs.

As with so many historical accounts it is impossible to say how these three young men came to such a tragic end. The question remains, if they were going out for the day on foot to another area, why would they have left their haversacks behind, with all their personal belongings, including the items they would have needed for the day, in an unsecured tent ?

On the same page of the Bridlington Free Press and Chronicle which reported on the three young men, was a small account of another tragedy. The body of eighty-two year old Mr Robert Teale, from Nottingham, had been found at the water's edge. The report vaguely states that he was found on a Bridlington beach, but there was no actual date given. I can only glean from references from other dates in the report that it must have been on April 14th. The newspaper states that his death was recorded as misadventure, adding that Mr Teale had died from asphyxia due to drowning. The coroner was satisfied that he had not entered the water deliberately.

Four deaths within such a short space of time must have been considered unusual. Or would they ? Since the sea is such an expert killer, that when a body is found usually no other suspects are required.

Were missing youths cut off by tide?

The riddle of the empty camp at Danes Dyke and the disappearance of three Halifax youths who went to camp there during the Easter week-end was no nearer being solved by the finding of the body of one of the youths on the beach at Primrose Valley on Monday.

The body was that of William Rupert Barrett (19), of Eldrath Road, Halifax, and his companions, who are still missing, were Ian Reynolds, of Wyvern Place, Halifax, and Stewart Greaves, of Saville Parade, Halifax.

They should have returned to work on Wednesday of last week, and when they did not do so the parents of two of the youths went to Flamborough and notified the police.

This led to the discovery of their tent in a wood at Danes Dyke, about 20 yards back from the cliff edge. With it was bedding, a hurricane lamp, and other equipment, and three laden haversacks which had not been used for several days were nearby.

Police, with dogs, and aided by a helicopter, searched the cliffs, and following the finding of Barrett's body the search was concentrated in the Reighton, Primrose Valley, and Hunmanby areas until Wednesday, when the search was called off.

In the absence of any clues it can only be presumed that the youths may have been returning to their camp along the beach and that they were cut off by the tide.

DEAD MAN WAS FREQUENT VISITOR TO BRIDLINGTON

The body of a man found at the water's edge on Bridlington beach was identified about a week later as that of Mr. Robert Arthur Teale (82), of 34 Servia Avenue, Leeds.

At the resumed inquest on Thursday of last week, the Coroner for the East Riding, Mr. H. W. Rennison, recorded a verdict of death by misadventure.

He said that Mr Teale had died from asphyxia, due to drowning, but he was satisfied he had not gone into the water deliberately.

When the inquest was opened the previous day the body had not been identified.

Mrs. Nora Elizabeth Parkin, 44 Runswick Drive, Woolaton, Nottingham, who gave evidence of identification, said the police had shown her a photograph, which she recognised as that of her father.

Before his retirement he was employed as a clerk in the Leeds Corporation Transport Department. He lived alone, and enjoyed good health. She last saw her father alive on 24 March. Her father knew Bridlington well, and visited the town frequently every year.

YOUTH DIED FROM DROWNING

After taking formal evidence, Mr. H. W. Rennison, the East Riding Coroner, adjourned the inquest at Filey on Friday of last week on William Rupert Barrett (19), an apprentice tool maker, of 34 Eldrath Park, Halifax, whose body was found on the beach at Primrose Valley on Monday of last week.

Dr. G. A. Dibb said that he examined the body found on the beach and formed the opinion that death was due to drowning.

"He had obviously been in the water for some hours," the doctor said. "There was no obvious sign of injury."

William Barrett, a pattern maker, of 34 Eldrath Road, Saville Park, Halifax, said he identified the body as that of his son.

Barrett and two other youths had been missing since they went to Danes Dyke for an Easter camping holiday. When they did not return home the police were informed, and a camp the youths had established at Danes Dyke was found.

There has been no trace of Ian Reynolds (19), of 38 Wyvern Place, Halifax, and Stuart Graves (19), of 28 Saville Parade, Halifax.

Live Broadcast UFO Sighting

Of all the archive reports I uncovered from 1966, one of the most interesting came from Radio 270, Yorkshire's first offshore pirate radio station.
I learned about the sighting while talking to a retired coastguard officer. He told me that in those days he worked from Hornsea lifeboat station, just down the coast from Flamborough. He said that he and his colleagues regularly listened to Radio 270, which broadcast from a converted Dutch fishing boat named 'Oceaan 7'. This boat was usually anchored about three miles off the coast, between Scarborough and Bridlington and only operated for around fifteen months in total, although early test transmissions began on June 4th 1966.

The coastguard told me about one unique broadcast, that he recalled from sometime around early 1966, one which he has never forgotten. He said that he and his colleagues were listening to the broadcast one evening as usual, when the radio DJs suddenly began to tell listeners about a UFO which was hovering above them. He says they listened intently and heard them describe, live on air, that a glowing sphere was above their ship. Talking excitedly, the DJs told listeners that this sphere of glowing white light, was directly above their ship's mast. They were unsure of what they were witnessing, but seemed to think that it was quite low in the sky.

On May 21st 2015 I decided to see what I could learn about this alleged UFO broadcast and began to research some of its past presenters. The first man I contacted was Chris Dannatt and he was very helpful, but I think he suspected the story was not authentic. His remarks actually threw me off-balance a little, as they not only potentially wrecked the story, they also cast a shadow on other information I had been given by the coastguard about another incident from 1998. However, the following day I received a phone call from Dannatt who had been doing a little research of his own.

"Hello Paul" he said, *"I've been asking a few questions for you about the UFO broadcast you told me about yesterday. It turns out you were right. I spoke to Paul Rustling who also worked for Radio 270 and he says he remembers that it was widely talked about at the time. Apparently one of our DJs Alan West, wrote about it."*

This was good news for me and I immediately scoured the internet for information about Alan West. I found that he had co-authored a book published in 1973 called *'Close Encounters: The Strange Truth About UFOs'*. I purchased a copy the same day, but unfortunately there was no mention of the pirate radio UFO account. At least now I knew for a fact that the UFO story reported by Radio 270 was real. After my initial enquiries many more people connected to the station contacted me to say they remembered it. The general opinion was that it happened sometime in the summer of 1966.

Sometime later, the retired coastguard also told me that he recalled a report from a lightship, which was effectively a floating lighthouse moored at Spurn Point, just south of Flamborough. Their crew had reported seeing an unidentified object in the sky on the same night in 1966. He remembered hearing that the official explanation at the time, for at least one of the two sightings, was a weather balloon.

AIR AND SEA SEARCH OFF FLAMBOROUGH FOR AIRCRAFT

A massive air-and-sea search was launched off Flamborough Head after an R.A.F. Lightning jet fighter, piloted by Captain W. Schafner of the U.S. Air Force, disappeared while returning from an exercise with a Shackleton to R.A.F. Binbrook in Lincolnshire.

The air control section of the Northern Rescue Control Centre, alerted Flamborough coastguards after the aircraft disappeared from radar scanners tracking its progress about five miles to the south of Flamborough Head at 10.30 p.m. on Tuesday night.

The Shackleton accompanying the fighter dropped flares to try and locate it, while Flamborough coastguards alerted Bridlington, Flamborough and Filey lifeboats, who set off with two launches from the R.A.F. Marine Craft Unit at Bridlington to search over a wide area.

Shipping join in

The search took place in very rough seas in an area from five to 10 miles off Flamborough Head, with Flamborough and Filey lifeboats searching in fixed set areas, and Bridlington lifeboat taking a zig-zag course.

All shipping in the area joined in the search, including the Dutch training ship Princes Margrite, and the coaster Stormont.

At day break a helicopter from R.A.F Leconfield and another Shackleton took over the air search, while the three lifeboats and the two launches returned to their stations after about 10 hours at sea.

Later on Wednesday morning an American "jolly green giant" helicopter and a C130 Hercules sea rescue plane from the American Air Force base at Woodbridge, Suffolk, joined in the search.

116

MISSING AIRCRAFT

I spent time looking into the story of XS894, an RAF Lightning fighter aircraft which crashed into the North Sea on September 8th 1970. It was ten miles out of Flamborough and was allegedly pursuing a UFO. I discovered that a few other interesting incidents had occurred during, just before and just after the crash, which add to the mystery. I am unaware of any other researcher who has looked as deeply into this matter and found these possible connections before. Had this been the case, it may have added more weight to the incredible story at the time.

I also researched the crash of ZA610, an RAF Tornado that disappeared from radar in 1985 and went down about sixteen miles off Flamborough Head. Then there was ZE732, another Tornado, which vanished from radar in 1998 while it was twenty miles east of Flamborough Head. Many references can be found on the internet that suggest the tragic loss of ZE732 was somehow UFO related.

I make no claims within these pages as to how or why these and other military aircraft were lost. I am simply sharing previously unknown information for the reader to form their own opinion. If the information points towards 'events of high strangeness' this is because unexplained incidents were reported at the same time. At the end of the day, these were genuine tragedies with no definitive explanation as to why they happened.

XS894 - The Lightning Incident

During my research into the case of the lost RAF Lightning I was fortunate enough to work with fellow investigator Tony Dodd. Tony has since passed away but he was instrumental in bringing the story of the Lightning into the public eye. Much has been written over the years about the alleged UFO incident involving this aircraft and I have no information that can prove or disprove what was said to have happened. However, I have tried harder than most to find unusual incidents leading up to the tragedy, that may indicate that something was not quite right in the days and weeks around September 8th 1970.

In 2005 I received two typed letters, both unsigned and hand-delivered, which placed another twist on the story. Their contents were brief and to the point, but suggested that there was no UFO incident at all.

They told of a Cold War encounter that, if true, was no less interesting. The letters stated that the Lightning incident took place at the height of the Cold War when Russia went to great lengths to test its military capabilities and our own. They went on to say that just off the East Yorkshire coast on the edge of our territorial waters, Russian factory ships were patrolling the sea. It was suggested that not all of these ships were fishing vessels and that some were monitoring the coastline. The Lightning was the fastest aircraft in the world at that time and it is well documented that XS894 was piloted by Captain William Schaffner, an exchange pilot from the US Air Force. One of the letters actually stated that he was in the UK to test new flight-suit technology.

I later received another unsigned letter, dated October 29th 2005. This one was post-marked with the city of Leeds and contained the following six lines: *"At the height of the Cold War, [Russians] operated submarines off this coast to 'sniff' [RAF] Fylingdales. When the divers got down they did not find the occupant and one report said that Russian divers had jacked up the canopy and removed the remains for the flying suit technology."*
(An image of this letter can be seen on the following page)

So according to this information, did Russian divers somewhere off the the East Yorkshire coast, close to our territorial waters, reach the submerged wreckage of the Lightning first - or were all these letters simply red herrings, designed to throw me of the UFO path ? It is not my intention to revive this story to simply attach another twist to it. However, if new information surfaces, it is only fair that people are informed. I realise that the account of the Lightning pursuing a UFO over the North Sea caused a lot of upset for the family and friends of Captain Schaffner. I wish to make it clear that this is not my intention, but I do believe new information needs to be made available if it is accurate and fits into the same time period that the aircraft crashed.

I contacted Tony Dodd and told him about the letters and to his credit, he accepted what I had to say about their content as a possibility. Tony genuinely believed that a UFO had something to do with the crash of the Lightning that night in September 1970 and even though some of the information I had found contradicted his own research, he still agreed to help me.

At the height of the Cold War, Russins operated submarines off this coast to "sniff" Fylingdales.

When the divers got down they did not find the occupant and one report said that Russian divers had jacked up the canopy and removed the remains for the flying suit technology.

Later Tony told me that he no longer wanted to be directly associated with the story of the Lightning. He said he had to distance himself from it because of death threats towards himself and his family and he advised me that I should also carefully consider what I was getting involved with. I think the death threats were real and regardless of whatever theories we subscribe to, there appears to be something very sensitive surrounding the loss of XS894. It was hard listening to Tony as he told me about his fears surrounding his involvement, because I felt that he had somehow touched upon the truth of the case.

I know from documentation that on the night of September 8th 1970, RAF Lightning XS894 disappeared from radar scanners at about 10.30pm, as they were tracking its progress some five miles off Flamborough Head. A Shackleton patrol aircraft, which had been accompanying the Lightning, dropped flares in an attempt to locate the missing fighter, but without success. Later reports say the search took place in very rough seas and that it was concentrated within an area between five and ten miles off Flamborough Head. The Flamborough and Filey lifeboats searched in fixed box areas and the Bridlington lifeboat took a zig-zagging approach. All shipping in the vicinity helped in the search, including the Dutch training ship the 'Prinses Margriet' and the UK trading vessel the 'Stormont'.

At daybreak the following morning the search was resumed in earnest. A helicopter from RAF Leconfield and another Shackleton were dispatched and two RAF rescue launches, based at Bridlington, joined in the search. According to The Bridlington Free Press newspaper from September 11th, an American 'Jolly Green Giant' helicopter, along with a C-130 Hercules aircraft from the US Air Force base in Woodbridge, Suffolk, also arrived to help with the search. During this time the local coastguard contacted Flamborough, Bridlington and Filey lifeboat stations, who were also introduced into the search.

On and around September 8th, residents of Bridlington, Scarborough and other towns further up the coast, reported seeing strange lights. On the 9th a trawler named the Ross Kestrel reported seeing flares in the search area, but on investigation nothing was found. My friend Tony Dodd, the researcher, told me that lots of UFO activity was being reported before and after the aircraft crashed. He said that people holidaying in Scarborough at the time, had claimed they saw a military aircraft involved in a UFO encounter over the North Sea. One witness reported seeing a huge disc-shaped object around 6am one morning, as it hovered over the sea off Scarborough's coast.

Another report from the night of September 8th, stated that a couple were out walking with their daughter and dog, along the coastal path at Alnmouth Bay in Northumberland, when they heard a strange humming sound. They are said to have later reported the strange occurrence to the police and MOD personnel.
They had apparently been walking for about ten minutes when they first became aware of a high pitched humming sound. They saw their family dog cock its head to one side and begin to growl, but they found it impossible to work out which direction the sound was coming from. They said It seemed to be everywhere. The sound lasted for between ten to fifteen seconds and then five minutes later, they say the sky lit up like sheet lightning. Although they described it as somehow different, in that it took about ten seconds for the sky to return to normal.
There followed a three minute period where the lightning flared up many times, but was only visible for one or two seconds each time - and the flashes of light were completely silent. They said that there was one final burst of sheet lightning, which lasted as long as the first, but the high-pitched shrill sound was much worse, because it actually made them feel their ears ringing. Later the family called into the local police station to report what they had seen and experienced.

This was one of many similar incidents that night, reported to both the police and RAF Boulmer, which is close to where the family claim to have had their strange experience. Although they had been out walking in the north of the country, almost a hundred miles away from Flamborough Head, it is on the same stretch of coastline and such a distance is nothing to a military aircraft - or perhaps another unknown.

A Flamborough couple, who wish to remain anonymous, told me that early one evening in September 1970, they observed five orange balls of light out to sea. They lived in one of four isolated bungalows, at the very top of the cliffs overlooking Thornwick Bay, which gave them unrestricted views out to sea. Unfortunately they were unable to give me an exact date for their sighting, but it seems that regardless of what people might want to believe, unusual activity *was* observed before and after the incident. Besides these visual reports of lights out at sea and the unsigned letters I had received, I also uncovered other information which added a further twist in the story of the lost Lightning.

On the afternoon of Thursday August 27th 1970, just twelve days before the Lightning incident, the Bridlington Free Press reported that an RAF rescue launch, out on a routine exercise from a unit based at Bridlington, suffered hull damage after hitting an unknown submerged object. The officer in command of the launch said at the time that they were well clear of all known obstacles when it struck something beneath the water. *"It must have been an unknown underwater obstacle,"* he remarked.
The launch was so badly damaged that it had to be beached on Bridlington's North Shore, otherwise it would have sunk. On inspection the boat was found to have a hole, measuring twenty foot by twelve inches, ripped into its hull. RAF personnel later worked to remove the vessel's port propeller and shaft, which had also been damaged in the impact. The launch was later towed to Whitby for repair.

As part of my research I spoke to many people about the damaged RAF rescue launch. I wanted to know the exact area of sea that it came into contact with the unidentified submerged object. In fact, I learned that it was positioned out in Bridlington's North Bay, less than two miles from Flamborough Head. This is an area of sea used on a daily basis by commercial fishing boats and pleasure boats.

R.A.F. launch holed by unknown submerged obstacle

A launch from the R.A.F. Marine Craft Unit at Bridlington is being repaired at a Whitby boatyard this week after a 20 ft. long by one ft. wide hole was ripped in its wooden hull on Thursday afternoon of last week.

What caused the damage is not clear. The officer in command of the launch said: "We were well clear of the sewage pipe when we struck something; it must have been an unknown underwater obstacle."

The launch was returning to Bridlington Harbour from a routine exercise when the accident happened. It tried to carry on to Bridlington Harbour, but the stern began to sink so the crew turned in towards the crowded north shore and beached the vessel.

Mr. Charles Wray, of 10 Westmoreland Grove, Bridlington, a beach inspector, told the Free Press: "There were lots of people swimming in the water and the launch had to blow its siren loudly to warn them to get out of the way."

After they had beached the vessel R.A.F. personnel removed the port propellor and shaft, which were damaged by the impact. Repair work was carried out on the damaged hull later on Thursday afternoon and evening, and the crippled launch was towed into Bridlington Harbour by one of its sister launches on the 3 a.m. Friday tide. Later it was towed to Whitby boatyard.

Holidaymakers watching as the R.A.F. launch was beached.

The rescue launch could not have hit a random outcrop of rocks below the surface, since the sea-bed drops away gradually there. They would have been well aware of what was below them. In fact it is free from obstructions, so quite how the launch came to have a gaping hole in it's side is a mystery.

The above account may be pure coincidence and as I write this forty-five years on, it is impossible to say with any certainty that any of the incidents are connected. If we were to believe in coincidence, then all of these events simply happened without any connection whatsoever. Mystery solved.

Moving ahead to the afternoon of Sunday September 6th 1970, less than two days before the loss of the Lightning, a young man and his family were enjoying a day on the sea. The man, with his three sons and a family friend, were all in their small speedboat, just north of Barmston beach, eight miles south of Flamborough. His wife was watching from the beach as they were all enjoying themselves on the water. Little did any of them know, that soon the boat would hit something beneath the surface that was so solid, the boat would capsize. The impact with the unidentified submerged object shattered the boat, throwing all five of them into the water. Reports later said that the boat had disintegrated after coming into contact with something beneath the waves.

They had been in the water for about thirty minutes, when they were spotted by a couple in a pleasure cruiser named Glenrose. The couple saw wreckage littering the surface of the sea and as they got closer, they could see the girl desperately clinging to a wooden seat from the boat and the man with his three sons hanging on to an inflated inner tube. At the time they commented that the man appeared in very bad shape and thought that he might not have lasted much longer.

The following day The Bridlington Free Press reported that the man, who was from Leeds and had piloted the boat at the time of the accident, was still too shocked to discuss what happened. Speaking to the newspaper, the man's wife, who had been watching from the shore, insisted that they had been travelling at low speed when they hit the object and were thrown into the sea. Through social media I was able to contact the man who had lost his speedboat over forty-five years earlier. I politely asked if he could add any other information about the accident, but he never replied.

Five rescued after speed-boat had hit submerged object

A LEEDS man and his three young sons and a girl clung for nearly half an hour to an inflated inner tube and a wooden seat after their speedboat had hit a submerged object and capsized off Barmston on Sunday afternoon.

On Monday afternoon Mr. Keith Woodley, of 12 Allerton Grange Vale, Leeds, was still too shocked to speak to the Free Press about his ordeal but his wife, who was not in the speed-boat at the time, said: "My husband, our three sons, and Miss Christine Oyston (18), of Plotion Way, Low Grange, Billingham, who is a friend of ours, left the South Cliff dinghy park to go to Barmston.

"I stayed on shore with the car and trailer. They were going along at a slow speed when they struck a solid object and were flung into the water."

Surrounded by wreckage, Mr. Woodley and his three sons Kevin (5), Philip (3) and Paul (2) clung to the inner tube while Miss Oyston, who is a non-swimmer, held onto a wooden seat from the speedboat.

There they remained for about half an hour until Mr. Sidney Desforges, of 382 Priory Road, Hull, arrived in his motor-cruiser.

With him were Mr. and Mrs. Jack Bolton of Thornton, Bradford, and Mr. and Mrs. George Bayes, of Whetley Lane, Bradford.

Noticed wreckage

Mr. Desforges told the Free Press: "We were returning to Bridlington Harbour in my cruiser, the Glenrose, from a day's fishing when we noticed wreckage strewn over the surface of the sea off Barmston.

"We went to investigate, and saw a girl clinging to what appeared to be a wooden seat. We threw her a rope and as we pulled her towards us she shouted 'save the kiddies' We saw a man and three small children clinging to an inflated rubber inner-tube.

"The smallest child was laid across the inner-tube, while the two other children, wearing life-jackets, were with the man in the water.

"We went alongside and pulled them aboard. The man seemed in pretty bad shape; in fact I do not think he could have lasted much longer, but as soon as the children had stripped out of their wet clothes and put blankets round themselves they seemed fine. We brought them back to Harbour and they were taken to hospital."

Treated for shock

The five people were treated for shock at Lloyd Hospital and discharged.

Mr. and Mrs. Woodley and their three children returned home from their caravan at Wallace's Holiday Camp, Cayton Bay.

With them they took their badly damaged speed-boat which was towed back to Bridlington on Monday morning.

Salvage claim?

The boat was towed back to Bridlington by Mr. Anthony Tanfield, of Dairycoates Service Station, Heassle Road, Hull, who was going down to Hornsea in his 14-ft. runabout boat when he saw wreckage and the nose of the submerged speedboat.

Mr. Tanfield believes that he has some right to a salvage claim from the boat's insurers for bringing it back to Harbour.

I doubt that a connection has ever been drawn between the damaged rescue launch and the speedboat accident before and perhaps no one has ever stopped to consider whether they actually hit an object or whether an object hit them. Either way, I have no evidence to prove that any of these incidents are connected to the loss of the RAF Lightning in 1970. The mystery objects below the surface were never identified and to the best of my knowledge, no boats have struck any unidentified submerged obstacles in the area, before or after. The area of sea just off the Barmston coast is flat and sandy, much like the bay of Bridlington. It could be argued that all three accidents were pure coincidence and I am in no position to dispute that. Yet at some point I think even the most sceptical mind has to pause and consider the possibility that something highly unusual happened around the time RAF Lightning XS894 crashed off Flamborough Head.

Each of these accidents are a mystery in themselves and have never previously been reported as part of the puzzle, but when they are placed alongside the loss of the Lightning, in such close proximity by date and location, the mystery deepens. This remains a controversial incident which continues to be discussed forty-five years later. If nothing else, once again the area seems to experience events that happen in clusters. I have noticed that long periods of time can pass when nothing happens, then without warning or reason a series of events occur within a very small time-frame. Can this all be put down to coincidence ?

On February 9th 2015 I visited the Bridlington Lifeboat Station. I needed to be sure that the dates and approximate times for the above accounts were correct. Log entries for September 8th 1970 showed that the Bridlington lifeboat was launched at 22.36pm and returned the following day at 9.25am - so they had spent a total of eleven hours out at sea searching for XS894. The log stated that visibility at the time was between five to ten miles - so good visibility. The wind speed was listed as force six - which is twenty-two to twenty-five knots and a rough sea. The station officer was very helpful and assisted me by checking the 1970 log a month before and a month after the Lightning crash. There was no record of lifeboat call-outs for either the damaged RAF rescue launch of August 27th or the speedboat accident on September 6th. Other call-outs were listed, but none seemed to refer to these incidents. I am unsure what this tells us because the local newspapers reported these incidents as they happened.

The RAF Lightning incident had allegedly involved strange balls of light around the aircraft, so with that in mind, I took the opportunity to speak to the station officer. I asked him about the lights that were often seen off the coast of Bempton and Flamborough. The orange spheres of light had been reported along the coast in almost every year that I researched, from the past to the present day. He said that although he had never seen them personally, he was aware that many reports had been made about them over the years, adding, that in some instances they could never get to the bottom of what they actually were. I detected a genuine interest in the information I had found, but I knew, due to his position, he would have to remain impartial.

The descriptions of these lights are all very similar from reports over the years - which are quite different to the explanations dreamed up to explain them. The experienced pilot who encountered a UFO while flying over the burial mound of Willy Howe in 1996 also spoke of his interaction with an orange ball of light. In many instances eye-witness reports speak of balls of light that look and act differently to anything we understand. Lightning XS894 allegedly reported a similar interaction with 'amber-coloured' lights before it vanished from radar in September 1970. I wonder how many more reports and incidents it will take before people's eyes are opened to the fact that the lightforms, whatever they might be, are real. The word 'coincidence' has its place, but I believe it is an overused word when dropped into multi-witness accounts as a sweeping explanation for things we simply do not understand.

Although not connected to any mystery I am aware of, it is worth noting that on September 22nd 1969, just over a year before the loss of XS894, an earlier RAF Lightning - XS926 of 5 Squadron - was reported to have spun out of control before it crashed into the sea, sixty miles off Flamborough Head. The aircraft was piloted by another USAF exchange pilot who ejected and survived. These are only a few of many aircraft which have plummeted from the skies off the coast of Flamborough and Bempton.

'UFO' And The UFOs

I pride myself on never revealing the identity of a witness if I am asked. This was the first request made to me by 'Alan', the pseudonym for a first-hand witness in an amazing sighting from September 1970.

Alan's story came just as we were in the final stages of editing Truth-Proof, but I knew instantly that it had to be included. I always suspected that he had a story to tell and his reluctance to share it earlier led me think he was very genuine about it, but also very cautious - especially about his identity not being revealed. Alan said,
"Paul this was my first encounter with anything like this in my life, and the only reason I was looking up at the sky that day was because I had been watching a new programme on TV called UFO."

As a child of the 1970s myself, I remembered the UK TV series well and like many kids from that era, I used to be glued to the screen watching. The first episode of the Gerry Anderson series 'UFO' was aired on September 16th 1970, just seven days after the crash of RAF Lightning XS894 off Flamborough Head. This places Alan's account within the time-frame of other UFO activity reported in the area at the time. Of course, it is ironic that the marker used to date Alan's sighting was a TV show called UFO.

This is Alan's full report in his own words:
"In the early 70s, I was always watching the sky, as you do. Well I did anyway. I remember it was a clear day with some big white cumulus clouds around. That's when I saw them. Six shiny spheres moving very slowly through the sky in an easterly direction. I shouted for my Mum to come and have a look. I'd have been maybe four or five at the time, but even at that young age I knew I was looking at something different to anything I had ever seen before. I guess she knew from the urgency in my voice that something was wrong and moments later, Mum arrived outside to see what all the fuss was about. She looked over to where I was excitedly pointing, [then] turned around and ran back inside for the binoculars.
I just could not take my eyes off them. Seconds later Mum rushed back with the binoculars and proceeded to watch them for a few minutes, before they disappeared behind a group of large clouds. She was so

mesmerised by them she totally ignored my pleas for the binoculars to be handed to me. She did however draw what she saw and as she was a brilliant artist, she used to design fashions etc., I got a detailed description what she saw.

We lived in [Bridlington] at the time and the objects were slowly heading towards Bempton/Flamborough and although it was difficult to calculate the exact distance, we think they were roughly three to four miles away. They were absolutely huge. I could clearly see six perfectly round objects that appeared to be travelling at around the same height as the clouds. I could tell they were shiny and very big, but Mum's drawings and description of what she saw through the binoculars was incredible.
She said they were round metallic discs and so big that she could actually see their underside. The metal - if it was metal - was shiny but not chrome-shiny. More maybe polished pewter or aluminium. But it was the centre underneath that was the most amazing sight to see. She said each one consisted of a raging angry looking fire of oranges and deep reds. Something like you would expect to see boiling away in a volcano. There was no noise or apparent rotation from these things and they were so large we would have been able to tell. My Mum got the best view through the binoculars. She estimated that each one would have been several hundred feet in diameter. They were just amazing to see, moving in a slow horizontal line through the sky towards Bempton and Flamborough."

Alan's brilliant observation of the cumulus clouds gives us a rough estimate of the height these objects were travelling. Cumulus clouds are usually low-level and no more than three thousand feet high. Given the estimated size of the objects it seems inconceivable that Alan and his mother were the only two people to see them that day. Yet this is not the first time that UFOs of a staggering size have been reported over the North Sea. In 1998 an object estimated to have been the size of a battleship was allegedly tracked by radar and pursued by military jets. This was reported in the UK press at the time, which stated that radar at RAF Fylingdales, North Yorkshire had picked up a giant UFO, estimated to be nine hundred feet long and travelling at incredible speed out over the North Sea.

It would be wrong to say that the UFOs witnessed by Alan and his mother were in any way connected to the tragic loss of an RAF aircraft. Yet they both saw something that, by even today's standards, defies explanation and adds fuel to the mystery of whatever was appearing in our skies that September in 1970.

SIGHTING OVER
BRIDLINGTON
1970

Tornado Vanishes Off Radar

On Monday June 15th 1998 an RAF Tornado F3 crashed into the North Sea off Flamborough Head. Aircraft ZE732 vanished from radar whilst on a routine training exercise over the North Sea and sent no Mayday message. The jet's flight recorder was located two hundred feet below the surface of the sea on the following day and was recovered a week later. The official report states that ZE732 was practicing intercept manoeuvres with two other Tornados, with a Hawk trainer aircraft as their target. They had successfully completed one intercept, at around 14,000ft, then the Hawk was said to have repositioned at the lower altitude of 2,000ft.

The official accident summary states that during the steep descent to intercept the Hawk, the Tornado crew had misjudged their rate of descent. As they realised the error, recovery was not possible and their aircraft crashed into the sea. Both men were tragically killed in the accident. A search and rescue operation was launched immediately, involving RAF Sea King helicopters, a Nimrod patrol aircraft on reconnaissance and lifeboats from Filey. One of the lifeboats found a body and wreckage approximately thirty miles north-east of Flamborough Head, the second body was never found. I found no mention in any of the reports that they had found either the pilot or the navigator in the search. It was said later that it was not possible to identify the body, although with the advent of DNA testing, I would have expected that it may have been possible, unless there were other reasons of which I am unaware.

Sadly, my enquiries into this and other tragedies have occasionally received a hostile response. It seems that to some, I have been disrespectful by asking such questions and although I apologise for any upset my work may have caused, I have always asked with respect. At no time have I tried to deliberately steer anyone into believing that something happened that did not. The official explanation given for the tragic loss of Tornado ZE732 may after all, be the correct one.

In February 2015 I paid another visit to the Bridlington lifeboat station. The officer on duty remembered me from earlier visits in the previous year. He was very helpful and allowed me to see the information they still held for June 15th 1998. Their log showed that, in the search for RAF Tornado ZE732, a lifeboat was launched at 1pm and returned at 12.35am the following morning. Visibility was one to four miles, with a gentle breeze of seven to ten knots. The log showed that wreckage had been located twenty miles off Flamborough Head, although the official report had indicated it was thirty miles. Then plotting its position on a chart, we found the wreckage was about seven miles from the offshore Cleeton Gas Field.

In 1998 there was much speculation online that the loss of this military aircraft was somehow connected to UFOs over the North Sea. Many unidentified aerial objects were reported around the time of the incident, although I have no evidence to offer as proof that something of this nature actually took place.

Of the many UFOs that were reported around the UK in 1998, one report stands out. In April 1998, the Daily Mail and Telegraph newspapers reported that the Royal Air Force and Netherlands Air Force had pursued a giant UFO over the North Sea. It was said to have flown in a zigzag pattern at speeds of over 17,000 miles per hour and tracked by RAF Fylingdales Radar Station in North Yorkshire. Reports said that RAF and Dutch fighter aircraft were sent to intercept the object as it rapidly moved away north-west, towards the Atlantic Ocean.

This report may have no bearing on the tragedy of ZE732 at all, but it adds much to the mystery of unusual activity over the North Sea during 1998. This, combined with reports on local TV news channels, which said that the RAF were reluctant to talk about the accident, helped to deepen the mystery, as a veil of silence seemed to be dropped over the incident.

Search Goes On For Tornado Wreckage

Bridlington Free Press
June 18th 1998

By Claire Davidson

THE black box of the RAF Tornado which crashed into the sea 20 miles off Flamborough on Monday will hopefully be recovered by a salvage vessel today.

The F3 Tornado, of the 29 Squadron based at RAF Coningsby in Lincolnshire, was returning from a training sortie with two other aircraft before it disappeared from radar screens shortly before 1pm, sending no mayday message.

The flight recorder of the Tornado, which was carrying a pilot and a navigator, was located at 200ft under water in the North Sea on Tuesday. It is hoped that the recorder will indicate why the plane crashed so suddenly on a routine flight.

Monday's rescue operation led to the recovery of one body.

Bridlington and Filey

● A Tornado F3 similar to the one that crashed.

lifeboat crews were alerted to the incident, which happened at about 1pm, and raced to the area, joining two Sea King helicopters from Leconfield and one from RAF Boulmer, a Nimrod and a NATO AWACS reconnaisance aircraft.

Fred Walkington, coxswain of the Bridlington lifeboat, said the crew of six men launched the lifeboat at

● Bridlington lifeboat - involved in the grim task of recovering wreckage. .

about 1.30pm and arrived at the area about one-and-a-half hours later.

He said both crews carried out search patterns and as the search widened one of the helicopters spotted some wreckage.

He said: "The fog was down to below 50 yards visibility and it was very difficult to do the search.

"We did everything we could to locate the unfortunate men and didn't know whether they were alive or dead.

"The helicopters had to pull out early because the visibility was very poor. We came away at about 9.30pm and Filey came away at about 10pm. Both the lifeboats had to come away at very low speeds to conserve fuel because they had been searching for so long at full speed."

The lifeboats retrieved a large amount of wreckage from the scene and returned it to land.

The rescue operation was co-ordinated by the Humber Coastguard and staff at RAF Kinloss in Scotland.

A spokeswoman from

RAF Kinloss said: "The weather had been ropey until late afternoon on Monday and in the early evening rescue 131 RAF Sea King and the crew of the Nimrod spotted wreckage a couple of miles from the search area. However, as they moved to recover it the mist rolled in again.

"Filey lifeboat went to pick the bits of wreckage and while they were collecting panels I believe they came across a body."

The aircraft crew were named as pilot Sqdn Ldr William Vivian, 33, and navigator Flt Lieut Derek Lacey, 33. Both were from Cheshire and married with young families.

A fuel tanker from RAF Leconfield was escorted to North Landing in Flamborough by police, fire brigade and the Humber Coastguard to refuel one of the Sea King helicopters involved in the search.

The refuelling took place late on Monday afternoon. When it was complete the helicopter returned to the search area.

The fire brigade was present to ensure the refuelling was done safely and the police and Humber Coastguard were asked to attend to keep members of the public away from the area.

Due to the mist at Flamborough the tanker was taken to the car park at the Humber Coastguard office in Bridlington in case the helicopter needed to return.

● Left: A RAF Sea King rescue helicopter lands at

Dark Object

Whilst discussing the loss of the RAF Tornado with local fishermen, one of the older men seemed to recall that he had heard of something else strange that happened around the same time. His memory of the incident was vague, but he remembered some of the men talking about black UFOs. He said they had been witnessed on more than one occasion from boats up and down the coast and near an area of sea-bed known by them as 'the ten wrecks'.

Armed with nothing more than the vague recollections of an old fisherman, I was not confident that I should place the information alongside the report of the lost Tornado - without being guilty of creating a mystery out of nothing. I had a pile of questions that needed addressing and few places to turn for answers. I was also aware that the location of some of these crashed aircraft was in an area of the North Sea where, on rare occasions, fishermen have found themselves in a state of confusion. I had been told about this by people who had experienced it first-hand. Their confusion seemed to be due to problems with their compass readings, which occasionally displayed discrepancies while on the same stretch of water.

I wondered what could be capable of creating such a magnetic anomaly out at sea, but gathering information was very difficult. It was there, but as soon as I began to expand on my questions, then ask the fishermen why they thought this might be happening, I hit a wall of silence. My own uncle spent all his working life as a navigator and second officer in command on huge oil tankers. He once suggested to me that there might be an outcrop of iron ore, just below the surface, which may be responsible. Although it is a fair to say that there could be many explanations for the anomaly which are equally plausible.

I had so many unanswered questions; compass anomalies, UFOs, crashed aircraft, I began to wonder if it all was just a fisherman's tale. If these stories were true and had occurred on land instead of the sea, the area would be fenced off with a big sign saying 'HAZARD'.

The next day I decided to pay another visit to the Bridlington lifeboat station. If there was any truth to the black UFO sightings, some clue might be contained in their log. No matter how small the reference, it might back up the stories I had been told.

As expected, records showed the lifeboat call out for the June 15th Tornado incident in 1998. Then looking at entries for the months before and after that date, to the surprise of the station officer and myself, there was another entry for July, less than one month later. The reference on the log had just one word. It simply said OBJECT. The details stated that a lifeboat was called out to investigate an area of sea five miles off the coast. A fisherman from Hornsea, just south of Flamborough, had reported seeing a 'black object' drop from the sky sometime after 9pm on Sunday July 12th 1998. He described it as 'large and dark' in colour.

I later discovered that whatever this object was, it remained on the surface of the water for some time. A little later, at around 9.45pm, the coastguard contacted Bridlington lifeboat rescue and a thorough search of the area began in an attempt to try and locate the mystery black object. A rescue helicopter was also called in to assist in the search, but nothing was found and by 12.44am the search was called off. There were no ships in distress and no aircraft reported missing. The dark object had vanished.

So what could have suddenly descended from the sky on July 12th and remained visible for a short time, then just slip below the surface of the North Sea ? Many UFOs had been reported throughout the months before and after the Tornado crash, but I think this report has gone undetected by other researchers, past and present. The short report in the lifeboat station log highlights that unexplainable things *were* taking place in the area back in 1998 and were considered important enough for the launch of a lifeboat and dispatch of a helicopter in the search.

My next task was to visit the Bridlington library archive, where I found a copy of the Bridlington Free Press dated July 16th 1998. It contained a short article on page 25 entitled 'Mystery Object' which stated that a mysterious black floating object had been spotted by a fisherman. Was it pure coincidence that this large dark UFO had been seen and reported, less than a month after ZE732 had vanished from radar or that people had seen a similar dark objects prior to the crash ? Finding information like this is only possible by asking questions and searching archives. This is how I discovered that the dark object was also seen on more than one occasion. If the information suggests possible links or connections, then it has to be considered, regardless of how unusual it may first appear. Although I cannot and will not say that any of these incidents *are* connected to one another, I continue to find unusual information and simply lay it out with an open-mind.

Bridlington Free Press July 16th 1998.

Mystery·object

A MYSTERIOUS black floating object spotted in the sea off Hornsea sparked a three-hour search by Bridlington Coastguard and Bridlington Lifeboat.

The search took place last Sunday night at 9.44pm after a fisherman saw a black object fall out of the sky and enter the sea.

At 12.44am the search, which also involved a rescue helicopter, was called off after no traces of the object.

The Bridlington lifeboat station officer told me that in 1998 their original reports would have been made out on paper. These have all since been transferred to a computer database, but he was of the opinion that back then, more details would have been provided on their paper reports than would be made electronically today.

The station kept log books for the years before and after 1998 - but 1998's log book was missing. The officer told that he had no idea where the old logs would be now. I realised that writing about seeing a log in the lifeboat station is not be the same as actually having proof. So with that in mind, I sent a Freedom of Information request in to the government's Maritime and Coastguard Agency. I gave them the exact date of the incident so there could be no confusion. Below is part of their reply back to me:

MCA - *May 5th 2016*
"Dear Mr Sinclair,
Your request for information has been dealt with in accordance with the
Freedom of Information Act 2000. Unfortunately the MCA does not
retain detailed information regarding call-outs from as far back as 1998,
and so we no longer hold any call-out records specifying involvement of
the RNLI Bridlington Lifeboat on 12/07/1998."

Undeterred I decided to send the same FOI request to the RNLI and to
my surprise, a few days later I received a reply via email. Here is part of
their reply:

RNLI - *May 11th 2016*
"Hello Paul,
Bridlington All-Weather Lifeboat launched at 22:15 on 12/07/1998.
Weather was cloudy with poor visibility, sea state 3 with a swell of 1
metre. This was their only launch on this date. Report is as follows:
LOCAL FISHERMAN HORNSEA CONTACTED HUMBER COASTGUARD
TO REPORT A LARGE BLACK OBJECT FALLING INTO SEA 5 MILES
OFFSHORE. COASTGUARD UNIT MET INFORMANT TO HELP
IDENTIFY POSITION. BRIDLINGTON LIFE BOAT LAUNCHED AND
DIRECTED TO A POINT 5 MILES OFFSHORE ON BEARING
INDICATED BY INFORMANT. HELICOPTER FROM RAF LECONFIELD
ASKED TO COVER SEARCH AREA. COASTGUARD CHECKED LOCAL
RADAR AND RAF, NO REPORTS OF MISSING PLANES. SEARCH OF
AREA WAS UNABLE TO FIND ANYTHING."

In April 2015 I placed an article in the Hornsea Gazette asking for
readers to come forward with any unusual stories they had from East
and North Yorkshire. A retired member of Hornsea Coastguard saw my
post and contacted me. He remembered the original incident but said
that he had to be very careful about what information he divulged. I
cannot say whether he knew more about the dark object, however, he
did inform me that a work colleague had described seeing a huge, low-
flying black triangular object, moving very slowly over some fields. He
also said that military vehicles were speeding up and down the roads
and road blocks were being set up. Although he could not remember the
exact date, he was sure it happened in the middle of 1998.

The Loss Of ZA610

A Sequence of Strange Events or
Nothing More Than a Tragic Accident ?

On Saturday December 12th 1985, six RAF Tornado jets were on routine exercises over the North Sea, together with two Buccaneer aircraft. The jets were working at thirty minute intervals with the Buccaneers that night on air to air refuelling exercises. Tornado ZA610 of No 617 Squadron was paired with Buccaneer MQU13.

ZA610's air crew were Flight Lieutenants Barnard and Sheen, both were experienced pilots with almost two thousand hours of flying experience and between them the men had over a thousand hours experience of Tornados.

An MOD/RAF Board of Inquiry report states that ZA610 took off from RAF Marham in Norfolk, fifteen minutes earlier than their scheduled departure time. The report does not give a reason for this, but they were scheduled to take off at 17:15 to rendezvous with Buccaneer MQU13 by 17:30 hours off Flamborough Head, approximately a hundred and forty miles north. Visibility was said to be good and there was a thin cloud layer at about four thousand feet.

Problems began for ZA610 when they could not establish radio contact with the Buccaneer aircraft. Another Buccaneer crew advised them to try an area radar frequency and when that was unsuccessful they tried yet another frequency. The crew of Tornado ZA610 acknowledged this suggestion and were never heard from again.

Prior to this, Buccaneer MQU13 had completed refuelling practice with their first Tornado and were on a southerly heading to rendezvous with ZA610 at an altitude of two and half thousand feet. Ground radar showed that MQU13 was behind ZA610 by about five nautical miles and had confirmed visual contact with lights at their 11 o'clock position. The crew stated that the lights appeared to close in and pass down their port side.

Buccaneer MQU13 then began a port turn on an easterly heading and lost sight of the lights. Rolling out of the turn, they had a second visual from their 7.30 position and after another port turn onto a northerly heading, they made visual contact once more from their 9.30 position. Reports state that after passing through a ninety degree turn, ZA610 had rolled out on a northerly heading and passed behind the Buccaneer at a distance of about one nautical mile. It has to be assumed that the lights seen by the Buccaneer were those of Tornado ZA610.

Radar tracking confirmed that ZA610 had started to climb to seventeen hundred feet. Eight seconds later they moved to the right and then vanished from radar. Although the move to the right could indicate they had started to descend, radar should have been able to track their position to as low as two hundred feet above sea level. Item 7 of the MOD/RAF Board of Inquiry report states that radar records clearly show ZA610 *was* the visual contact that Buccaneer MQU13 saw from their 11 o'clock position, but suggests that the crew's description of aircraft lights closing and passing down their port side to have probably been a 'night-time illusion'.
Does this mean that MQU13's visual sighting of lights off their port side were not picked up on radar - the same lights that were *confirmed* by radar from their 11 o'clock position moments before ?

On Saturday December 14th, The Filey Mercury newspaper reported that Tornado ZA610 had disappeared from radar screens about six and a half miles off Flamborough Head. Yet on December 17th, a Bridlington trawler named 'Betty FR68' had actually located the Tornado in the water, sixteen miles off Flamborough Head. So it appears the aircraft had travelled almost ten miles undetected. At the time, other newspaper reports gave different distances off the coast for the crashed aircraft, although after speaking with the trawlermen myself, I believe the Betty's location of sixteen miles to be the most accurate.

The Tornado accident summary states that it was not possible to determine the cause of the accident and the most likely possibility was loss of control, following either 'pilot-induced oscillation or disorientation'. It goes on to state that a less likely cause or contributing factor was 'technical defect' leading to loss of control. The summary also suggests that the crew probably did not eject from the aircraft.

The story of Tornado ZA610 has not changed over the past thirty years and this would have remained so, if not for my research into strange events and happenings around East and North Yorkshire. It was in the archives of Bridlington library that I made a discovery in a Bridlington Free Press newspaper article, from Thursday December 19th 1985. This discovery led to a mystery.

Entitled '*Body Mystery*' the short article states that on Thursday December 19th 1985, the body of the Tornado's navigator had been found by the Bridlington trawler 'Betty', sixteen miles south-east of Flamborough Head. The article explains that, thirty-six miles to the east of the first, a second body was found in an ejector seat. This is confirmed by a report from The Scarborough Evening News published a day earlier, which also states that two bodies were found in ejector seats on the same day. The story becomes even more intriguing when we see that both newspapers state that the second body was *not* thought to be that of Tornado ZA610's pilot.

If a person had made up this story to create a conspiracy, I very much doubt people would believe such an unusual set of circumstances. Yet this is what was reported in late December 1985. Although the newspaper reports may be accurate, I just wonder how the story would be viewed if I had reported it here, without having the original newspapers to support my words.

Bridlington Free Press - Dec 19th 1985

Body mystery

Two bodies, including that of the co-pilot of the RAF Tornado that crashed last week, have been found off Bridlington.

Mystery still surrounds the identity of the other body; it is not the plane's pilot.

Local trawler, the Betty, found the first body with an ejector seat, floating 16 miles south east of Bridlington yesterday. It was identified as that of Flt-Lieut John Sheene (36), a married man from Ixworth in Suffolk.

The second body was found 36 miles east of the first, by a Dutch trawler. It too was found with an ejector seat but it is not that of the pilot.

My continuing research led me to Bridlington's small fishing harbour, where thirty years earlier, the crew of the trawler Betty FR68 would have worked. I was hoping to find more information about the tragedy of the Tornado and learn more about the men who had made the discovery. My first port of call was the harbourmaster's office, where I learned that the Betty had been scrapped sometime in 2012. Then I was advised that there was a good chance some of her former crew may still be working on the harbour. This was more than I could have hoped for. A first-hand account of the events from 1985, as seen through the eyes of the trawlermen who were there, was what I really wanted. A walk around the various cabins on the harbour that day proved uneventful, since tides dictate trawlermen's work hours, all the boats were out at sea.

As there was no one around, I realised I would have to wait another day. So from there I went to Bridlington lifeboat station, carrying my folder containing the small amount of information I had gathered so far. I thought they would have a log of some kind dating back to 1985, but I was hoping to find a detailed account of the search and rescue for Tornado ZA610. One of the lifeboat officers read through the information I had unearthed, then I told him about the second body which had been found on the same day. When I mentioned that it was not thought to be the Tornado's pilot he said nothing, but I could tell from his reaction that he thought I was mistaken.
To back up my words I showed him the newspaper clipping from 1985. Now he was interested. The chances of anyone finding a second body in an ejector seat and it being the wrong man, seemed impossible to me. It appeared that the lifeboat officer agreed, as he read more of the information I had taken with me. Indeed, he echoed my thoughts, but sadly could offer me no documented evidence for the crash. We looked at a wall plaque at the station, which listed incidents for the years before and after the crash of ZA610, but strangely, there was no reference of any events for December 1985.

I began to wonder why such a major search and rescue event in the local area would not have been documented. After all, it was their lifeboat that was involved in the rescue operation. It *had* to have been logged somewhere. My subsequent visits to the station revealed that a computerised log did exist showing the search for the aircraft, but showed nothing of any significance for 1985. According to The Filey

Evening Mercury at the time, lifeboats from Bridlington, Scarborough, Filey, Whitby and Flamborough were *all* involved in the early stages of the search.

Over the next few weeks I gathered additional bits of information, but I still needed a key to get inside the mystery. With that in mind I set off once again to Bridlington harbour, hoping that on this occasion I might find someone willing to talk to me.

It was August 2014 and a cold autumn day, yet the sun was shining and the last summer holidaymakers were enjoying a day by the sea. All the harbour cabins consisted of dark blue, painted wooden door, behind which was a small working area. As I drifted around the harbour looking into the cabins, I thought they looked like dull and depressing places to spend a day working. Making eye contact with some of the men in the cabins, I was hoping for a nod or some kind of acknowledgment that would enable me to bring up the questions I wanted. For the most part, these men seemed distrusting of unfamiliar faces walking around their place of work. This was something I had also encountered when researching events around the East Yorkshire Wolds. Then it occurred to me. Looking at these men I realised that most of them were quite young and would not have even been of working age back in 1985. I began to think it was a lost cause.

Then as I rounded a corner to view the final row of nine work huts, I saw a fisherman hard at work. He was coiling ropes out in the open air. He wore jeans with nothing above the waist and was a giant of a man. At around six foot five and lean, he was formidable looking to say the least, but then he was exactly what I had been looking for. As I approached, he looked at me from under his brow, smiled and said,
"Hello Paul."

The fisherman was named Tom Quinn and a few years before, he had taken a break from working the sea and had taken a job as a labourer for a large construction company. Over the years I had worked as a joiner on many building sites around Bridlington, so we had already become acquainted. We exchanged a few words about life and work, then I got to the questions I wanted to ask. I asked Tom if he knew of anyone on the harbour who might have information about a Tornado that crashed almost thirty years earlier off Flamborough Head. I told him what I had found out so far and he listened with interest. Then a

141

huge grin appeared on his face and for a moment I thought I was about to receive a sarcastic comment.

"It was me Paul. I was part of the trawler crew who found that plane. I pulled the navigator from the water."

At first I thought he was joking, but he was deadly serious.

I could not believe that out of the thirty-five work cabins on Bridlington harbour I had found a first-hand witness, but Tom began to tell me of his memories of the day they had gone to sea that December in 1985. He said that morning he had noticed the local post office and newsagents were displaying a news board outside their shop, showing the image of a Tornado with information about the crash. He said he thought it would have been Saturday December 14th.

"I can remember seeing the news-board Paul. It said 'Tornado Down - East of Flamborough Head' and I thought to myself, 'that's right where we are going to be'. It was just a passing thought, because the chances of us coming across the aircraft in the vast area of sea that we work, were slim to say the least."

Tom explained that he left Bridlington harbour that morning aboard the Betty with two crew mates. He told me that the area of sea that they were going to fish was east of Flamborough, about a hundred and eighty feet deep and flat and sandy, with no known obstacles. *"We were fishing for queenies,"* he said. *"That's scallops to you Paul. We had fished that area for years and there was nothing there but sand."*

Tom said that back in 1985 the depth sounder on board the trawler gave out a paper graph print-out of the sea-bed beneath them. They knew that area of sea very well and nothing of any significance had ever showed up on the sounder before.

"We were about sixteen miles east of Flamborough Head," Tom continued, *"when the nets suddenly jumped. The boat jolted violently as it hit something big on the sea-bed that should not have been there. It stopped the Betty in her tracks and for a moment we were all a bit stunned by what had happened. We rushed into the wheel house and could not believe our eyes when we looked at the print-out from the sounder. It was just a mass of lines mapping out a large, dark shape on the sea-bed.*

There was nothing we could do except haul the nets to the surface and hope that no real damage had been done. At this point we were more concerned about our fishing gear and getting it back to the surface undamaged, than what had caused it. After all, this was our livelihood and no fish meant no wages."

As they began to retrieve their nets from the sea-bed below, it soon became apparent that something more than shellfish and seaweed would be accompanying them. The first glimpse of anything unusual was the swaying red and black silk of a parachute as it rose from the depths. Then to all their amazed eyes, the full extent of the tragedy unfolded, as the body of the Tornado's navigator, still strapped into his ejector seat, came to the surface entangled in their nets. Tom explained that the navigator's parachute must have been trailing in the depths below them and the trawlers fishing gear had become caught in it. In the process of pulling up their nets, in addition, they believed they had inadvertently pulled the navigator and his live ejector seat clean out of the aircraft. Later that day, when a naval vessel had arrived on the scene, their crew also thought that this is what must have happened.

At the time, it was thought that before being caught up in the trawlers nets, the navigator should still have been inside the cockpit of the aircraft. However, the canopy must have been up for the parachute to have been loose in the water. Of course, these were only observations made on the day, before any detailed report had been made. How the parachute came to be loose in the water is not known. One possibility is that the aircraft's canopy fractured on impact, but it is something we can never know.

The MOD/RAF Board of Inquiry report later said that examination of the wreckage and the severity of the navigators injuries indicate that it had been a relatively high speed crash. This may lead some to assume that Tornado ZA610 had broken up on impact, but this conflicts with Tom's recollections of the size of what their trawler's depth sounder had located. His comment to me may also add weight to this theory, when he said, *"when we hit this thing the nets jumped and the boat jerked so hard we thought it was going to rip the back end off."*

His remarks do seem to indicate that the trawler had come into contact with something much larger than just an ejector seat. A Tornado has a duel ejection seat mechanism, meaning that if one person ejects, then the other is automatically ejected also. If the ejection seats were still within the submerged aircraft, then they could <u>not</u> have been activated by either occupant. If they were, there is an automatic sequence of events; the canopy is jettisoned, the seat ejects upwards and out after a period of thrust, the main parachute is deployed and the seat then separates from the occupant. There is an inflatable life-raft and survival kit below the occupant which is deployed on contact with the water. In some instances, so I am told, it may be possible to manually deploy the parachute - usually after manual seat ejection, such as for aerobatic displays.

Tom Quinn told me that he tried to cut the ejector seat free of the fishing nets. His two crew mates were so shocked by the find that they were unable to assist. He said that at first they were unsure what to do, as none of them had ever experienced or could have ever anticipated such a situation. However, a short time later Tom made radio contact with a nearby naval ship, the Hunter-class Minesweeper HMS Brecon, and he informed them of their discovery. He said that it seemed almost instantly that they were surrounded by helicopters and military boats.

The first vessel on the scene was the Brecon. It had been searching the area for days along with four other navy vessels; HMS Leeds Castle, an off-shore patrol vessel, HMS Edinburgh, a destroyer and HMS Bildeston, another mine hunter. Also engaged in the search were a Wessex helicopter and two Sea King helicopters from RAF Boulmer.

Four crew from the HMS Brecon boarded the trawler and they assisted Tom in freeing the ejector seat from the fishing nets. Before they arrived, Tom had already radioed out on channel seventy-one. He made radio contact with the Brecon and told them he had been trying to free the ejector seat from his nets. He said they gave him a harsh warning telling him not touch the seat again unless instructed to do so.

Tom laughed, as he recalled the minesweeper's approach. He told me that the men aboard were waving and shouting at him. He said, *"I waved back, not realising they were frantically urging me to step away from the live ejector seat."* They later told him that the seat had enough explosive in it to blow the back of the trawler clean off.

How did the Brecon crew know that Tom's discovery was potentially dangerous ? Does this indicate that they already knew the Tornado crew had not ejected from their aircraft ? If so how ? Or was this simply a precaution to avoid another accident ? If the bulk of the aircraft was below the surface and the aircrew had not ejected, where was the pilot ? These were all questions I put to Tom over the many months we discussed ZA610.

He explained that by the time the Brecon had arrived the trawler had drifted away from the aircraft's original location, although they were still in the immediate vicinity. The MOD/RAF accident report may be entirely accurate of course, and I am sure every effort was made to learn how the aircraft had crashed. It is a pity that no one ever asked to see the original print-out from the trawler's depth sounder.

On their arrival on board the Betty, the first thing the Brecon's crew wanted to know was how much contact Tom and the others had had with the navigator's body and ejector seat. Tom asked why, but it seemed that these men did not answer questions - they only asked questions and expected answers. He told them that he had been in close contact with the ejector seat and the navigator for a number of hours. It was then decided that one Brecon crew member would attempt to free the seat from the fishing nets and Tom Quinn was asked if he would assist. He was told due to the risk of radioactive contamination, contact should be kept to a minimum. At this point Tom was still trying to take in everything that was happening. He said it was all so surreal - and now they were talking about radiation ?

He agreed to help and was given a pair of thick rubber gloves that went past his elbows. He asked what they were for, since he already had gloves which he thought were quite suitable for the task, but his own gloves were thrown over the side.

"*Radiation!*" The Brecon crew member said in a stern voice. Tom repeated the word out loud, somewhat puzzled.

"*Yes radiation*" said the Brecon crew member, pointing to the ejector seat. "*There is a possibility that the seat and the navigator are contaminated with radiation and you and your other crew members could also be at risk.*"

Tom and the two trawler crew were then told that if they began to suffer nose bleeds, nausea, vomiting or if their hair began to fall out, or they noticed any other strange physical abnormalities, they should seek medical help immediately. They were also ordered to discard their catch of fifty or so sacks of shellfish, because they were also at risk of radioactive contamination.

I thought it seemed strange to throw potentially radioactive material back into the sea, but this is what Tom said they told him. I wondered whether the use of the word 'radiation' was standard procedure when an aircraft crashes. I do know that some aircraft's instruments can have radioactive properties and that dust from these can be harmful. Then I tried to imagine if it would still being present after five days below the North Sea. Why were no notices ever issued to other fishing vessels, so they could avoid fishing in that area of sea. Or why not a temporary ban on fishing in that area for a period of time ? Something as serious as potential radiation contamination, in productive fishing waters, must be important.

Tom Quinn and his crew mates were now in the middle of a strange set of circumstances, in an even stranger situation. This is something Tom has ran through his mind many times over the years. He told me that the men from the Brecon must have known about the risk of radioactivity when they boarded the trawler, because they brought a Geiger counter with them. He remembers them using it, but he did not know for sure whether any dangerous levels of radiation were found. Maybe this is standard practice in such circumstances.

Months later I received a message from a student helicopter crewman, who had been on board one of the Sea King helicopters during the search. His message was brief and to the point, but he says they spent a day looking over the search area, including time spent refuelling on HMS Leeds Castle. They found nothing except a slick of petroleum, oil and lubricant and as far as he was aware, no health and safety warnings had been issued.

As previously stated, the trawler's sounder had revealed a large part of ZA610 on the sea-bed, less than two hundred feet below them. According to Tom, the crew from HMS Brecon had also thought the same. This was not an official comment, but part of a verbal exchange between the crew of both boats on the scene at the time. Although, if this was the case and the accident summary says it is thought that the crew of ZA610 did not eject, where was the pilot's body ?

Maybe the question will forever remain unanswered. Yet in the vastness of the North Sea what are the odds of finding a second body on the same day that the navigator was discovered and it not be the pilot ? The Scarborough Evening News from December 18th clearly states that a

Dutch trawler had discovered a second body in an ejector seat. Yet they were thirty-six miles to the east and not part of the official search. The newspaper report also said that a Ministry of Defence spokesperson claimed that the remains were not believed to be that of ZA610's pilot, but were believed to be from another jet that crashed more than a year earlier. It seems to be an incredible coincidence that they just happened to find a second body, also in an ejector seat, on the very same day that Tom Quinn and his crew mates had found the first.

Scarborough News - December 18th 1985

MYSTERY BODY
TRAWLED UP

RAF investigators face a grisly mystery following the discovery of two bodies, both strapped to aircraft ejector seats, off Flamborough Head.

One of the bodies has been positively identified as that of Flight-Lieut John Sheen (36),

the navigator of the RAF Tornado jet which disappeared off Flamborough Head on Thursday.

That body was trawled up by the Bridlington fishing-boat the Betty last night near the area where an aviation-fuel oil-slick was found 25 miles west of Flamborough Head on Friday.

Flight-Lieutenant Sheen's body was landed at Bridlington and then taken to the Tornado's base, RAF Marham (Norfolk), where it was identified.

The second body, also strapped to an ejector seat, was trawled up in the net of a Dutch fishing-vessel 36 miles east of the first. A Ministry of Defence spokesman said that the remains were not believed to be those of the Tornado's pilot, Flight-Lieut Michael Barnard (32).

The remains were lifted off the trawler by an RAF helicopter and flown to Great Yarmouth, where it was hoped they would be identified later today.

The spokesman said that the remains were believed to be from another jet crash which happened more than a year ago. He declined to elaborate, saying: "Until the body has been identified it is pointless to speculate." But he confirmed that no aircraft had gone

missing in that area in recent months.

The spokesman said that little or no wreckage had been found with Flight-Lieutenant Sheen's body, apart from his ejector seat, and that the search for the body of Flight-Lieutenant Barnard was continuing.

After the Betty's crew had given the men from Brecon a breakdown of the sequence of events up to their arrival, it was agreed that Tom and one of the Brecon's men would attempt to remove the body from the ejector seat. Tom and his crew mates were then told that *they* would have to return with the body and ejector seat to Bridlington Harbour. When Tom asked why, he was told that HMS Brecon had no mortuary facilities on board. I suspect that it is also possible they did not want to risk transferring a live ejector seat to the minesweeper.

According to Tom Quinn, the navigator appeared to be still strapped into his seat and was wearing a full immersion suit. These are all-in-one suits, presumably worn over standard issue underwear and have elasticated neck and wrists with an attached foot-sock. They are designed to give air crew maximum protection against the elements should they need it.

Tom told me that the navigators right hand appeared to be "embedded" in part, into his chest, as though he had been trying to release a clasp. Despite learning about the procedure for ejection from the aircraft, I still wondered whether there might have been a manual parachute release. This could account for Tom's observation of the navigator's hand position. Tom said that the HMS Brecon crewman thought the navigator had been trying to remove himself from the aircraft as it sank. Although that remark was made to Tom on the day, there is nothing in any official document to suggest this was the case.

The MOD Board of Inquiry report suggests that ZA610 had broken up in a high impact crash into the sea and thirty years on, all we can do is speculate. We may never know the full facts, but if this is correct and the crew of the Betty had located the bulk of the aircraft on the sea-bed, perhaps ZA610 did not impact with the sea in a high speed crash at all. The MOD report says that when Buccaneer MQU13 lost their visual sighting, neither of their crew saw signs of an explosion and nothing that would indicate a crash had taken place.

Tom Quinn has never been a man to hold back, neither now or thirty years ago and he told me that he put a few questions to the crew of HMS Brecon about what he was observing. Tom said,
"I asked why the navigators underwear was around his neck."

This visual fact could not be denied and has remained the biggest mystery for Tom for the past thirty years. The navigator was still belted into the ejector seat, he had his boots on and the immersion suit. From the shoulder area down the suit was badly damaged, either from contact with the trawlers fishing nets or the crash, but it was still in one piece. So how could underwear, which were not ripped, have got around his neck without the immersion suit being removed ?

"That's what I saw Paul. I know it sounds impossible, but that's what I saw."

Tom was told to disregard what he had observed without being given an explanation, then the body was removed from the ejector seat with great care. Photographs were apparently taken and Tom assisted one of the Brecon crew to remove the navigator's flight-suit.

I have since spoken with Tornado pilots who tell me that it is not unusual for them to wear fabric of some kind, beneath the elasticated collar of the flight suit, to make them more comfortable. So I wonder if this is what Tom had seen and he had simply been mistaken at the time. Although he still insists that he knows what he saw, that detail will forever remain a mystery.

Section 9 of the MOD/RAF Board of Inquiry report states that substantial amounts of airframe and engine wreckage were salvaged from the sea, along with pieces of the navigator's ejector seat. Local newspapers reporting on the crash at the time said that the navigator was found in the ejector seat. Tom Quinn had remarked on the condition of the seat, saying that it was in remarkable condition. These two descriptions seem poles apart, but many things surrounding ZA610 sound unbelievable. My talks with Tom took place long before I submitted my request for the full Board of Inquiry report. My witness has simply shared with me, his observations and memories of that tragic day.

After the body was removed from the ejector seat, the local mortuary in Bridlington was informed and instructed what to expect. A local funeral director, F. Kneeshaw and Sons, were waiting for the trawler's arrival at Bridlington Harbour. On arrival the body was handed over to waiting MOD personal and, as far as Tom Quinn knew, it was transported by vehicle to RAF Marham for a positive identification. Yet if the body was taken by the MOD, quite why the funeral directors were there is unknown. Although Tom became less involved once they had reached the harbour, he told me that he recalled them receiving word from the funeral directors, who expressed concern about the body being potentially radioactive. It is worth noting that on December 18th the Eastern Daily Press newspaper, of Great Yarmouth, reported that a body was flown ashore by helicopter for positive identification. This was the second body found, thirty-six miles further away, by the Dutch trawler.

So, according to Tom Quinn's first-hand account, it appears that a large part of Tornado ZA610 lay on the sea-bed sixteen miles off the coast, east of Flamborough Head - the same area of the North Sea well known for other aircraft accidents and mysteries.

A short time after the crew of the Betty had found the aircraft I am told that the crew of another trawler named the Alatner, which had been fishing out of Grimsby, were paid £1000 a day to locate the wreckage of ZA610. The Alatner had a much larger set of trawling gear, so could cover a wider area of the sea-bed - so it is assumed they were considered more suitable for the search operation. They also had a naval salvage expert on board. Yet this remains a puzzle, since it had been established that the Betty had already found the bulk of the aircraft on December 17th. The Betty's crew were unhappy about this since they believed such lucrative pay should have been theirs. However, the MOD/RAF report states the Tornado's 'black box' or ADR (Air Data Reference unit) was not recovered. Perhaps this is one of the reasons why the Alatner was used in the search. It could also be that in the days after the aircraft's discovery, strong tidal currents had moved and broken up the wreckage, although it is not possible to say for certain at this late stage.

The above comments do prove that Tom Quinn's recall of the tragic events of thirty years ago is very accurate and some interesting facts from an archive in Great Yarmouth, back up Tom's account of the Alatna being brought into the salvage operation. I discovered a newspaper report from December 20th 1985 which states that a charted trawler named the Alatna "will resume the search, with a naval salvage expert on board" - presumably scheduled for the following day. It is also known that two other fishing boats from Bridlington Harbour picked up wreckage, thought to be from the Tornado, ten miles south east of

Flamborough Head.

At the time, a spokesperson from the national Search and Rescue Coordination Centre, at Pitreavie in Fife, Scotland, said that the RAF were anxious to recover the Tornado's 'black box' in order to help establish the reason for the loss of the aircraft. Although the official accident summary report makes no mention of the black box ever being found.

Scarborough News - December 19th 1985

Five minesweepers hunt Tornado wreckage

The second body of an airman found off Flamborough Head on Tuesday has still not been positively identified.

It was found after the body of the navigator on the Tornado jet which went missing a week ago was trawled up by a Bridlington fishing-boat. Both bodies were still strapped to ejector seats.

It is thought that the second body may be from a civilian aircraft which went missing over a year ago.

Five Royal Navy mine-sweepers are continuing to search an area 25 miles east of Flamborough Head for the wreckage of the missing Tornado. There is still no trace of the pilot of the aircraft.

A spokesman at the rescue co-ordination centre at Pitreavie (Fife) said today: "The RAF is anxious to recover the black box, the aircraft's flight recorder, which could be a great help in establishing the reason for the loss of the aircraft."

He said that the five Navy vessels would be leaving the area in the next few days to give crews their Christmas leave. The search would be resumed after Christmas.

Bid to lift Tornado wreckage from sea-bed

The wreckage of a missing RAF Tornado jet has been found lying in 180 ft of water 25 miles east of Flamborough Head.

The Royal Navy's mine-counter-measures vessel Brecon located the wreckage at the weekend. An oil-slick on the surface was found to be aviation fuel and the Brecon used sonar and underwater television equipment to pinpoint the wreckage.

There is still no trace of the aircraft's two-man crew.

The Tornado disappeared on Thursday night on a training flight from RAF Marham, in Norfolk. A big air and sea search was mounted to find the aircraft involving Royal Navy ships, RAF aircraft, and six lifeboats, including those from Scarborough and Filey.

A spokesman at the rescue control centre at Pitreavie (Fife) said that a salvage vessel would now be brought in to attempt to recover the wreckage from the sea-bed.

On Saturday the Bridlington fishing-boats Contesier and Sunningdale picked up wreckage thought to be from the Tornado about 10 miles south-east of Flamborough Head. That wreckage is now being examined by the RAF.

Conflicting Reports

On Monday December 16th 1985, the Scarborough Evening News reported that ZA610 had been found lying in a hundred and eighty feet of water, twenty-five miles east of Flamborough Head - and not sixteen miles east, where the trawler Betty had located it the next day. It reported that the Royal Navy countermeasures vessel, the HMS Brecon, had located the aircraft on the 16th using sonar and underwater TV equipment in order to pinpoint the wreckage. The article goes on to say that there was still no trace of the pilot or the navigator. Yet this was printed a full day before the Tornado's navigator was actually found by Tom Quinn and his crew mates.

Can we believe from this report that the HMS Brecon had actually 'pinpointed' the location of ZA610 on the 16th - and that they could see enough with their equipment to establish that the pilot and navigator were not inside their aircraft ?

The next day the same newspaper printed a retraction by the MOD's spokesperson, which stated that their report of the HMS Brecon finding the wreckage on the 16th, had proved false (see image below).

If their first article is to be believed, I wonder what the Brecon had found on the 16th ? Was it something *resembling* a Tornado aircraft ? This is curious, since it was the HMS Brecon that first arrived on the scene to assist the crew of the Betty, to retrieve the navigator's body, the following day. In addition, a spokesperson for the Search and Rescue Coordination Centre in Pitreavie said on the 16th that a salvage vessel was now being brought in to recover the wreckage from the sea-bed.

Renewed search for Tornado wreckage

Efforts have been renewed to find the exact location of the wreckage of the Tornado jet which crashed into the sea off Flamborough Head on Thursday.

The Royal Navy's mine-counter-measures vessel Brecon thought that it had found the wreckage yesterday, but that later proved false.

Today, four Royal Navy vessels were in the area 35 miles east of Flamborough Head where it is thought the jet went down in 180 ft of water. They were using sonar and underwater TV equipment in their efforts to find the wreckage.

Navy divers were hoping to recover the aircraft's flight-recorder, which could reveal why the £11m aircraft plunged into the sea during a training flight.

No trace has been found of the Tornado's two-man crew.

There was also confusion as to whether the two recovered bodies were taken to RAF Marham for identification or to the James Paget Hospital in Great Yarmouth, as newspaper reports from the time conflict. When I made enquiries at the Yarmouth hospital, I explained that I only wanted to know whether a body or bodies had been brought in - I wanted no personal details, no names, simply a yes or no. A few days later they called me back to say that a meeting had taken place about my enquiry. I was then told, in no uncertain terms, that they could tell me nothing about this.

The second body, which had been retrieved by the Dutch trawler, was stated to have possibly been from another jet that had crashed more than a year earlier. On December 18th an MOD spokesperson was quoted in the Eastern Daily Press as saying that it was a possibility the second body had nothing to do with Tornado ZA610. He concluded by saying that he understood there had been other air crashes in that area of the North Sea over the past eighteen months. The MOD also said at the time, that little or no wreckage was found with the navigator's body, apart from his ejector seat. Yet this seems an odd thing to say when the Betty's depth sounder had mapped a large solid mass on the sea-bed.

More confusion ensued when The Scarborough Evening News reported on the 19th that the second body was thought to be from the crash of a civilian aircraft a year before. Yet the recovery had originally been reported by the MOD who stated that it was from a crashed jet, but no civilian aircraft has ejector seats. Surely the facts would have been thoroughly checked before they talked to the press ?

A breakthrough of sorts came, when I contacted an archive in Great Yarmouth. I had given them dates and a breakdown of the story, then a few weeks later they sent me copies of December 1985 newspaper reports in the post. I discovered that quite a bit of information in the reports was at odds with what had been reported in the Bridlington and Scarborough papers of the same time. Although this could simply be the way the information was interpreted at the time, I would like to believe that the MOD press spokesperson would have been telling the same story to all interested parties.

One of the most interesting pieces of information came from the Eastern Daily Press which stated that the second body had been identified as that of Dr Anthony Liston. He had been involved in a fatal helicopter crash on November 20th the previous year. The fact that Dr Liston's body just happened to be found on the same day that ZA610's navigator was found in the vastness of the North Sea, seems to be an amazing coincidence. Although I am only highlighting this information as it was published in the newspapers from 1985, in conjunction with first a hand witness account, I wish to stress that I am not disputing the official line.

Information surrounding the identity of the second body said that on November 20th 1984, a Bell 212 helicopter from North Denes Airfield, near Great Yarmouth, crashed on its approach to the Cecil Provine oil rig, about fifty miles east of the Humber Estuary. The wreckage lay in thirty metres of water, two hundred metres north of the rig. The accident report states that about 98% of the wreckage was found, in two diving operations over a two week period. It also states that the only significant part never found was the tail rotor. Of the two occupants in the helicopter, only the pilot's body was recovered at the time. Interestingly, the inquest into the death of the 212's pilot was held only two weeks before the loss of ZA610.

I wondered if, after more than twelve months submerged beneath the North Sea, there would be anything left to identify Dr Liston. His body had travelled a great distance in the water from the time he was lost, until the Dutch trawler found him. His body would have been subject to the very worst conditions imaginable, so I put this question to the trawlermen working out of Bridlington.
Their opinion was that the sea can dispose of a body quite quickly and that in the time that had passed, nothing would be left to identify. Between the sea life which can dispose of a body in a matter of months, to the savage currents below the surface, finding anything to identify seems highly unlikely. When the Dutch trawler found the body, other reports state that it was from a crashed jet the year before, but surely trained RAF personnel would have known the difference between a jet's ejector seat and a helicopter seat ?

When the Betty recovered the Tornado's navigator, he was still strapped to his ejector seat. The seat was still 'live' according to the crew of the

156

HMS Brecon, so he could not have successfully ejected from the aircraft. Also, for the trawler to have made their discovery, the aircraft canopy must have been open, perhaps damaged on impact or opened manually - yet the MOD/RAF accident report states that no traces of bird-strike could be found on the aircrafts windscreen or side-screens. A Tornado's canopy will jettison in one piece, taking it's side-screens with it. Only the windscreen remains attached to the aircraft. So if the Betty's crew did pull the ejector seat and navigator from the aircraft, it has to be assumed that the canopy was open and found elsewhere at some stage.

The crew of the Betty and crew members of HMS Brecon thought the bulk of the Tornado was on the sea-bed, in the approximate area that the navigator was found. These were not official views, but remarks made on the day based on the evidence the men had to work with. The trawlers depth sounder had mapped out a large dark mass and in the words of Tom Quinn; *"We looked at the sounder and could not believe it. It looked like the f***ing Eiffel Tower !"*
Clearly they had encountered something much larger than simply an ejector seat on the sea floor.

During my research into the loss of ZA610, I called the RAF historical records office to inquire if they had any information about the crash. I was told that all historical records were now crated up and ready to be sent to the National Archive, but that they would be available to view sometime in 2015. During the conversation the words 'Flamborough Head' came up and the man on the other end of the phone paused a moment. Then he commented that many aircraft had been lost in that part of the North Sea. He then said that the area of the sea around Flamborough Head was known to them as the Bermuda Triangle of the UK. I thought this was an interesting thing to say, even if it was just an 'off the cuff' remark.

In the past I have spoken with people who talked of experiencing strange compass readings while out at sea, between fifteen and twenty-five miles off the coast of Flamborough and Bempton. I wondered what could cause such anomalies.

The Admiralty Leisure Chart (number 129) names an area of sea, roughly eighteen miles off Flamborough Head, as having a local magnetic anomaly. A footnote on the map states,

"A local magnetic anomaly is reported to exist in this vicinity."

This may simply mean that nothing more is known about this unusual area of the North Sea, but the wording is interesting when considering that local fishermen have reported odd compass readings in the area - readings that they say only occur on very rare occasions.

Message 19

A short time after I began looking into the story of ZA610 I received the strangest call on our landline at home. It was mid-morning August 2014 when I answered the phone. A man on the other end told me to stop looking into events over the North Sea. Before I could ask who was calling the phone went dead and as I expected, the number was withheld. Puzzled but undeterred, I carried on gathering information.

Over the months that followed a few more odd things happened. After my first conversation with Tom Quinn I returned to the harbour many times to talk with him. I wanted the information he was sharing with me to be as accurate as possible. Not once in that time did Tom give me his phone number and I did not give him my number - neither mobile or landline.

It was during November 2014 that my wife decided to clear all the saved messages from our phone at home. There were about twenty in all from various people. We went through them one by one, deleting them once we had listened to make sure we had not missed anything important. Message number 19 was a real surprise.

It had been sent on Wednesday November 12th and we had to listen to it a few times to actually understand what we were hearing - although I knew instantly that one of the men talking was Tom Quinn. Somehow, someone had sent us a recording of Tom talking to other trawlermen in the harbour warehouse. It was a conversation about nothing of any interest to anyone, except the men involved and had nothing to do with ZA610. The recording lasted about two minutes and our number is ex-directory, but why would anyone send it to us ?

I made a recording of the conversation straight from the phone and took it with me to the harbour for Tom to listen. He confirmed right away that it was him talking and even recalled being in the warehouse on the day it was made. I have no explanation for how or why this recorded conversation ended up on our phone.

A few weeks later my wife and daughter and I were in the kitchen at home. I recall asking them if they knew where I had put my mobile phone, then I went to look for it. I found it in another room and brought it through to the kitchen. A few minutes later a voicemail came to my phone, which I listened to and immediately shared with my wife and daughter. It was a recording of all three of us talking in the kitchen that same morning. I am not asking for anyone to understand why this should have happened, but it did. This involved two different phones, one landline and one mobile and they both had recordings sent to them by withheld numbers.

I have no answers to the crash of ZA610, only questions. After reading this account you may think that it was nothing more than a tragic accident, but I cannot help but feel that there is more to discover. Over the course of the investigation I collected many newspaper reports from December 1985. I have not changed any of the dates or details as stated at the time to make the story seem any more mysterious than it is. My conversations with Tom Quinn are recorded first-hand accounts of the events as he saw them in 1985.

I have tried to be as respectful as it is possible to be, but to tell the account of ZA610 through the eyes of those men who were there that day, I have to tell it as it was told to me. Tom's story has never been told and although his version of events may clash with what has already been reported, no one is better placed than Tom Quinn to recall the facts, as he saw them, on that day in December 1985.

THE BERMUDA EFFECT

All through my research it was becoming increasingly clear that highly unusual events were happening within a thirty mile radius of Bempton and Flamborough, both inland and out at sea. Some were so strange that they appeared to be forgotten as quickly as they had happened.

On rare occasions local fishermen have experienced unusual problems with their radio and navigation equipment, but no one can give a definitive explanation why this might happen. More than one person has told me they suspect some kind of radio-jamming signal could be coming from the underground RAF base at Speeton, not far from Bempton. Others have suggested that some kind of interference from RAF Staxton Wold may be to blame, but this is all speculation as no one seems to have a clue. As mentioned before, drawing a line through a map of the area reveals, that the bases at Speeton and Bempton run parallel to the base at Staxton Wold, although I am not sure if signal-jamming could be the explanation, because these things occur so infrequently and should not affect a modern compass. It could just as easily be the result of a naturally occurring phenomenon that is not fully understood.

Once I had started to ask other fishermen, it became clear that many of them had encountered the same anomaly at one time or another. I shared the suggestion, made to me by my navigator uncle, that an unseen outcrop of iron ore below the surface might be affecting compass readings. The men I spoke to didn't think so, saying that if this was the case, then why didn't it happen more often when they were in the vicinity, instead of only once or twice during their many years at sea.

Ted Harwood is a fisherman with two boats at Bridlington Harbour. He told me of his own experience of the anomaly, from a time he had been out to sea in an area known as 'the ten wrecks', about sixteen miles off Flamborough Head.
"I cannot explain what made it happen. It was nothing short of weird. I can remember we were steaming along problem-free, when the compass readings suddenly went all wrong. We knew exactly where we were because we were going along in a straight line, so for example we are steaming east and for no apparent reason the compass says we are going north. It really was a strange one and I cannot explain it. It has

happened before to people but we just get on with it. It's just weird at the time 'cause you think 'what the hell?' We were about fifteen miles of Flamborough Head when it happened to us. It was only the one time, a few years ago. The compass worked fine before and after. Something just affected it in that area."

I later spoke with another seasoned trawler man who still works off Bridlington Harbour, about what Ted had told me. He said they had experienced similar things between twelve and fifteen miles off Flamborough Head. He also spoke about how another instrument had been affected, something they used to have on board called a Decca navigation system, which was an early equivalent to GPS. He said that on one occasion many years ago, they were steaming off to the east and reached between twelve and fifteen miles off Flamborough Head, when the dials on the Decca suddenly started spinning. They had no explanation why this happened and once they were out of the affected area, everything went back to normal.

One local writer said that this phenomena has actually been known about for many years, but is rarely discussed. He added that it could in fact be responsible for many strange phenomena. Yet, once I had informed him of my research for Truth-Proof he seemed reluctant to offer me any more information. When I spoke with the researcher Tony Dodd about RAF Lightning XS894, he thought the reason the pilot ditched his aircraft was due to suspected radiation contamination. The suggestion was considered ridiculous at the time, but if we consider Tom Quinn's account of a radioactive Tornado the idea suddenly becomes more interesting.

However, it is impossible to understand what is happening when these events are reported so infrequently and always after the event. Nothing that we can call evidence is ever left behind for study and even the fishermen who have encountered the phenomena are most often reluctant to talk.

Encounter At RAF Staxton Wold

Less than ten miles north of where the pilot had his aerial encounter over Willy Howe burial mound, is Staxton Wold RAF base. This remote radar station plays a key role in the military defence of the UK. It is the oldest operational radar station in the world and at one time worked hand in hand with RAF Bempton, eleven miles to the east. It is hard to believe that the bases never seemed to detect anything unusual in the sky in 1996, when the pilot had his incredible encounter with the orange light. They never seemed to detect the lightforms witnessed by countless fishermen over the years either. Yet I know from conversations with the owners of Grange Farm at Bempton, that UFOs *were* detected at RAF Bempton in its operational years. The owners were on good terms with base personal and were often told about objects that had been seen and tracked on radar. Although radar might clearly detect objects at great distances, in some instances the lightforms have been seen directly over both of these bases.

Strange lights have been reported in the skies around the area of Staxton Wold for many years and by the summer of 2007, my local interest in the unexplained had become quite well known. Sometimes local newspapers and TV stations would even contact me for an opinion on things of an unusual nature that had happened or had been seen. That September I received a call from a couple who lived near Staxton Wold. They wanted to tell me about something that happened a few weeks earlier. After only a few telephone conversations it became apparent to me that they felt the need to remain anonymous and if I were to apply the term 'genuine' to any story, their experience would be top of the list.

They did not want to go into great detail over the phone, so they invited me to their home near the bronze age barrow cemetery of Sharp Howe. They live close to a whole group of other unnamed burial mounds with uninterrupted views of the Wolds. I arrived and was greeted warmly. Then looking out onto the back of their property, I thought it must have been a wonderful place to spend outdoors on a summer evening. In fact, they told me that on warm nights it was not unusual for them to sit in the garden and relax with a glass of wine. Except, ever since they had their UFO experience, they said they could not relax like they used to and found themselves constantly looking to the sky.

163

They went on to tell me about what they saw on July 23rd 2007. Brian said that they had been out for tea and were a little later than usual driving home. They pulled onto their driveway at about 8.30pm and it was still quite light and very warm, as they stepped out of the car. They were met at the back of the cottages by Alan their neighbour, an off-duty police officer, who lived just a few doors away in an adjoining cottage. He had been closing up his free-range chicken pen for the evening when they arrived back and they spoke for a while. Just before 8.45pm Pat suddenly saw something that had appeared in the sky.

"What's that ?" She called out, as she pointed to something just above the trees. The other two looked and immediately focused on a bright orange ball of light in the sky that seemed to be just in front of the trees.

Struggling to understand what it was, Pat said she thought a plane was heading straight towards them. They all agreed and for a moment, fear instantly filled their minds. They imagined that the 'plane' was going to crash into the cottage and they began to step back as they tried to understand what they were seeing. Without warning, a second orange ball came out from the side of the first. It seemed to be moving around the first ball, yet remained on the right hand side. It was hard for them to explain and made no sense. The second ball was slightly smaller and Brian thought they were connected to each other, even though he could see a gap between the two. Once again this is a good example of our inability to understand precisely what we are seeing. As they looked on in amazement, a third ball came out from the side of the second ball. Now there were three and they were all shimmering in bright orange and in a perfect row. Alan suddenly said, *"This is weird,"* and he ran towards his cottage saying, *"I'm going to get Jane. She has to see this."*

The trees at the back of Staxton Wold RAF base are about sixty feet tall and both Brian and Pat think the lightforms were only a few feet above them. They said the lights were slightly in front of the trees and no more than two hundred feet away, making this a frighteningly close encounter. Alan arrived back with his wife Jane, just in time for her to see them. Seconds later the lights simply switched off. A few minutes afterwards they reappeared, slightly to the right above a nearby barn, then switched off again. A single light finally reappeared and after a few moments it vanished.

Brian said the lightforms were mesmerising and exciting to see and for a long time afterwards they could not think or talk of anything else. They estimated the size of the first light to be slightly smaller than a full moon, with the second light smaller and the third smaller again. The entire event lasted no more than five to ten minutes, but the impression it made on them all was life changing. From that day they decided they wanted to learn more about what they had seen. Brian is a retired electronics engineer and he has since set up video cameras on sweeping arms that monitor a large area of the Wolds, both day and night. Over the years that have passed since their first encounter, they have amassed many hours of footage and documented much information about the lightforms. Much of their evidence ties in with what local farmers have seen and experienced. Up to 2014 they had collected over two hundred separate sighting accounts, complete with footage. They are both in no doubt that the lightforms have some kind of awareness and they firmly believe that interaction takes place between witnesses and the lights.

In 2010 Richard D. Hall of Richplanet TV worked with me on a short documentary about the lightforms. Since that time Brian tells me that his phone has been monitored. With his extensive background in electronics he was able to make a device that is able to detect when his phone line is being accessed, but why would this be happening if these things are of no interest ?

From that one sighting back in 2007 Brian and Pat's lives have been changed forever. On one occasion in daylight, a large black car slowly passed their kitchen window. The driver appeared to be a very pale, blonde haired woman with a round face. Pat quickly moved to a second window to see where the car was going, but there was no car to be seen. Access to their home has only one entrance, so it was impossible for the car to have driven any other way than the way it arrived. The two kitchen windows are on a right angle, so as the car passed the first window Pat simply needed to walk fifteen feet over to the second window. Yet there was no car in view.

Brian and Pat decided to no longer go out after dark, not because of the disappearing car incident, but due to a scary encounter two years later in 2009. They told me that a lightform actually reacted to them both as they stood together and observed it. Out of respect, I can say no more about the events that unfolded that night, although their experiences are on-going and continue to the present day.

Lightforms can vary in colour, from pale yellow to blue and to a deep red and they do seem to have the ability to affect the mood of the observer. Are they simply latching onto our emotions or able to touch on something within us all ? I asked myself if the lightforms were perhaps projecting these emotions. Or if they were simply reacting to the emotion that the witness is feeling at the time, somehow heightening the experience, good or bad. The intelligence behind them is clearly on another level and it may be unaware of its effect on us.

We consider ourselves to be of superior intelligence to other life on this planet, yet we have no real understanding how our own actions and observations impact on other life, even if we think we do from our limited perspective. Could this be how we are viewed by the lightforms ?

I have interviewed many witnesses and it seems that an individual experience is always taking place, even within multi-witness sightings. Therefore, I would suggest that the lightforms may be affecting witnesses on an individual basis. This becomes even more complex if we look more deeply into what Brian said when he described his first sighting. He told me that the second ball of light seemed to be moving around the first, but that it also remained on the right hand side. This threw his mind into confusion. Is it possible Brian was receiving different messages at the same time - one that told him the second light was stationary *and* circling the larger light at the same time ?

It seems that some kind of mind interaction allowed Brian and Pat to see the events unfold the way they did, but perhaps their minds were not advanced enough to completely comprehend what they were actually seeing.

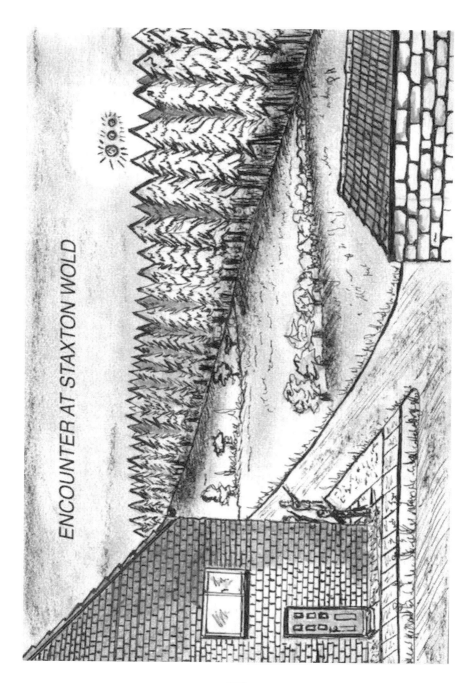

ENCOUNTER AT STAXTON WOLD

The Beings Of Staxton Wold

One of the strangest reports I have been given relates to a farm close to RAF Staxton Wold. The individual who shared this account with me is still employed there and does not wish to put his job at risk, so I am keeping the exact location private.

I was contacted by a farm contractor named 'Rob' and he told me that he had been working on the farm for a number of weeks with his son 'Paul' when he first heard of something strange being seen nearby. They were both in the farm canteen when one of the regular farmhands radioed in, saying in an excited tone,
"I have just seen one of them !"
Rob said that one of other farmhands quickly stood up, gave them an odd look, then picked up the radio and stepped outside. He said that another man who remained seated just appeared to be observing their response. Rob felt there was an air of secrecy surrounding this incident, but as the weeks passed, the regular farmhands eventually became more trusting of the contractors. At the time however, no one offered an explanation for this unusual radio message.

Rob then told me of his own sighting, which occurred once evening at the farm. Before they headed back home to Bridlington, Rob noticed two large white lights in the sky, one below the other. He called for his son to come and look and they saw the light at the top slowly begin to move downwards, just like the minute hand on a clock would move. It travelled from what would have been the 12 o'clock position to the 6 o'clock position and stopped. The light now in top position then repeated the sequence and moved downwards in the same way. Rob told me that the lights were interesting, but not enough to stop them making their thirty-five minute journey home.

The next morning Rob told one of the regular farmhands what they had seen and it was at this point the sense of secrecy that Rob had felt, was dropped. The farmhand, who was from nearby Folkton, asked Rob if he remembered the day that one of the men had radioed in with a strange message. Rob told me that he nodded in agreement, adding that now the farmhand was talking in a whispered tone, which seemed odd because no one else was there. *"I will tell you now because I trust you,"* said the farmhand. *"He saw a being, a little man."*

Rob said that he thought the man was joking at first and he was just being wound-up, so Rob just laughed out loud. The farmhand snapped in reply, *"Okay forget it. If that's how you're going to be, just forget it."*

Rob apologised as soon as he realised that the man was not joking at all and was in fact, deadly serious. The farmhand relaxed and began to tell Rob that other regular workers had all seen glimpses of 'small beings' around the farm. This was in 2013, so it was not some ancient tale handed down through time.

Rob admitted to being very sceptical, but due to the secretive way in which he was told, he believed the farmhands had seen something. Rob made the mistake of telling them about someone he knew who would be very interested in these sightings. He told them that this man had been making regular visits onto the Wolds for many years to film lights, similar to the ones Rob and his son had seen the previous evening. That man was me, but the farmhands made it clear to Rob that they would not share what they had seen with me or anyone unconnected to the farm.

When the story began to unfold it became apparent that they were all involved. Rob was told that even some of the farmers wives had claimed to have seen glimpses of the beings. They claimed to have seen them around the fields and farm buildings for what were fractions of a second. He was told that it was not unusual to see deer, rabbits or pheasants at all times of the day in the surrounding fields and woodland, but the farmhand said these things were different. Sometimes while out in an open field, they would just catch a glimpse of legs flashing past the tractor and then see nothing more. At other times, when walking around a corner in different parts of the farm, the thin outline of a small person could be seen. It would then vanish in less time than it takes to blink. Rob said that it would not have been so credible, if it was not for the fact that *all* of them claimed to have had some kind experience with these unknown life forms. The fact that they were all so secretive and guarded about it made it even more believable.

I do not expect anyone to simply accept these accounts as the truth, since I have no way of proving what Rob told me. I have tried to learn more about these sightings, but people are very reluctant to talk.

However, what I find interesting is that stories of strange beings are nothing new to this area and if we look back through time, we find comparisons.

Close to Staxton Wold is a burial mound known locally as Elf Howe and stories attached to this mound tell of goblins and elven-type beings that haunt the location. I have one report of a walker hearing voices around Elf Howe, even though there was no one else in the vicinity at the time. Today, due to over-farming, Elf Howe barrow has sadly been reduced to nothing and only traces of its once impressive size are now visible, although there are clear views of the surrounding countryside.

In the same area is Sharp Howe, an ancient barrow cemetery where many strange things have been seen - including the 'Flixton Werewolf'. It is a very lonely place, overlooking much of East and North Yorkshire. A short distance away to the east of Folkton village is the burial mound of Spell Howe - also known as Speech Mound - it is thought to have been used as a communal meeting place where issues of great importance were debated. Twenty miles inland is Fairy Dale, another area said to be inhabited by small beings. So it is clear that stories such as those told to Rob are nothing new to the area.

Perhaps the most famous of them all sits between the villages of Burton Fleming and Wold Newton, less than four miles away Elf Howe. This is the where we find the burial mound named Willy Howe, said for centuries to be inhabited by little people. Willy Howe has more than one story involving encounters with strange beings attached to it. The farmer who owns the land where the burial mound is situated tells me that it attracts visitors all year round, sometimes by the coachload. Not bad for a place where the only advertisement is its name on an Ordnance Survey map.

It is hard to explain why these locations have carried such stories throughout their history. To simply disregard witness accounts of small beings, because they do not fit into what we understand, is a repetitive mistake that stops us learning from the past. I believe the science of interconnecting ley lines could hold some of the answers and may be the key, if these phenomena prove to be interdimensional in nature. I think the early settlers on the land were more in tune with these unseen energies than we are today. True they were not as scientifically or culturally advanced, but they were also in tune with the land that provided them with food and shelter and they regarded its very essence as a living thing. They built their burial mounds and huge earthworks in these places because they knew they were important - places where amazing things happened and continue to happen today, at times giving us a glimpse into another world.

In folklore the small beings are often described as being dressed in strange clothing and footwear. In some recent accounts this does not appear to have changed. I was told about an elderly man from the village of Burton Fleming who used to walk his dog close to Willy Howe, this was something he had done for a number of years. One morning in 2006 he says that he observed a little man standing beside the burial mound. It was a clear daylight observation and the small being is said to have stared back at him as he passed. The man described the being as less than two feet tall and wearing what looked like a leather waistcoat, with baggy brown trousers and an unusual hat. He was convinced the being's skin was brown with age and although he was close close enough to see detailed features, he thought his eyes were black and very shiny. The experience unnerved him so much that he has not passed the burial mound alone since then.

These events are so rare and undocumented that huge gaps in time can pass between such encounters. It took a lifetime for this elderly man to have his one brief encounter with the being, before that he regarded the stories of Willy Howe as nothing more than fairy tale. I wonder how many more stories like this remain untold ? I have never heard of anyone who has found physical evidence of the little people, in the form of footprints or something left behind. So could we be looking at apparitions or glimpses into another world through a portal and not something in the physical realm as we know it ? Perhaps they possess the ability to only occasionally slip into our sphere of existence.

Of all the locations on the Wolds I would say without doubt, Willy Howe is the most interesting and atmospheric. I contacted the landowner in 2014 to ask his permission for a visit. I had been many times in the past, but wanted to gauge his opinions of the place. After a short conversation he agreed to let me visit the burial mound, but asked me why I was so interested. When I told him I was looking into strange and unexplained happenings around the area, he was very interested. To my surprise he asked if I would come and talk with him at the farm that same day. I was met by a very welcoming retired man, who was as full of questions about the unexplained as I was. He told me that over the years people had come from all over the UK and abroad to visit Willy Howe.

He knew most of the stories attached to the mound but sadly had none of his own to add. I admired his honesty and open-minded approach. He explained that he had been at the farm since 1964 and had spent lots of time around the mound. He had never personally seen or experienced anything unusual, but told me that he did want to. He knew of people local to the area who had seen and experienced strange phenomena and he brought out a folder which contained a drawing. He said this was what an elderly woman, who lived close by, had seen one night at the back of her remote farmhouse. He gave me a short account about how the woman had heard a knock at her door.
When she answered she saw a man standing there and recalled that they spoke for a while. The next thing she remembered was seeing a huge object hovering over the field at the back of her home. Below it she could see a long tube, almost like the trunk of an elephant, which was scouring the land below. The following image is taken from the lady's original painting.

The Cottam Wood Spaceship

I was given another first-hand account by a farmer, now in his seventies, who lives in the tiny village of Cottam, some thirteen miles from Bempton. Myself and my friend Steven Ashbridge were in the area in 2006 hoping to get some film footage of the lightforms. It is true to say that our early visits to some of the more remote areas did cause a little concern. As strangers arriving and standing around the edges of fields in the early evening until late, we must have looked suspicious !

On one such evening, two large four by four cars pulled up on the single-track road where we were standing. One man got out of each vehicle and walked towards us. One of them said,
"Do you mind telling us what you are doing, as you look suspicious ?"
They were polite but wanted answers and I remember smiling and saying, *"You will probably laugh when we tell you, but it's the truth. We are here because of the strange lights that have been seen in the area."*

The two farmers looked at each other and smiled. How much of that was relief that we were 'okay guys' and how much was simply a knowing smile about what I had just said, we will never know.
"Oh we would not laugh, we have seen them," was the reply.
They were genuinely interested and wanted to know what we had seen. I told them about the couple who lived near RAF Staxton Wold who had been documenting the lightforms and about the things we had seen which first sparked my interest. I told them about a farm labourer I had spoken with named Denis Woodmansey, who lived in the nearby village of Langtoft. They knew Denis and they listened as I told them about what he and his wife had seen and experienced.

The Woodmansey's UFO encounter surprised the farmers and I think this goes to show how guarded people can become after such an experience. So much so, that they even hold back from telling friends, even within close-knit communities.

Denis and his wife reported that they were followed home by a 'huge white light' which scared them both half to death. Their terrifying ordeal began on the outskirts of Rudston village, as they travelled back along the lonely B1253 road to their home six miles away. They said that at times the light seemed so bright and low that it almost appeared to be touching the back window of their car. Their frightening experience did not even end when they arrived home. When Denis and his wife entered the house they both ran upstairs to take refuge in a darkened bedroom. They both swear that this glowing UFO was now hovering above their house and they felt as though it was observing them.

After listening to what I had to say, the two farmers, who I will call Bob and Sam, just looked at me. Then Bob told us that he did not need convincing. He said he had already seen them with his own eyes. Then he pointed over to a farmhouse in the distance saying, *"You see that house over there, well that's my home. At the back, can you see that wood ? Well the small wood and the land around it belong to me."* Both Steve and I looked over to where he was pointing and I suspected that he was about to tell us of an experience of his own.

"When I was a young man I saw one. [I was with] my wife, my daughter and our daughter's boyfriend, now her husband. It was over there above the trees, in the early 1990s. We were driving home and my daughter phoned us. It was when [mobile] phones were like bricks. She said, "Dad, Dad you have to get home. There is something above the farm. I think it's a spaceship."
As we got closer to the farm, sure enough we could see this circular thing. It was very low in the sky. It had lights like Christmas fairy lights all around the edge of it. Apart from that it was black, but it looked amazing. As we approached the farmhouse it began to slowly move out towards the woods at the back of our home. My daughter was standing with her boyfriend looking up at this thing in the sky. Me and my wife got out of the car, then all four of us just stood there looking up at this amazing thing that just sat in the sky in silence. It was now over the trees, which were no more than thirty to forty feet high. Apart from all these rotating lights around the rim of this thing, it was black. I decided I wanted to see more of it so I ran towards the wood to get a better view. My wife was shouting and pleading with me to stay with them. Looking back now it sounds ridiculous, because she was shouting, "Bob, Bob, come back. It will take you."

As I approached the edge of the wood this thing began to move away very slowly. It was only just above the tree-tops. Now I was right below it, walking through the wood looking up at this incredible thing that moved no faster than walking pace. It was only when I was more isolated in the small wood, that I became aware of a sound that seemed to be coming from it. It was about forty feet above me and I just could not believe my own eyes or ears. The sound it made was like that of a gentle breeze. It was even fainter than that, but that's the only way I know of describing the sound. I followed the object all the way through the wood until I reached the outer edge that looked onto open fields. It stopped for a moment, I don't know for how long, and then began to move back along the tree-tops towards the farmhouse.

My wife was still shouting for me to come back, she was genuinely frightened, but I was in awe of this thing. When I arrived back at the farm it continued on its journey over the single track road and across the open fields until we could see it no longer."

Bob first told me this story back in 2006 and I have spoken to him about it only once since then. After our initial conversation he seemed very reluctant to share the account again, even though it was his own first-hand account and was a real event.

I have come to understand that this is the nature of these phenomena, even when the truth of what has been seen screams in your face. People either take what they see or experience as something very special and life changing - or they do what ninety-nine percent of the population does and simply file it away into a dark corner of the mind. Reason and comprehension do not even come into question. It's a definite process, after which, the memories seem very reluctant to be revived. I know from first-hand experience how hard it is to play over in your mind something that cannot be understood.

Since our first meeting with Bob and Sam I have visited the area often, at all hours of the day and night and although I would not say we have become friends, we are like trusted acquaintances with a mutual interest.

COTTAM
WOOD
ENCOUNTER

177

The Easterby Sighting

In August 2014 I called the homes of a few local farmers in the area to let them know I would be parked on the nearby lanes that evening. There had been a few reports of unusual activity in the area so I thought it might be worth setting up cameras. I called them out of respect, because in the past there have been suspicious looking vehicles parked on their land and it helps them avoid having to investigate. I told one lady that I would be visiting their land until the early evening and before I hung up, the lady asked if Peter had called me.
She meant Peter Easterby, a local farmer who had apparently had an unusual sighting of his own some weeks before. Although he had not called me, I said I would contact him soon.

Peter owns land that until the 1950s, used to be the airfield for RAF Cottam, a base which no longer exists. When I did call Peter's number no one answered, but that evening I drove up to their farm and parked on a strip of land just inside the boundary. This vantage point gives three hundred and sixty degree views of the Wolds, the coast and RAF Staxton Wold to the north. It is a location that my friend Steve and I had used on investigations for many years. At about 9.30pm we could both hear the sound of a car approaching. We do not tend to get out to look on these occasions, because the vehicle is usually hidden beside a small group of trees. That way, most of the time, we remain unnoticed.
To my surprise the vehicle slowed down and turned onto the private road just where we were parked. It was actually Peter Easterby and his wife Sue. They were with their teenage son Harry and were returning home after a meal out. They stopped and asked us if we had seen anything unusual. I told them we hadn't. *"Well we have,"* replied Peter. *"It was a few weeks ago. Saturday July 12th to be exact. You see that mast over there in the distance ?"*

Peter was pointing to a very tall and thin white mast, that was not there the last time we visited the area.
"That mast has not been up that long. It was when we were coming home that night when we saw it. We were roughly here - this spot where we are parked right now. I stopped the car and Harry jumped out to lock the gates. It was still quite light so I think the time would have been about 9.45pm."

Peters wife and son both nodded in agreement.

"It was a very clear evening, with not a cloud in the sky, so we definitely know we saw it. I pulled onto the road, Harry jumped out and there it was in front of us. I looked at Sue and said 'can you see that ?' We both just sat there in disbelief. Shock I suppose. We could not believe what we were seeing. It just should not have been there. I repeated, 'can you see that ?' and Sue said she could. So did Harry who was standing and looking down the road and asking us if we knew what it was. None of us could explain it. To this day we have no idea what it could have been. Whatever it was seemed to be slightly to the left of that new mast. We all agreed it was in front of the mast and definitely lower. I would have said about two thirds up. Sue thought it was rising between the gap in the trees. It was definitely rising and coming towards us."

I interrupted Peter and spoke briefly about the mast. We estimated that it was about a hundred and fifty feet high, so the object they saw must have been around a hundred feet above ground level.

"It just appeared between the gap in the hedgerow," said Sue. *"I am sure it was rising from the ground and coming towards us."*

Her son and husband both nodded.

The drawing below depicts the object with the mast in the distance. The land behind the hedgerow drops down at about thirty degrees towards the mast, which is about a quarter of a mile away. The object was sighted somewhere between the mast and the hedgerow, so in actual fact it must have been much lower to the ground than originally thought. Peter went on to describe the object as best he could.

"It was all white, glowing white and about the size of a jumbo jet. No kidding, it was massive and it was just there in the sky, sideways on, slowly moving towards us."

I asked if it had wings of any kind or if any sound could be heard.

"No. It was just a great big white tube, as big as a jumbo jet without any wings and no sound at all. It was definitely not an aircraft."

The three of them all agreed what they had seen that evening. I had no doubt in my mind that they were telling me about a close encounter with something real and unknown. One question worth asking is why other people did not report seeing such a huge object, after all it was still light. But the area is so remote and on some evenings we can spend up to five hours at that location and only see two or three cars pass. So unless you were actually on their farmland, I do not think it would have been possible for anyone else to see it. Also, the Easterby's sighting only lasted a short time, so the chances of passing vehicles being close enough at the time are slight. Another point worth mentioning is that the object appeared to be rising, so it is possible that it was much closer to the ground or may have even landed below the incline, before they arrived back home. Perhaps it was their presence that disturbed it. When I asked about how it left the area, similarities to my own sighting from 2002 sprung to mind.

"It never flew away," said Peter. "It was like one moment we could see it, the next it had gone. Just vanished. For reasons I cannot explain it spooked us and left us feeling unsettled. As soon as we got home Harry went around the house closing all the windows and from time to time he would go back to the windows to check if anything was there. It really did catch us all by surprise."

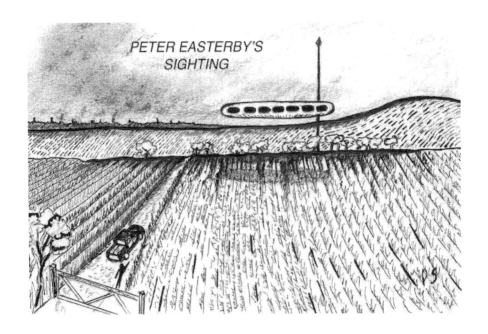

PETER EASTERBY'S
SIGHTING

Sighting Over Sledmere Field

I believe Peter Easterby's sighting had some connection one of my own in 2002. There were lots of similarities that suggested it may have been the same object or one very similar, once again proving that location is key. I asked the Easterby family to try and write down separately what they recalled about their sighting. I never said at the time, but I suspected they would all have seen and experienced something slightly different to one another. It is worth noting that many sceptics who view multi-witness accounts look for these inaccuracies, which can then often be used to discredit the witness. My own theory, which points to an interaction between a UFO sighting and the witnesses perception of it on a personal level, has never been considered before.

If the majority of people who have seen and experienced these phenomena are telling the truth, then in some cases this has to be what is happening. The starting point in the Easterby's encounter would be that Peter, his wife and son all agree they saw the giant white object over their farmland. The second step would be that they all agree on its actual position above the land and approximate height when compared to the mast. From there the visual recall begins to change. Peters wife Sue says the object came slowly up and into view between a large gap in the hedges and she thought it was moving towards them. Peter says he could see a row of windows in the object, which implies that he got closer to it than his wife and son. We know this was not the case, as they were sitting side by side in the vehicle. It is hard to understand what is taking place during these experiences, but I do believe after the initial group sighting, the experience becomes more personal.

Now compare the Easterby's sighting to my own from August 2002. I was travelling back home from York with my work colleague Chris Short and were near Sledmere, just four miles away from Cottam. In many ways it was this sighting that inspired me to begin looking into the area's interesting past. I contacted the Bridlington Free Press to share my story and this is what they reported:

Bridlington Free Press *(August 29th 2002)*

'UFO SEEN OVER FIELD'

"A Bridlington man is hoping readers may be able to solve the mystery of a possible UFO sighting. Paul Sinclair is convinced that he and a colleague saw an unidentified object [on August 21st] hovering above a field near Sledmere as they were driving back to Bridlington last Wednesday. Now he is hoping that other people may have seen the mystery object, which he described as a 'white glowing oblong', and may be able to explain it.
Mr Sinclair said: "We both saw it and at first we thought it was a plane. It was very big and was just stationary in the sky. We watched it for about a minute-and-a-half and then it just disappeared." Mr Sinclair and his colleague spotted the object in a field just outside Sledmere, at around 4.15pm."

The following month the same newspaper published a second report, from a couple who claimed to have seen the same object in the same place - but *twelve years* before our sighting.

Bridlington Free Press *(September 26th 2002)*

'WE'VE SEEN A UFO TOO'

"A couple claim to have seen a UFO at the exact spot that another Free Press reader spotted one - only 12 years earlier. In August, the Free Press reported that Paul Sinclair of Bridlington saw a white glowing object hovering above a field near Sledmere, which then suddenly disappeared. Since then, John Smith has written to the Free Press to say he and his wife saw a similar object on the same stretch of road in the summer of 1990 during a journey to Bridlington.
Mr Smith, of Heber Street, Goole, said: "As we travelled along I noticed a flash of silver in the sky above the car and told my wife to look at the glider. I then immediately said 'no it's not a glider, I don't know what it is'. Mr Smith said he stopped the car, got out and saw a large silver disc in a field, hovering above some trees. He said: "There was no sound whatsoever and after a minute or so it just disappeared - not appearing to move from its position - more as if a curtain had been drawn round it. Although this was twelve years ago, your recent story is an identical sighting."

182

The object seen by Peter Easterby and his family in 2014 sounds very similar to the one Chris Short and I witnessed at Sledmere. The distance between the two locations may not be a factor but it has to be considered. Cottam is only four miles from Sledmere, which is such a small village, so the locations of the two sightings must be very close to each other.

So between the Easterby's, the Cottam Wood farmer and his family and Chris and myself, we have three separate sightings witnessed by eight people. Although there was gap of twelve years between them it seems that something is definitely going on in this area that none of us understand.

In 2010 I took part in a short documentary with Richard D. Hall of Richplanet TV. We focused solely on the Wolds Lightforms and after it was released, I received fifteen calls from people living in the surrounding area, who all told me they had seen the same objects. One man from Walton-on-Thames, just five miles away from Sledmere, told me how he had observed a large amber light and small beings, in the paddock at the back of his home.

A short time after our Sledmere sighting, my work colleague Chris refused to talk about it any further. Yet, on the journey home after seeing the object we talked of nothing else. The next day at work, during tea break, I spoke about what we saw, telling a few people of our experience. Chris agreed with what I was saying but he seemed reluctant to offer any views of his own. It appeared as though some in-built defence mechanism was already at work inside his head, stopping him talking about it. I have noticed this 'numbing' process on many occasions and it seems to take effect after a nights sleep. Chris Short's reaction the following day is a prime example of the closing down of memories after an event. During our sighting we actually pulled over in the van to watch this glowing white tube. It was a bright sunny day and we had much more than just a fleeting glimpse of something unusual over that field in Sledmere. Yet the truth of our sighting seemed somehow to be 'tightening up' in his mind, to the point where now, he will no longer speak about it.

The human reaction to phenomena of this nature most often seems to be one of denial. I wonder how much of that is also due to media conditioning ? The subliminal drip of ridicule that screams denial when faced with an unfathomable truth. Or perhaps some advanced intelligence places a firewall in the mind of the witness that can never be breached ?

SLEDMERE SIGHTING
2002

Time Stops In Bessingby

On Monday April 20th 2014 I interviewed a lady from Bridlington named Lesley Buttle. She wanted to tell me about a close encounter she and two other women had with a UFO back in 1977. This sighting was reported and documented at the time.

Lesley told me that she worked as a cleaner for a manufacturing company named Britax PMG, on the coast at Bessingby. She was on her way to work that day with two other women named Liz Jennison and Margaret Mooney. It was winter and about 4.30pm in the afternoon of January 21st 1977. Lesley said that it was starting to get dark when they noticed a patch of low white cloud or mist, over some nearby garden allotments. The rest of the sky was clear so they stopped, as they were puzzled by this fuzzy cloud. They stood to watched it for a short time trying to make sense of what it was, when it slowly began to clear. To their amazement they could now see a huge oval-shaped craft hanging low in the sky over the allotments.

Lesley says their instant reaction was extreme fear. For some reason the three of them were so terrified, but to this day Lesley cannot understand why this wave of fear came over them. The object was very close and making a strange humming sound. This made the hair on their arms and bodies stand up and their skin feel tight and prickly.
"It was not a nice feeling," remarked Lesley. She said the craft was white or light grey with a darker band around the middle, which she was sure had seven illuminated windows. It was also spinning very fast but the windows were not spinning. This is something that still confuses Lesley even now, but they all agreed that the object looked huge as it hovered above the allotments.

The three women estimated that if they had been up close to it, the craft would have been as big as a double-decker bus. Although from where they were standing it looked no bigger that the size of a family car. Lesley thinks that if they had stood beneath it, the object would have been circular. Her reasoning for this was that the windows were small and seemed to curve towards the edges, as though the whole thing was round. As they stood there watching the object they all began feeling sick and dizzy, which heightened the fear they all felt. Then without warning the spinning and humming sound stopped and a green luminous tube began to descend from the middle of the craft.

I asked Lesley if she thought it could have been green beam of light, rather than a solid structure, but she confirmed that it looked like a tube. The fact the sound and spinning had stopped when the tube descended is an interesting observation, which may indicate that the sound was associated with the spinning. Yet the craft remained in the same position and did not need to spin to remain in the air.

Lesley said the green tube was very close to the ground and if they were closer, she thinks they would have been able to reach up and touch it. They saw material from the allotments rising up into the tube, which after a few minutes began to slowly retract back into the craft. The three women were observing all of this as it happened, but were glued to the spot, as though trapped in fear. Once the tube had retracted the humming noise started up and the object began to spin once again. Moments later the entire craft vanished into nothing more than a tiny speck of light and was gone.

By now all three women were shook up by what they had experienced. They were shaking and crying as they walked away and made their way to the factory. The three of them spoke about what they saw in hysterical tones. Looking back now Lesley thinks the object affected them all, both mentally and physically, for weeks and months after the sighting. The first thing they had to do when arriving at work was 'clock in' to begin their shift. It was at that moment that the three of them realised that all their watches had stopped at 4.45pm. They all had wind-up analogue watches, so whatever they had been through earlier was able to affect the mechanics of their watches. Once inside the factory it was clear that things were not right.

The factory clock had stopped at 4.44pm and the machines on the factory floor had all stopped working too. They began to tell everyone at the factory what they had just seen and experienced, but no one would believe them. They were laughed at for suggesting that everything had stopped because there was a spaceship in the sky near the factory. Lesley told me that an engineer finally got the machinery up and running again, but that everything ran backwards.

For days and months after their encounter, all three women suffered from severe head pains and bouts of dizziness. Lesley remembered that people came out to interview them about what they had witnessed. She also said that Bridlington Town Hall was open the following Sunday - she thinks this was something to do with finding out who owned the allotment where the object had appeared to take things.

A short time later the women learned that some men had arrived who took samples of earth and did tests on the area the object was seen. A few times afterwards the three of them were questioned further, but due to the traumatic effect the experience had on them, they decided not to talk about it any more. The ridicule they endured from friends and other factory workers was bad enough, without added pressure from unknown outsiders.

I was able to track down two witnesses who saw a green glowing UFO in January 1977. One of them at the time was an eight year old boy named Tim. Now in his mid-forties, Tim told me about seeing a green oval-shaped object as he was playing with friends, close to the golf course on Bridlington's south side. The distance between the Britax women's encounter and Bridlington golf course is only approximately half a mile. I do not have the exact dates for the two encounters, but I do know they were seen in the same month. Tim told me that at first, he and his friends were puzzled by the green glowing object hovering in the sky, then for some unknown reason a kind of fear came over them and they began to run. He swears that the object followed them home and was there in the sky above his house when they arrived.

Another report from January 1977 came from a young man who had been walking home from a night out at the time. Phil Morris told me of how he observed a green glowing UFO close to where Bridlington fire station now stands. He told me that back in 1977 the area was an open field, over which he was making his way in the early hours, when the object slowly passed him. He said that it was very low in the sky and about the height of a first floor window. Phil also remembers other people talking about seeing the object and said that it was reported in the Bridlington Free Press the following week. This would have been the Britax women's encounter. Phil said he was relieved to find others had seen it at the time, even though he never spoke of it back then, for fear of ridicule.

It is unfortunate that back in 1977, no one was able to connect all three of these sightings together. It might have helped Lesley Buttle and her two friends come to terms with what they experienced, rather than them having to be the target of ridicule and sarcastic comments.

Below is a separate sighting report from the following June and on the next page is a representation of Lesley Buttle's sighting.

Bridlington Free Press - June 9th 1977

U.F.O. looked like 'aeroplane without wings'

A Bridlington man found himself staring into the sky in disbelief when he spotted a cigar-shaped craft which he described as an "aeroplane without wings".

Mr. Martin Blow was driving in Station Road and turned the corner into Midway Avenue, where he lives, when he saw a craft hovering at about 500 feet.

He said the unidentified flying object seemed to be as big as an airliner with a fin on the back, but no wings.

His father-in-law Mr. Raymond Newell and his wife Susan were also in the car at the time, Mr. Newell thought the strange craft was an airship at first.

Mr. Blow added: "There were no clouds. It's a complete mystery. I don't believe in spaceships, but I've got to admit it was a bit funny."

Mr. Philip Fargus, of the U.F.O. Research Association, said that he was very interested to hear of another unusual sighting in the Bridlington area.

His members have been taking statements from people who reported sighting an object which landed near an allotment in Bridlington at the end of January. It was said to have been collecting soil samples.

The Ministry of Defence stressed that it had no planes without wings and nothing which looked anything like a saucer. A spokesman said that it might have been an experimental commercial venture.

188

LESLEY BUTTLE'S ENCOUNTER

TOOTH AND CLAW

The Flixton Beast
A Passage Through Time

Ten miles from Danes Dyke and less than one mile from Staxton Wold is the village of Flixton. Many believe that Flixton is home to a werewolf - a creature which has been seen and documented in the area for a period of more than nine hundred years.

I am not suggesting that we accept the notion of a man, who is ruled by the moon, who then becomes a monster and actually roams the countryside of North and East Yorkshire. However, stories of this mysterious creature have continued to surface throughout local history to the present day. Many accounts suggest that it frequents old graveyards, where it is said to make a terrifying appearance from time to time, and some modern researchers seem happy to support the idea. But I wanted to dig deeper into the past to try and find reasons why tales of a werewolf have made such a lasting impression on the area.

When I began researching the story I was aware that, even in a book as open as Truth-Proof, accounts of such a creature may be a step too far to accept. I thought that devoting a few pages to the 'beast' story, along with reports of 'big cat' sightings, would be enough. However, like all mysteries, the deeper you dig the more you find.

Locally there are references to wolves, dogs and hounds to be found in many of the place names close to Flixton. The village of Hunmanby or Hund-manby (meaning hound man) being one such example. There was once a part of Flixton known as Wolf-land, which some locals still refer to. There is also a water course on Staxton Wold named Hundykes (Hound Dykes) and a local burial mound named Wolf Howe (Wolf Hill). In one old document I uncovered during my research, I discovered a reference to 'wolves and wild beasts' which were 'infesting' the land at that time. Although I wonder what kind of beasts could be more dangerous than a pack of hungry wolves ?

It is interesting that these place names have ended up with such canine connotations, and although they may have originated from ancient references to wild wolves, I do not feel it is bending the truth to suggest they may also refer to the Flixton Beast.

I spoke with a contractor I have known for many years, who works for a group of farms in the immediate area around Flixton. He said that he thought it was strange that the farmers all know about the Flixton Werewolf, but were very guarded about discussing it. It is true that new information on the beast has always been hard to obtain. In fact much of what is known is often recycled information, containing the same errors throughout. This is equally so in current research.

Many reports of the Flixton Beast often refer to an ancient 'refuge' or shelter, which existed in Flixton during medieval times, but as entertaining as this research is, it falls short of the truth. Ancient shelters of this type were early versions of the modern hospital, known in medieval times as 'spitals', where the needy were cared for by nuns or monks. These refuges were also used as places of worship and by travellers needing a safe haven from wolves, which were plentiful on the Wolds at that time.

With a little work I discovered there were two of these medieval hospitals or refuges, built locally. There was one was at Flixton named Carmans Spital, which was founded a thousand years ago by a knight named Acehorne, Lord of Flixton, during the reign of King Athelstan. The other was the Spital of St Mary and St Andrew at Staxton, which was overseen by Bridlington Priory and stood where Spital Corner is today.

Until now, it seems that no one has realised that both Flixton and Staxton each had their own refuge, less than a mile apart and within the same timeframe. The refuge at Flixton is the one most widely written about and although the names of the two have often been confused, I suspect the name 'Carmans Spital' arose because of its links to the beast. In the low lands just north of Flixton, a short distance from where Carmans Spital once stood, are the remains of an even more ancient settlement that goes back eleven thousand years. Today this is known as Flixton Star Carr and its early inhabitants are thought by some archaeologists to have been animal-worshipping shaman.

Some ancient accounts of the beast tied in with information I was gathering locally. One elderly Staxton resident, named Edwin Cooper, told me that there was a medieval refuge, which once stood on an area of land now named Spital Corner. It is thought that Spital Farm was built on the actual foundations of the refuge, although the farm is now The Spital Inn and Restaurant. There is also a small stream running nearby named Spital Brook. So it seemed that name 'Spital' was a common thread, which I began to notice more and more during my research.

In mid-2015 I contacted the owners of The Spital Inn and Restaurant, to ask if they knew the interesting history of their home and business. Indeed, they knew their land had a very ancient past, so were happy to speak with me. I visited them a few weeks later and was greeted by a very pleasant and down-to-earth lady, who told me they had owned the property for the past fourteen years. Then she told me of the time her husband had been digging a pond in their garden and had actually unearthed human remains. All worked was stopped and a thorough archaeological dig was arranged and documented. The findings stated that fifteen ancient Roman bodies had been found on the site and a geophysical survey of the land revealed that it was once the site of a Roman marching camp.

It was becoming clear to me that this small part of North Yorkshire had a rich and interesting past and was a place that held many secrets. The lady then kindly showed me the deeds to their property which referred to the nearby medieval refuge, which had once existed on the site. The document stated that it existed *"to protect travellers, least they be devoured."* I thought this was an an astonishing reference, and although a 'beast' was not mentioned, some kind of threat was clearly being inferred.

I sometimes wonder whether some researchers today have omitted the finer points of their research, just to enhance the myth of a story. Or perhaps they simply do not work hard enough to gather the available information. In the end, I believe it may well be a mixture of both, because modern accounts of the Flixton Beast do suggest that something of a paranormal nature is manifesting around the area at times.

Flixton lies west of its neighbouring village of Folkton, but the two are so close, it is hard to know where one starts and the other ends. To the north is some low lying land which, thousands of years earlier, had contained Lake Flixton, complete with its own small islands. The lake has long since gone and all that remains is wet farm land with raised areas which indicate where the islands once were. Lake Flixton is better known today as Flixton Star Carr.

The medieval site of Star Carr is near the village of Seamer. It was discovered in 1947 by a local amateur archaeologist named John Moore and was first excavated in 1949. Since then the site has become known throughout the world and is considered to be of great historical importance. Although I never imagined that a Mesolithic archaeological site would have anything remotely connected to ancient stories of a werewolf.

I first became interested in Star Carr while retracing the steps of the Flixton Beast. As I began learning more about it and the ancient artefacts which had been uncovered there, I noticed its close proximity to alleged sightings of the werewolf.

During excavations at Star Carr, among other finds, were twenty-one red deer skull-caps, complete with antlers. They had been fashioned with primitive flint tools and worked in such a way that they could be worn on the head by those inhabiting the land thousands of years ago. Some archaeologists have suggested they were worn as camouflage when hunting, while others believe they were used for ritual practices.

I found the archaeologist's observations very interesting. Did this mean that some of those early people of Star Carr could have actually been shaman ? My mind instantly drew comparisons to the Native American Medicine Men or Skinwalkers who believe, through the practice of ritualistic magic, that they can embody and become one with the animal whose skin they wore. The people of Star Carr would have most likely been superstitious and they probably placed great importance on the spiritual nature of the world around them, certainly more than we do today. It is also possible that the primitive instincts of those early men and women was more suited to picking up on things of a paranormal nature, something that we seem to have lost the ability to do today.

The suggestion of shamanic practices struck a chord with me when I first saw images of the ancient skull-caps - especially when comparing them with ceremonial head gear worn by shaman in other parts of the world, where similarities can be found in the use of antlers, teeth and animal skins. It was a theory that, to my mind, suddenly connected these early people of the past to the present day - and made a connection to the Flixton Beast.

Stories of the beast have persisted over many hundreds of years and probably go beyond the written word. But I began to wonder whether sightings of the creature could be the result of some early shamanic practice. As though a trace or imprint had been left on the land from the distant past - a lingering remnant of a lost knowledge, used by those early inhabitants of Star Carr.

Either way, Star Carr is known as a place of mystery and magic and the surrounding land, with its ancient earthworks, are no less intriguing. In my opinion Star Carr and Sharp Howe burial mound, less than a mile away, may be prime locations where the Flixton werewolf stories first appeared.

Could the practice of shamanism have combined, in some way, with the essence of this unique location, to actually bring about the creation of the Flixton Beast ? If these ancient people actually understood how to tap into other dimensions through acts of shamanism, then who knows what they might have unleashed ? We already know that the refuge at Flixton has references attached to it of wolves and infestations of wild beasts. But could an inhuman creature have actually been manifested, through some kind of magical process, thousands of years before and continued to survive throughout this entire period ?

Of course modern science and logical thought would brush aside the notion that these early people had access to such power. It is something that modern man discarded long ago as superstition and nonsense.

Evidence of animal bones on the 'islands' of, what was, Lake Flixton, together with other artefacts discovered at Star Carr, do suggest that ceremonial sacrifice may have been taking place among these early inhabitants. Yet ritualistic practice and superstition are still as active today - in a deep secretive underworld, hidden from public view. Recent reports of witchcraft, as allegedly practiced at Irton Moor near Scarborough, and the alleged dark practices of RAF Bempton during the 1970s, are prime examples. So was this ancient knowledge handed down though time by a select few ? There is at least one account which states that the Flixton Beast was under the influence of a 'magician', although I have so far failed to locate the origin of this information.

Scientific advances and progress in this material world have suppressed ancient knowledge, to the point where science is thought to have the answer to everything. Yet if the inhabitants of Star Carr *were* practicing shamanism, then who can say what unknown forces may have been brought into our reality ? However, I do not think it is possible to understand shamanism from a scientific point of view. Magic cannot be explained or assessed in a laboratory.

These are my own theories and opinions and I am not asking for anyone to accept what I say as truth, but the Flixton Beast has been seen on many occasions.

I spoke to a modern-day shaman about sightings of the beast and she had the opinion that it was more likely to be a spirit or apparition. She told me that the only way she could find out more, would be to go into an 'altered state of consciousness' to try and communicate with it. It is said that in these altered states, a traditional shaman can become one with the animal whose skin and bone they are wearing. If such things are true, then perhaps the Flixton Beast *is* a remnant of an ancient knowledge, created by the shamen of Star Carr as they journeyed into other realities. I then wondered about Carmans Spital, the refuge at Flixton which protected travellers from savage beasts on the Wolds. Could it have been named 'Carr-man Spital' because of this legend ? Perhaps the *Carman Beast* is a more appropriate name ?

No Witnesses

Between 2012 and 2015 I spent many days visiting the tiny villages of Flixton and Folkton. I even decided to set up camp up in the area where the last sighting of the beast had taken place.

Regardless of whether we think there is any truth to the stories or not, sitting on Flixton Wold at night, surrounded by nothing but darkness and one's own imagination, is incredibly scary.
I wanted first-hand information from the residents of Flixton. Although

most of the people I spoke to had never heard any stories of a werewolf and when I asked, they just looked at me as though I were an alien.

I recall talking with one man named Carl, who was restoring the old village blacksmith's building. He thought I was making the stories up and he openly laughed into my face. However, he did try to help by pointing out a large white house nearby and saying that if anyone knew about these things, it would be the man who lived there. That same day, I was able to speak with the owner of the white house, but he also told me that he had never heard of the Flixton Werewolf and was quite dismissive of my questions.

I did not give up and eventually, I was lucky enough to speak with a few elderly residents of Flixton. Although two of them, who I met a few times over a couple of years, denied all knowledge of the beast at first. It was as though they were waiting to see how much information I could unearth before imparting what they knew. There were those who knew of the stories but did not claim to have seen the creature, but they had known of people in their living memory who said they had. Eventually and on more than one occasion, I was able to speak with some residents at length and from there, the story of the Flixton beast slowly came to life.

The church warden from the neighbouring village of Folkton was very helpful. I told him about the accounts of this mythical creature having roamed local graveyards and he was quick to set the record straight. He pointed out that both villages were side by side - so close in fact that they merged into each other. He told me that he knew of a burial site outside of the village, on Flixton Wold, where only one gravestone remained. In his younger years he remembered there being more, but he doubted that anyone today would even know that it was once a graveyard. As for the werewolf and stories of the creature appearing in the graveyard at Flixton, he said they were nonsense. Then he said, *"There is only one cemetery in Flixton and the first burial there was in 1922."*

I felt this statement instantly deflated any credibility that held these stories together *and* any respect I had for the researchers who came before me, who had previously connected accounts of the beast with the non-existent Flixton graveyard. However, a few weeks later I found myself back in the area looking for clues that might bring the story into the light.

After an uneventful morning, I decided to have lunch at the Foxhound Inn at Flixton. It is a busy pub that attracts customers from outside the area due to its reputation for good food. I had never imagined that my research into the history of the area would have been noticed, but as I sat there, waiting for my meal to arrive, a thin, red-faced man in his late 70s, came towards me.

"You're the chap who's been asking about that old story of the black dog aren't you ?"

I nodded and looked around, wondering if I was being set up. He seemed genuine enough, so I said yes.

"Well I can tell you it's real. I saw it once when I was a young lad."

I could not quite believe he was telling me this. I had been all around the village speaking with locals and almost all of them did not want to comment - yet here was a witness.

"I saw it up past Seller's Off Barn, way up top, amongst that burial mound called Sharp Howe."

Hearing the words 'burial mound' was like flicking on a light switch inside my head. It seemed that all was not lost. The man then went on to tell me about what he saw as an eleven year old boy. His encounter would have been in around 1948, while he was close to the ancient graves of Sharp Howe, less than a mile out of the village.

"I don't know what it was. I was with another lad, he's dead now, but he would have told you the same thing if he stood here with me. We were up there one summer. It was still light and we were just messing about like young lads do, when we saw it. This bloody thing just crouched next a tree. It was covered in dark brown hair and lean, sort of bone and muscle. I cannot say how tall it was, because it was sort of squatting down and looking at something in its paws or hands - I don't know what they were. I have never seen a dog sit like that, but this was no ordinary dog.

We froze for a few seconds in shock, staring at this bloody thing. That's when it lifted its bloody head. It had a dog's head, but it was no dog. I am sure it had seen us. It must have, because it was looking in our direction. It just stared, with these big reddish-brown eyes and to this

day I can still feel the fear it put into me. We turned and ran, we didn't even look back. But I will never forget it.
No one wants to talk about it, but I know what we saw was real. It put me off going up there for good. It's been seen a few times since then, but it is just so unusual that if you say you have seen it, you just get laughed at. People also think it's bad luck; a sign that something bad is going to happen."

I find it hard to understand why this savage beast of legend, never leapt forward to attack the two boys, but I suspect the man's own childhood encounter helped to shape the belief that the Flixton beast was a real flesh and blood creature. I recalled what the shaman had said to me and wondered if the man had actually seen an apparition, instead of a living, breathing creature. Perhaps he and his friend had experienced a brief glimpse into another dimension back in 1948 ?

I already knew of the group of burial mounds named Sharp Howe, which is up on high ground and less than a mile out of Flixton. I had never associated them with stories of the Flixton werewolf before, but the old man told me that for as long as he could remember, Sharp Howe was known as an ancient graveyard.

This had to be the location of the ancient cemetery where stories of the Flixton Werewolf first began. It felt good to find this information and finally learn something about the origins of the story, although proving the existence of such a creature would be close to impossible.

My belief is that we are dealing with a genuine unknown, much the same as the orange lightforms seen on land and out at sea. I am sure that phenomenon is interdimensional in nature and so perhaps is the Flixton Beast.

Tracks of Power

I had already begun to realise that ley lines appeared to be present in many locations where unexplained events were taking place. These unseen tracks of power were always somewhere to be found. Perhaps the land around Flixton was no different. Subtle hints within the information I was collecting suggested that there was a link - an interdimensional highway perhaps ?

Old maps of the area show a landscape littered with burial mounds, standing stones and other earthworks. I wondered if these ancient structures were built on interconnecting energy lines, to give them a better connection to this great unknown. It cannot be coincidence that this area is rich with reports of unexplained phenomena. Sharp Howe is only a short walk from the farm where workers often see small beings,

and it is very near to where Brian and Pat have their experiences of the lightforms - it is as though the area acts like a magnet for the unexplained.
I had already discovered there was an area of land which, in Flixton's distant past, was known as Wolfland, but how much of this was due to the presence of wild wolves or an actual werewolf, is unclear. Yet for such a tiny part of the world to be referred to as Wolfland, the human connection to these beasts must have been very powerful.

Edwin Cooper from Staxton told me that, in days gone by, packs of hungry wolves roamed the Yorkshire Wolds. He had said this was the reason why the spital had been built and not for protection from some mythical beast. He also told me that it was built a mile away in Staxton and not Flixton. So I wondered if earlier research had deliberately placed the Staxton refuge at Flixton, purely to give the story more substance - like a white lie, told only to add more weight to the legend of the Flixton Beast. Whatever the motive, it did not really matter. I had gathered enough evidence and witness statements to be of the opinion that something unknown to science has existed in this area for as long as man has documented his experiences.

I had already established that there had been two spitals in the area, one at Staxton and one at Flixton. Old maps clearly show Spital Farm, which stands on the foundations of one old refuge - but the farm is in Staxton, not Flixton. If earlier researchers had done more than just skim the surface of the available data, they would have discovered the evidence for themselves. Flixton had its own refuge, Carmans Spital, which stood on the site of the old Flixton House. Staxton had the Spital of St. Mary and St Andrew, which stood on the site of Spittal Farm, where the Spittal Inn and Restaurant stands today.
Either way, the details are a tangle of confusion and very little is known about Carmans Spital, except through ancient texts and little more than references to confirm its existence have survived to the present day.

A Strange Biology

If we allow ourselves to play with the notion that there *is* something of substance to the Flixton Werewolf, what could that mean ? What are the implications if we accept that accounts, written over hundreds of years, actually have some threads of truth attached to them ?

It would mean that we have to admit this phenomenon exists and that it operates outside of human understanding. This is something I believe we have to accept, if we are to truly learn any more about it.

Accounts of the Flixton Beast have all been very similar in nature, from ancient times to the present day. They tell of a creature which is able to walk on two legs and has some resemblance to a man in body shape and movement. Not all the reports have described a wolf *man*, although many accounts seem to suggest that it is male - although I cannot see how a person could perceive this. Once again, I find myself asking whether something is happening within the minds of witnesses during their experience - something that gives them the feeling of a male presence. It may be that the creature it is neither male nor female and that it may even exist outside of what we know as a life form.

The beast has been documented as having glowing red eyes and a long curved tail, which gives it more of a demonic appearance. I would lean more towards the word demonic, rather than werewolf. Overuse of the word 'werewolf' plunges our minds into the world of films and silver bullets - and this is clearly not the case.

Glowing red or amber eyes seem to feature in accounts of paranormal creatures from all over the world, so the possibility that we are dealing with something which does not belong to the physical world we know, seems to outweigh the suggestion of a flesh and blood creature. What biology or internal mechanisms could give something the appearance of eyes that glow ? We know that some insects are able to glow in the dark and some sea creatures produce their own bioluminescence, but the Flixton Beast is none of the above. Yet this is what witnesses continue to describe.

Creature In The Field

During my research I visited Flixton Sawmill to speak with some of the staff. They seemed happy to talk to me about sightings of large black cats from around the area, but for the moment I wanted to concentrate on sightings of the Flixton Beast. I was given the number of a former employee named Dave Hartley and told that he might be able to help. A few days later I was able to speak with Dave and after explaining my interest I discovered that he did have a story to tell – one which has never been aired outside of a few friends and his family.

As a boy in the 1970s he lived at Binnington, less than a mile from Flixton. Dave told me that he saw the creature in a cattle field. He remembered it had glowing red eyes, which now seem like a prominent feature in sightings. Dave told me that it was pursuing the terrified cows across the field and in their panic, they were forced into a large open ditch, where apparently many of them fell and died.

Like the handful of local witnesses from Flixton and Folkton, Dave wishes that he had more of a story to tell. I thanked him, but was beginning to realise that, over the years, many people have known about the werewolf, but very few would speak openly about it.

I began to wonder if there were any patterns in the appearances of the beast. As with accounts of similar creatures seen in other parts of the UK, the Flixton Beast seemed localised to a specific area. I wondered if these areas had anything in common or whether sightings were dependant on the seasons or weather conditions. But some stories of the beast were so old, that unless dates had been kept it would be impossible to find any patterns. It could also be possible that the creature appears when people are not around. However, I believe that the location and some element or condition of the location, allows and sustains this phenomenon.

Dave Hartley knew of an elderly farmer who lived between Flixton and the village of Seamer. The farmer told him that he was out one night on the Carrs (wetlands), close to the railway line near the Seamer land drain, which runs under the A64 road. He told Dave that he needed to pass through a gate, which had a latch on the other side of it to keep it closed. As he reached out with his hand over the top of the gate to release the clasp, a clawed hand covered with fur came out from the darkness and actually grabbed hold of the farmer's own hand.
The old farmer swears this happened, although he had nothing more to add. There was no beast with glowing red eyes, just a clawed hand that grabbed hold of his in the darkness.

After listening to Dave and the others share their recollections, I wondered how many other stories were now lost in the past. Many people who have come to settle in the area know nothing of the beast, so if it was just a legend to attract people and create a talking point, then surely more people would know about it. Yet just the opposite has happened and the Flixton Werewolf has almost become like a guarded secret.

It Ran On Two Legs

One early morning in November 2013, a man who I have renamed James, was out walking his two dogs in a field which runs parallel to a three mile stretch of the A1039 road in Flixton. Just north, on the low lying land, is the archaeological site of Star Carr. The higher ground, due south, leads up onto Flixton and Staxton Wold with the RAF remote radar base situated at its highest point.

James told me that while he was walking along the edge of the field with his dogs, about five hundred metres away due south, he could see what he thought was a small pony.

I have been to the location myself and estimate that the ground rises to about forty-five degrees. This was the same area I camped out overnight in early 2014. At the top of the field is a three-bar wooden fence with woodland behind that, leading up onto Flixton and Staxton Wold.

James told me that his dogs suddenly froze rigid, with their eyes fixed on the 'pony-sized' animal lurking at the top edge of the field. An interesting point here is the dogs. Could they actually see or smell the creature or did they sense its presence ? James said that this reaction was unusual, because his dogs always liked to chase rabbits and other wildlife, even if they had no chance of catching them. Then he realised something was not right about what he was seeing.

James said that the creature then began to move away from the tree line and down towards him. It was at that moment he realised that it was up and running - on two feet. He told me that it seemed to have the body of a dog, but ran upright. James said he became very scared at this point and wasted no time in moving through the hedgerow and onto the grass verge by the roadside. Still the animal continued to head down the field towards him.

James can recall that a car passed by and he was not sure whether this actually distracted the creature, but for some reason he watched it turn in a half-circle and run back up into the wooded area. He believes the car might have saved him from a very close encounter.

There is another account from the 1970s, which tells of the Flixton Beast allegedly leaping out at a timber wagon, as it drove along the same stretch of road. The details are vague but the report has been featured in books and is widely talked about.

On April 27th 2015 I decided to try one last time to gather a little more information about the Flixton Werewolf. It really was a hard task trying to decipher the genuine stories which had survived time, from the rubbish written in recent years. I knew for a fact, that any historic stories connected to the beast were held in the heads of no more than ten people from Flixton and the surrounding villages. I was reliably told that everyone else had either passed away or would never tell.
I contacted a man I had spoken to previously, to ask if he had any further details to add to an account he had already given me. To my surprise he invited me to his home. He wanted to relate another account which had never been talked about, outside of a handful of close friends. I don't know if he did this simply because of my relentless efforts to uncover information or if he just felt the stories needed documenting.

Encounter After A Night Out

The man told me of an encounter which took place in 1967. Two young men from the village had been on a night out to the coastal town of Filey. They were returning home on a motorbike when the terrifying encounter took place. Both men have since passed away, but the man told me that his two friends never changed their story from the day it was first told. He said it would often crop up in their conversations because of the impact it had on their lives.

It was apparent, as I listened to him recall the story, that the man believed his two friends were telling the truth and they had seen the Flixton Werewolf in 1967. He said, *"They stuck to their story for over thirty years and it never changed. Any doubt we might have had when they first told us passed in that time. They definitely saw it."*

They were travelling back home in the early hours, on the lonely A1039 road that runs through Flixton. In the 1960s the road had small drainage ditches running intermittently on either side and was lined with hedgerows. Beyond them were the Wolds on the left and the marshland of the Carrs to the right. In those days I imagine the area must have been even more desolate than it is today.

As their motorbike weaved along the country road from Filey, through the village of Muston and on towards Flixton, their the headlight caught a pair of eyes in the distance. Red eyes. The driver took a hand off the handle bars and began to point and gesture to his passenger that something was on the road in front of them. As they got closer they both saw the strangest looking creature they had ever seen and they could not believe what they were looking at.
It was covered in dark hair and was crouched down in a ditch, staring at them with its glowing red eyes. Although it never moved, they said it looked as though it was about to spring forwards and they were terrified. They said it looked huge and its eyes seemed full of anger and rage. It was in the form of a man with, what looked like, a dogs head on a broad muscular body. Without having anything else to compare it to, they said it was a werewolf. Even though the terrifying encounter lasted no longer than it takes to pass by on a motorbike, they felt anger pouring from it, as though it was angry at having being seen.

It was strange listening to an old man recall such a story. He said that as a young boy living in the village, he remembered that many people knew the stories of the Flixton Werewolf. Now he wishes that he had listened more to his grandparents and other older people when they talked about these things. Most of these stories have now gone to the grave with these people.

Today, there are only a handful people left in the village who are Flixton born and bred. They are the only ones who might have anything more to add to these historic accounts of the werewolf. The man I spoke with did not have a story of his own to tell, but in the absence of a first-hand account, I feel that any recollections of encounters with the beast, must be documented.

I had spoken to the same man four times over a three year period, because I knew he had more information. For whatever reason he was reluctant to share it, until he finally told me about what his two friends had seen in 1967. His family go back over five generations in Flixton and before that they came from the surrounding villages. He said that years ago, the subject of the beast came up in conversation many times, but this was when the village really was a place where people were born and died. Now it was rarely, if ever, discussed. The above account may be the last historic encounter with the Flixton Werewolf in living memory that we will ever learn of - although time will tell.

I cannot not help feeling that there is something very real about these accounts, yet I am still unsure. I cannot imagine that they have no substance, but having said that, I also cannot see how a flesh-eating beast, as depicted in films, can be roaming the Wolds and woodlands of North and East Yorkshire.

If the stories are true, then the beast appears to have an awareness of the people who have seen it - but if it is some kind of apparition, is it able to reach out and touch the physical dimension we exist in ? My personal opinion is that it is just as aware of our presence as we are aware of it. It is difficult to explain, but perhaps the creature's physical presence may be stronger at different times, due to factors we do not understand. Maybe this is where the moon has an influence ? My own view is that from time to time, the creature has the ability to briefly look into our sphere of existence, but just like oil and water, the two sit side by side but do not interact.
Its strength of presence and reactions whilst visible may even depend on those who see it. Weather, the seasons and even temperature may play their part. I do not think we should discount anything out of hand, since we simply do not know the true origins of this creature.

It is interesting to note, that unusually large black cats have also been seen all around this area for many years. These big cats are not native to the UK and, in many instances, their descriptions do not sound like any known cats from around the world. I have also found that they are often seen close to burial mounds and earthworks. These ancient locations have to be part of the mystery. The burial mounds of Sharp Howe, Elf Howe and Willy Howe, as well as others too numerous to mention, may ultimately hold the secret. These ancient landmarks are as important as the actual events that unfold around them. Stories of small beings, sightings of UFOs and other unexplained phenomena have been documented throughout human history around these places. Once again I feel that location is key and must be a starting point when looking for an answer.

To understand more about the Flixton Werewolf it may be that we have to step away from 'the beast' - whose terrifying appearances have become imprinted on our minds to such an extent, that it is hard to see anything else.

I began looking to other villages for similar accounts of those reported at Flixton. I found an interesting story of a similar beast from the village of Goathland in North Yorkshire, which is less than nineteen miles from Flixton and twenty-eight miles from Bempton. Due to the relatively short distances involved, I wondered if it could even be the same creature.

In the North the creature is known as the Gytrash and it seems to come in many shapes and sizes. Over the centuries it has been reported to appear in the form of a goblin, a horse or a large fearsome dog with a mane like a lion. Once again, the glowing red eyes feature in many accounts. One description of the Gytrash took my mind instantly to the encounter James had in late 2013. He said, *"it stood at the edge of the tree line and at first I thought it was a small pony."*

A small pony ? So could the Flixton Werewolf and the Gytrash be the same type of interdimensional creature ? There are similar stories from Lincolnshire of a creature which resembles the Gytrash and the Flixton Werewolf. They call it the Shag-Foal and the descriptions are similar in every way but name. However, without further research I cannot write with any conviction of creatures seen in other areas, but there are similarities. Wherever possible, I have tried to keep all of my research to within a thirty mile radius of Bempton and Flamborough, with the exception of some aircraft crashes. Although I have noticed one curiosity in the accounts of the Lincolnshire Shag-Foal which takes me out of my thirty mile radius. It is said to frequent a coastal area near Freiston, known as Spittal Hill - the site of another old refuge/hospital.

The Flixton Beast is also associated with a refuge/hospital and is close to the coast, but the similarities do not end there. Both locations have a brook or stream running nearby and both locations have accounts of a strange beast. I have noticed that moving water seems to be present wherever similar unexplained phenomena occurs. Legends of werewolves in Germany talk of a connection to brooks and running water and stories of Dogmen that come out of the deep woods and forests of America, all have similar connections.

So we have markers; the phenomenon often appears to have a connection to moving water and the location tends to have ancient earthworks close by - which have attracted human interest for thousands of years. Perhaps ancient humans marked the areas, either knowingly or unknowingly.
I personally believe it is the land itself which holds the power, not necessarily the components of the earth, but something above or below which acts as an outlet for these unexplained events. I also think it would be worth studying ley lines in these and other areas, to establish whether there could be any further correlation.

Howling In The Woods

On the August 5th 2015 I decided to visit Flixton and Staxton Wold for the day. I was with my good friend Dean who had a personal interest in the Flixton Beast and its Danes Dyke connection.

For three years Dean worked as security guard at the Bridlington Links Golf Course, which runs alongside Danes Dyke. As part of his job, he would spend many hours patrolling the golf course and he recalled a very scary experience he had there one night. He told me that while he was standing there in the darkness, he was listening to a creature among the trees. He said it was howling and running through the woodland and he admitted to feeling very scared at the time, which is rare for Dean. Since his job involved working through the night, on an all year round basis, feeling scared was not an option.

He said that whatever it was made a choking, howling sound like he had never heard before or since. It gave him a chilling feeling as he looked in the direction of the woods towards Danes Dyke. It only happened once in all the time he worked there, but it had such a lasting effect, that after he had learned of my research, he wanted to spend time with me at Flixton and Staxton.

Walking through the Wolds, even in daylight, is quite an experience and due to their elevated position most places in the woods are very hard to access. Most of the time we were walking up thirty to forty degree inclines, amongst a mixture of mature trees, thick brambles, nettles and all other plant life. The woods give you the feeling that you are entering a very ancient place. It really is an amazing location to walk around. I still do not buy into the notion that some long lost breed of dog/man is actively roaming these woods, but the energy of this area and surrounding lands are key to the appearances of the Flixton Werewolf over the centuries.

Our visit was only days after I had been contacted by a thirty-three year old woman from nearby Cayton village. She got in touch to tell me she had seen something very unusual on the night of July 30th 2015. It is interesting to note that her sighting occurred on the night of a blue moon.

Creature At Spital Corner, Staxton

The witness was returning home from a day out in York with her husband and two small children. Her husband was driving them along the A64 road as they reached the traffic roundabout at the junction of the A1039, next to Spital Farm. I have tried to keep this next part of the account as close to her words as possible.

"As we approached the roundabout I saw something. At first I could not believe what I was seeing. It registered, but even then it was just so unbelievable, that it shocked me to silence.
There was a huge, dark, shaggy dog-like creature on the traffic roundabout. It was so big, that it just looked unbelievable. At first I thought it was on all fours, but after thinking it over in my mind, I now realise that it was bent over, with its head quite low to the ground. Its back was long and muscular and it had a huge bushy tail that curved down to the ground.
The road was quiet and the roundabout is always well lit, so I was able to get a really good look at it as we approached. After visiting the location a few days later to take pictures for comparison, I have no doubts that this thing was as big as a small pony. It was much larger than our own German Shepherd dog. I would say it was bigger than any dog, if I am honest.

I still struggle to believe it, but if all this does not sound crazy enough, I noticed that this thing had a defined stomach and looked muscular. Its face was unusually long and pointed like a German Shepherd dog. I think it was standing on two feet bending over towards the ground, with its hind legs slightly bent. It must have been eating or looking at something. It was just the strangest animal I have ever seen. I never said a word to my husband until we had gone around the roundabout and were on the Seamer Road heading for Cayton. I was in shock and felt frightened, I really did - even though I was in the car.

Once we were off the roundabout, I told him he had to stop the car and turn around. Then I tried to explain what I had just seen, which was not easy, as I was struggling to believe it myself. At first he laughed and thought I was joking, but a few seconds later he realised I was serious and agreed to turn the car around. I looked back at the sleeping children and told him to lock the car doors, as we slowly approached the roundabout again.

It was well lit with street lights, but dark in the middle due to being planted with established trees, shrubs and long grass. I felt that I needed to see the creature again and show my husband. Sadly I could not do that, because as we drove around, we saw nothing, but I know what I saw."

On August 6th 2015 the witness contacted me again to ask if I would visit the area with her, since she could not get the sighting out of her mind. We met the next day beside the Spital Inn and Restaurant, then walked around the area of road where she had seen the huge dark creature. I thought she was perhaps trying to find a logical explanation for what she had seen and was looking for something that might indicate she had been mistaken. As she talked to me about her experience I asked if she had seen the creatures eyes. She told me that it did not have glowing red eyes, a feature which now appears to be common in such sightings.

She also told me that her father-in-law had ridiculed her story and insisted that she must have seen a large stag and not a monster. Even her husband thought she had imagined it. I suppose these kind of responses are the reason why people refuse to talk about such encounters. Before her experience the witness had no interest in stories of the Flixton Beast, but she has since visited the area on six separate occasions. Nearby is a large densely packed woodland which stretches as far as RAF Staxton Wold. It rises steeply from the road below to five hundred feet above sea level. The witness has even explored these woods, during daylight and night time hours, in the hope of finding answers.

It must become unbearable for many people when an experience plays out in their mind, over and over without answers or explanation. Especially when the few people they share it with usually laugh or tell them they are mistaken. But a stag does not have the face of a dog or a defined stomach or huge bushy tail. In fact, the witnesses description sounds nothing like a stag at all. Once again, experiences like this are so far removed from human understanding, that we often look for other explanations that might fit. Due the size of the creature and its location, I suppose a male adult deer could be the only alternative.

I think that events of this nature, like some other accounts shared in Truth-Proof, can often cause an uncategorised trauma within witnesses, and they end up suffering in silence due to fear of ridicule. On the other hand, it would be just as insulting if we were to question a person's religion, which I feel is something else that has no real proof. However, I am grateful the witness contacted me so quickly after her sighting. If she had not, her story might have been lost forever.

The Danes Dyke Werewolf

I cannot end the strange subject of Lycanthropy without mentioning another event that seems to defy explanation.
Close to Flamborough and Bempton is the ancient earthwork known as Danes Dyke. The area is known for its ghost of a white lady and sightings of strange balls of light encountered by walkers at night - and it was on the main B1255 road into Flamborough, that one man had a terrifying encounter, with what he could only describe as a werewolf.

At 3.30am on April 16th 2014 there was a blood moon in the sky. Tom Stone [not his real name] had been working a night shift at Bessingby Industrial Estate and was heading home on the B1255. This road is unlit and would have been very desolate at that time of the morning.

Tom was driving towards the brow of a hill with the entrance to Danes Dyke on his right hand side. As the road dipped down ahead of him he suddenly caught the brief flash of a pair of eyes in his headlights. When the road levelled out what Tom had seen a few moments before was now in full view. He became overwhelmed with shock and amazement as the full beam of his headlights suddenly lit up the figure of a large hairy man, who was down on all fours. Tom was now terrified.

He said it was just crouching at the roadside and was staring at him as he passed in the car. He had no idea what the creature was, but the closest thing he could compare it to, was the werewolf from the movie "An American Werewolf In London".

I did make various attempts to interview the witness, but like so many other people who have experiences beyond understanding, he declined.

I was able to speak to several people who knew Tom, to ask about his experience, but the story slowly closed down, to the point where no one would talk about it. Apparently, Tom's wife had said that he never usually bothered to wake her when he returned home from work, but on that morning he did - simply because he was so shaken by the experience.

I am not sure whether the moon played any part in what happened at Danes Dyke, but there was a blood moon in the sky that night. On the night the creature on the traffic roundabout was seen near Staxton, there was a blue moon in the sky. All this could be nothing more than coincidence, but it is something to consider when documenting sightings.

I do not think for one moment that there are people changing into huge and terrifying werewolves at the sight of the full moon. I do however think, that somewhere within this mystery, it does have a part to play.

A Flamborough farmer once told me of an elderly man, who lived close to Danes Dyke, who'd had a frightening experience with what he described as a pack of animals. He was not even able describe what he saw because they were running through the woodland in darkness, but they sounded like wild rampaging animals.

Another man from Bridlington told me that on three separate occasions at Danes Dyke, he had seen a huge black dog with glowing red eyes.

In February 2015 I spoke about the Flixton Beast to two elderly men from Bempton. To my surprise one of them told me he had heard of a similar thing near to Bempton. He said that many years ago there was a man who had claimed that he *was* a werewolf, who had actually been killed and then buried in a field in Bempton. He said that locals had given him a Christian burial and placed a single unassuming stone over his remains.

I am unable to add any more to these accounts of beasts and werewolves. They seem to conflict with everything we believe and make no sense. If you were the kind of person who laughs and ridicules those who claim to have seen such things, imagine if it happened to you. They really do challenge a person's whole belief system.

Just like the big cat sightings, they are rare and often shocking one-off encounters, but do I think they are real ? Do I believe that something has genuinely been seen ? Yes I do. Do I think they are flesh and blood ? I'm not so sure. Logic would tell us that the area of Flixton is not large enough to sustain a living, breathing mammal of such size, over such a long period of time.

One thing I *am* sure of, is that unless all of these stories and accounts of the Flixton Beast through the ages are lies, we have to accept that some quality of an unknown nature has been imprinted into the geography of East and North Yorkshire.

Although, after talking with locals and people from the surrounding areas, I am convinced that something real has been making terrifying appearances in this remote area, far longer than documented history, but no single element of the phenomena points us in a direction we can understand. On one hand, the evidence that something is occurring is overwhelming and on the other, we have nothing to show to the masses that would be acceptable as proof.

THE DANES DYKE
WEREWOLF

215

The Big Cats Of East And North Yorkshire

Sightings of 'big cats' have been reported around East and North Yorkshire for decades. They seem to appear around certain locations for brief periods of time, then just go off the radar. In fact all of the locations covered in Truth-Proof have, at some point, been the subject of big cat sightings.

The Bridlington library holds archive newspapers that report spates of big cat sightings in the area from the 1970s through to the present day. There are multiple witness accounts which suggest to me that these cats were and are, very real – even though they seem to slip in and out of reality, like ghosts.

On July 22nd 1976 the Dangerous Wild Animals Act was introduced in the UK to regulate the keeping of certain kinds of dangerous exotic animals. It cannot be denied that this change in the law would have forced irresponsible owners of such pets to release them into wild. This is thought to be one of the reasons why such animals are sometimes seen roaming the British countryside.

I seriously doubt that there could be self-sustaining populations of big cats living in the UK, but the sightings have continued long after 1976. So either I am wrong or they are still escaping or being released. Maybe they are surviving much longer than they should or indeed, they are something else entirely.

The question that they are something else is not often raised. Yet some of these cats appear large enough to take down a human being, but we hear no accounts of this happening. In fact, lots of younger people explore forests and woodland, so surely a big cat would consider them as a potential meal. In terms of size, a big cat would not distinguish between a child or a deer, so why is this not the case with the cats that are reported here in the UK ?

The Ruston Parva Lioness

The cats which have been reported do not appear to show aggression towards witnesses. This may be perfectly normal for those the size of a Labrador dog. They would probably avoid human contact in their natural habitat, unless cornered. I would however place a lion in a different category, because a lion would almost certainly attack a human. For that reason, logical thinking has to be ruled out when we read reports of a 'lioness' seen around Ruston Parva and Woldgate in 1994.

The accounts of multiple witnesses, who saw the cat at close quarters, say that it was a lioness. This is where logical thinking plunges into the illogical. They either misidentified the animal (although what other mammal resembles a lioness ?) or the witnesses were all lying independently of each other - another explanation that does not seem possible. Unless it *was* what they all claimed it to be. A lioness.

However unlikely that may sound, when the facts are laid bare, it has to be accepted that these people were telling the truth. How that fits into what we understand, I do not know. We either have independent witnesses who were all lying and leaving themselves open to public ridicule or they are telling the truth. I would go with the latter, since I just cannot see what a person would have to gain from creating such a story.

If we assume that many of the big cat sightings were due to some being released from captivity after the 1976 Act came into force, surely those who *had* been kept in captivity would have lost much of their fear of humans - perhaps even associating our presence with being fed. Yet this does not seem to be the case, because these big cats seem to be even more elusive than those in their natural habitat. Although it seems that no sooner than an argument is put forward, than another is offered to discount it.

The fact that these cats are sometimes seen by the roadside or running along a field close to a road, makes perfect sense. Main roads could be associated with food for them. It is not unusual to see pheasant, rabbit or even deer, dead at the side of the road. Crows and magpies worked out long ago that roadkill is an easy meal, so why not a big cat ?

The cats are usually described as either black or beige and about the size of a Labrador Retriever. The exception being the Rudston lioness reported in mid-1994. If we believe these cats to be pumas or jaguars, which in their natural habitat can expect to live between ten and fifteen years, then it would not be unrealistic to say that in the UK, a big cat with no known competition could live considerably longer. Of course, any captive cats would already be of a certain age before they were release, but with abundant food they could live on for a few years more.

The fact these big cats are witnessed by so many, but for such short periods of time and then to simply vanish, may have more to do with the location – as though it somehow contributes to their appearance. It is the same with other unexplained phenomena, like the lightforms, which can simply appear, disappear then reappear. Whatever the origins of these big cats happens to be, I firmly believe that something of an interdimensional nature is taking place around this area and at times we are seeing glimpses into another reality. Appearances of the Flixton Beast, which span over nine hundred years, are no less unusual. Its appearance at Sharp Howe barrow cemetery, just outside of Flixton village, is significant in that the location may connect to ley lines all across the East and North Yorkshire Wolds.

In the village of Rudston, within the village churchyard, stands the Rudston monolith. At twenty-five feet high, it is the tallest ancient standing stone in Britain. From Rudston, ley lines appear to connect to other locations where many 'events of high strangeness' have taken place. It is also the location of many big cat sightings.

During the early 1990s there were many reported sightings of big cats, but the locations were not random places, they were localised to a few specific areas. The sheer number of recorded sightings, from different witnesses, were too numerous to claim they were misidentifications. In August 1994 the Bridlington Free Press newspaper ran two separate articles, side by side, about just one of the sightings. The location was Ruston Parva, just eleven miles from Bempton and the sighting was of a true big cat - a lioness no less.

The newspaper reported that sightings of the 'mystery beast' had been flooding in. It was seen first by the six year old daughter of local resident Sue Hutchinson. The little girl was overheard talking with her sister about something they could see in the field. Her sister thought it

was a leopard but then the girl called to her father asking,
"What's that in the field ?"
The girls' mother Sue and her husband Vic had been in another room at the time, but were already becoming curious about what the girls were discussing. Vic went to look for himself and grabbed some binoculars. Then he shouted for his wife to come and see. Sue took one look at the animal and said they had better call the police. It was clearly a lioness or a young lion and their sighting received a massive media response.

The animal was seen again in the same week by another man, who prefers to be anonymous. He claimed that he saw a big cat whilst driving to his place of work at Carnaby, just six miles away from Ruston. He said it was smaller than a lion, almost puma-size but slightly larger and beige in colour.

Police received sighting reports from Beeford village, which is ten miles south of Rudston, Nafferton village two miles south-west and from Hayton village, which is over twenty miles away. Similar cats were spotted in Wawne village near Hull in the south and in Burniston, twenty-files miles north. Some were even further away in different counties and up to eighty miles from Ruston.

How could the same cat have been seen in so many different locations over such a short period of time ? It seems an impossible feat for any animal. Some of the sightings were even within the same timeframe, which means the cat would have needed to be in two places at once. So unless there was more than one 'allegedly non-existent feline' appearing in different locations, some of the reports may not even be worth consideration.

It was thought that the cat had even slept in the garden of thirty year old Debbie Greenhouse, who lived close to Ruston Parva. She claimed that, although she had not seen it, a patch of overgrown garden had an area of flattened grass as though something big had been lying there or made itself a den. If this is evidence of the same animal, then physical traces of its presence were actually left behind.

Yet could all these sightings from August 1994 really be of a lone cat. Even with the huge territories that big cats cover in their natural habitat, I think it is doubtful. Genuine big cat experts stated at the time, that this collection of sightings could not have all been of the same animal. So we have to accept that a cluster of big cat sightings seem to have happened over a short period of time in 1994, but then just stopped. The cats simply vanished. If they were genuine sightings why were there no reports from other areas, as the cat travelled across land and changed locations ?

Yet the reports from Ruston Parva were considered to be so serious, that no less than twenty-seven police officers worked on the search, some of whom were armed, and a helicopter was flown in from RAF Leconfield to assist in the search. It was all considered to be a huge expense at the time and Humberside police stated that the search had cost them many man-hours - but it showed how serious the sightings were being taken. Without doubt they clearly thought that the big cat was real, even though it looked as though they were hunting a ghost.

Bridlington Free Press - September 28th 1995

Beast on prowl

A MYSTERY beast, dubbed the wildcat of the Wolds, is on the prowl again according to an astonished eye witness.

Amazed painter and decorator Alan Dickinson, 38, of Richmond Street, Bridlington, was travelling home through Woldgate at 4.45pm on Tuesday when he came face to face with what he believes was a lioness.

The beast, which was hunting just yards away from Woldgate Pony Trekking Centre came within 15 feet of Mr Dickinson's car.

"It was definitely a lioness," he said.

"I slowed down at the cross roads and a deer shot in front of me, closely followed by this lioness.

"I braked and followed the road round the corner. The deer had gone and the lioness was coming to a trot. It sat down and looked at me."

The sighting comes days after a woman, who refused to be named, claimed she saw a panther-like animal on the Bempton to Flamborough road as she was driving to work at 6.40am.

She told police the beast jumped out of a field of livestock and landed in the middle of the road in front of her car before clearing another hedge into another field.

Last year the reported sighting of a lioness in Ruston Parva sparked uproar and led to armed police staking out the village.

220

Armed police in village lion hunt

by Alison Young at the scene

ARMED police surrounded the fields of Ruston Parva yesterday following reports that a lioness was roaming around the village.

Residents were advised to stay in doors and a helicopter with heat seeking equipment was called in from RAF Leconfield during the drama, which erupted at 8am.

A villager, who has not been identified, alerted police after claiming he had seen a lioness wandering in fields, opposite Main Street.

Within minutes officers were on the scene and throughout the morning 25 support staff - including at least nine marksmen - flooded into the village.

They were joined by members of the press as villagers stood at windows watching.

Chief Insp Michael Kennington of Beverley Police said: "At 8am a resident was looking out of their window when they saw what appeared to be a female lion walking along the hedge.

"We are trying to get staff down here to go into the field and armed officers are out here as a safety precaution. Our main concern is for our safety and the public safety."

CI Kennington said no lion had been reported missing and officers visited houses in Ruston Parva to see if villagers had large dogs which may have been mistaken for a huge cat.

He added that there had been confirmed sitings of a similar large, unidentified animal roaming in the Pocklington area earlier this year.

A helicopter with heat seek-

ing equipment was called to join the search because it was too dangerous to allow officers into the fields.

"At this moment we are not prepared to search the field," said CI Kennington. "So we are getting a helicopter. It is so dangerous going into a field of corn, we may just stumble across it."

Driffield vet David Tunnicliffe of the Albany Surgery was on hand in case the cat had to be tranquillised or shot dead.

"When we were called out there was mention of darting it," he said.

"But from previous experience that is found to be impractical because you have to get very close up.

"In a field situation you may only get within 100 yards of it. An animal like that is likely to run away rather than attack any-

thing and you may only get one chance at shooting it."

Flamingo Land curator Neville Wilby was called in with a tranquillising gun to stun the beast, but if he could not get close enough police planned to shoot it.

The drama added excitement to village life in Ruston Parva.

Mary Skelton, who lives opposite the fields, joked: "This has been the highlight of my life in the last three years.

"I didn't see anything, I just saw the police vans and cars out there this morning. It will be a shame if anything happens to it."

Neighbour Susan Harper was watching the action with her children Jacqueleme, 11, Charlene, 11, and Charles, 10.

"This is a very quiet village and then all of a sudden this happens," she said.

"I daren't go out and have a look because the children will follow me."

221

The Rudston Panther

On Thursday September 29th 1994 the Bridlington Free Press reported that another big cat had been seen. Their article stated that Mr Bev Harrison, age thirty-seven, was driving to work at 5am on Tuesday September 27th. He was on the B1253 road, a mile out of Rudston village, when a large black cat suddenly appeared in front of his car.

He says there was no time to avoid it and he hit the cat so hard, that the impact tore the bumper off his Austin Maestro car. He was too scared to stop, in case the animal attacked him, but he felt sure that he must have injured the cat in the collision.

I have no reason to question Mr Harrison's account of what happened; after all he was the only person involved. What I find more intriguing than the actual collision, is what he says he saw moments before the incident. Mr Harrison says he saw a dead rabbit, a dog and a third animal he was unable to identify, at the side of the road. He saw the dead animals first and managed to miss them, but said he could not avoid hitting the cat, which suddenly appeared on his left and crossed in front of him.

None of what Mr Harrison claimed, made any sense. There were dead animals lined up on the road and a big cat – which he described as a jet black panther - had appeared from nowhere. He added that he had hit the animal so hard, that he thought the car might have even flipped on its side. He later contacted the police, although he was aware that he would be laughed at, due to what he said had happened. Mr Harrison could have avoided any sarcasm or ridicule if he had simply said he had hit a large black cat whilst driving to work. Instead, he chose to tell the truth about what happened, no matter how bizarre it sounded.

A tuft of animal fur was found beneath the car and was handed to the police for examination, although I have no information to say whether it had been tested or identified.

I find the set of circumstances surrounding this big cat encounter so amazing - with a collection of dead animals by the roadside and a 'black panther', which simply ran in front of his car causing enough damage to rip off the bumper. His description of the impact sounds more like he hit concrete than a big cat. It would be difficult for anyone offer an alternative rational explanation for Mr Harrison's encounter. Yet unfortunately, instead of simply accepting that this event might have happened as it was described, accounts such as this are often left to become nothing more than mild curiosity and amusement.

Panther strike sparks more 'wild cat' fears

A SHOCKED Rudston driver believes a wounded black panther could be prowling the Wolds after he ran into the beast while driving to work.

Bev Harrison, 37, of Nightingale Row, was driving on the B1253 a mile out of Rudston at 5am on Tuesday when the big cat suddenly appeared before him.

He hit the animal with an impact that tore the front bumper off his Austin Maestro.

Mr Harrison dared not stop for fear of being attacked by the injured animal.

"I saw a dead rabbit, a dog and a third animal I couldn't identify at the side of the road.

"I missed them but then the cat came out from my left hand side - it was jet black," said Mr Harrison, who is a factory operative at Malton Bacon Factory.

"I hit it so hard that at first I thought the car was going to flip on its side," he said.

"I didn't stop to take a look, I was scared, I thought I may have only stunned it and it could have gone for me," he added.

Mr Harrison contacted police, but fears many will laugh at his claim.

He recovered a tuft of black fur from under his car and this has been handed to police for examination.

Police have investigated several sightings of a black panther-type creature in East Yorkshire.

And a month ago a field in Ruston Parva was surrounded by armed police after reports of a lioness.

A spokesman for Malton police said: "He told us that he collided with what he described as a large jet black animal, larger than a Labrador, but long and thin."

Bridlington Free Press September 29th 1994

223

The Pumas Of Ruston Parva

In June 1997 sightings of a big cat surfaced once again at Ruston Parva. I have a few accounts from locals in the area, but the first one to hit the newspapers was that of Derek and Betty Chadwick from Bridlington.

The Bridlington Free Press reported that a large panther-like cat was observed by the couple on Sunday June 8th 1997. Mr Chadwick has since passed away, but I was able to talk about the sighting with his wife Betty, on January 25th 2015. She had kept four different newspaper clippings about their encounter, but said that they rarely talked about it after the story had initially reached the press back in 1997 - mainly due to the ridicule they faced.

Betty told me that nothing had changed and she did not need to refer to the clippings when relating the story to me. She said that both her and her husband were both definitely of the opinion that it was a big cat. *"My late husband and I were travelling through Ruston Parva, near Driffield, in June 1997. We were having a leisurely drive when we noticed what we thought was a calf, lying under a hedge. We thought it was odd since there were no cows to be seen around. We were both curious, so we pulled over to have a better look."*

Betty told me that when the creature stood up they realised it had a massive bushy tail which curved upwards and the centre of it touched the ground. She said, *"We knew instantly that it was no calf or dog as it began lifting up its tail to spray, just like a domestic tom-cat would to mark its territory. It was just so surreal. It just casually looked around as though everything was perfectly normal. We did think it had seen us, but it was in no hurry to get away."*

Betty told me that they watched it for about ten minutes. At the time her husband Derek had described it as being about four and a half feet long, not including the tail. Betty said that they both remarked on the shape and unusual length of its tail. She told me that the animal then just slowly wandered off to the hedgerow by the side of the field. I asked Betty if she remembered if the cat had any other markings on its coat. She said, *"It was just sandy-coloured. We thought it was a Puma, then it went through an opening in the hedge and disappeared into a wheat field"*

I asked her about the size of the animal and she said,
"I thought it was about the same height at the shoulder as an adult Labrador dog, but my husband thought it was slightly taller. Although it was a short distance away, I would think it was about twenty-six inches at the shoulder. My husband was quite knowledgeable about wildlife and was very convinced about this sighting. I just knew it was a cat that should not have been there."

Mrs Chadwick remarked that after the cat had gone, they both experienced an extraordinary build-up of energy that was somehow exhilarating. This reminded me about location being key to many of these events of high strangeness. The Rudston big cats are a prime example. Many more reports of big cats appeared around the same time that Betty and Derek Chadwick saw their sandy-coloured puma (pictured below). Most of them were in close proximity to Rudston and the East Yorkshire Wolds. Although some sightings were of a large black cat, the local newspapers at the time simply named it, *'The Wild Cat of the Wolds.'*

Couple tell of 'big cat' sight

A MYSTERIOUS big cat was spotted on the prowl near Bridlington on Sunday.

Derek Chadwick, 54, of Midway Avenue, Bridlington, was out for a drive with his wife Betty, 53, when they spotted the large sandy-coloured cat at about 10.45am near Ruston Parva.

Mrs Chadwick said: "It was definitely a big cat. We saw it in a hedge about 200 to 300 yards away. It got up and disappeared through the hedge into the next field. I thought it was about the size of a labrador but my husband thought it was slightly bigger."

The couple took pictures of the animal which are currently being developed. A police spokesman said: "We have had no more reports of a similar animal in this area."

The Cayton Panthers

There was another strange sighting of a black cat in 1997 in Cayton village, which is three miles north of Flixton. I say strange because, after doing a little more research, I was told that this cat actually vanished, right in front of one of the witnesses.

In the same year, reported sightings of a large black cat also came from nearby Staxton and Fordon. Then the sightings seemed to stop until 1980, when large paw prints, thought to be those of a big cat, were found in snow in the garden of a house at Staxton. Each print measured several inches across, were three feet apart and showed three pads, with no sign of claws. The police were called to look at them and were reported to have remarked that they looked far too big to be those of a domestic cat or dog. Experts believed they could have belonged to a lynx or panther.

I find it strange that even when experts identify such prints as belonging to a big cat, still the public at large do not accept that the animals exist. Perhaps the opinion of an expert only seems valid if it is what the authorities want to hear. Both local and national newspapers have reported sightings of big cats in the UK, with clusters of sightings occurring every decade, which always reignites debate.

The Bewholme Puma

I was given a first-hand account of a black panther sighting from 2000. It was seen on the outskirts of Bewholme village, close to Hornsea on the coast.

The witness was John Davies, who was riding his motorbike in the early morning of July 2000 when a large black cat ran across the road in front of him. He said that it was crouched by the road side when saw it from a distance, so he slowed down. At first he thought it was a large dog, judging by its height, although it looked unusually long.

John said that it turned its head to the side and he felt sure that it had seen him. Then it casually crossed the road in front of him and entered a field on the opposite side of the road. He says it had big, glaring yellow eyes and he thought it looked angry because it had been seen.

Yet what stuck in his mind the most, was just how long and lean the animal looked. He said it looked too long for its height. John did not hang around long enough to see where it went, because he thought it looked more than capable of attacking him.

John told me that he would never forget his panther encounter and although the animal had been reported by others, he chose to remain silent at the time, until he contacted me in 2014.

The Scarborough Panther

In May 2012 reports of a big black cat made the newspapers once again, this time in Scarborough. Similar sightings have been made around the Scalby Mills area of Scarborough for a number of years, where many UFO's are also reported. The Scarborough Evening News asked, *"Could A Huge Panther Be Prowling Scarborough's North Bay ?"*

Twenty-two year old Steve Johnson, said he saw a large black cat, as he had begun to set up for the day at North Bay's miniature railway. Mr Johnson was working on the railway's turntable when the strange creature appeared, just a few feet away from him in the undergrowth. He said he heard a rustling sound in the nearby bushes and then a few birds suddenly flew off. That was when he saw what looked like a big black cat. He said the animal was massive, much bigger than a domestic cat - but he began to doubt his own eyes, since the animal was so big and well built.

Unfortunately the newspaper article and others like it, are often biased against the claims of witnesses. Disbelief or ridicule tends to get in the way of the witness being taken seriously. This is how the media often are and conditioning tries to mold our thoughts so that nothing outside of 'scientific fact' is ever considered.

The Danes Dyke Cat

For many years sightings of a large black cat, the size of a Labrador dog, has been reported around Bempton and Danes Dyke, near Flamborough. There are also reports of a sandy-coloured cat, of a similar size, seen around RAF Bempton in the 1970s.

In the 1990s there were accounts of a big black cat, which was said to frequent a small quarry on Stonepit Lane on the outskirts of Bempton. This is next to Metlow Hill round barrow near Bempton Cliffs.

It has also been seen around Beacon Hill, an ancient settlement on top of Flamborough's cliffs. Sadly, Beacon Hill is now reduced to a fraction of its former size due to the excavation of gravel between 1956 and 1984. The man responsible worked continuously at the site for twenty eight years - this was the same man who discovered the Bempton Crater in July 1963. He also told me about a big cat that was seen there during the 1970s.

A first-hand account of a big black cat came to me from farm worker John Sleightholme. He was working the land around Danes Dyke in May 2014. He told me that he had already had a few fleeting glimpses of a large black cat over a three year period. He said it was down among the crops and thought it would have been impossible to spot from ground level, had he not been in his tractor at the time.

In 2014 a large beige cat was also seen on farm land close to Reighton Gap, between Filey and Bempton.
Around this time I also received reports of a big black cat, which many different people had seen around Staxton Wold, just a short walk from Sharp Howe barrow cemetery. One witness, who lives in the nearby village of Fordon, gave me a good description of the cat. He said it was the size of a Labrador dog, but much longer and jet black in colour. He also said it was very lean looking and thought it could have been something like a black lynx.

The same black cat had also been seen around a pond at the top of Staxton Wold, just off a single track road. Water is a scarce commodity on the Wolds during the summer months, so this location would have been perfect for a sighting of the cat. So in June 2014, I contacted the landowner and politely asked if I could film the wildlife around the pond. I was given permission and a few days later I set up my cameras in the thick bush surrounding the pond. The pond itself is about seventy feet by forty feet, but it was not possible to determine the depth, since the water looked quite muddy in colour. It is about twenty feet from the track and is well hidden within densely packed trees and brambles.

I visited the same location twelve times in 2014, both in the morning and early evening and each time I set up my cameras, in the hope of catching sight of this elusive animal. Apart from once hearing the movement of something quite large in the undergrowth and then a roe deer on another occasion, I saw nothing of interest. On my last visit I did photograph some animals prints which were quite close to the water's edge. The image below is one example, shown beside a phone for scale.

On one visit, just as I was leaving the area, I saw a young man walking his dog. I knew he had to be local, so I decided to stop and talk to him. I ask him whether he had seen anything unusual nearby and explained about the big black cat, which had been seen recently. He told me he had not seen it, but knew of its existence.

We were standing close to the entrance to his father's farm and the farmhouse was obscured from view by mature trees and a thick hedgerow. He went on to tell me that during the winter, when snow was on the ground, they would often see large prints that they were sure belonged to a big cat of some kind. Although he said that none of his family had seen it personally, they were sure it existed.

While I was actively trying to capture the Staxton Wold cat on camera, reports came in of another cat which had been seen in a small wooded area, close to Scarborough's golf course. It was described as lean, with a mottled coat and the size of medium dog. The main witness was a man who owns a large secluded house close the golf course. He saw the animal a number of times over a two week period during June 2014.

These sightings were backed up by a young man, who had been out for an early morning run before going to work. He told me that he had been running up a slight incline, then when he got to the brow of the hill he saw what looked like a thin brown and black dog, which was crouched at the edge of the field. The man was quite close so he got a good look at it. For a moment he thought the animal was just as startled as he was. Then it sprung up, took a step up into the field and ran along the field edge, before slipping into the undergrowth. He said that the step it had made was at least as high as a nearby stile between the fields. A few days later I returned with a tape to measure the height of the stile and found it was seventeen inches high. The man had already searched through images of different medium-sized cats hoping to identify what he had seen. The image he thought most resembled the cat he had seen was one of an Onza. This is a wild cat similar to a cougar and native to Mexico, but it is steeped in legend. In fact, its existence is still to be confirmed. It is ironic that as I was out searching for evidence of a big black cat in Staxton, a totally different big cat is seen with in the same timeframe, just six miles away in Scarborough. I wondered what the chances of this could be.

One link that seems to connect many of the big cat sightings is their close proximity to burial mounds and ley lines. I wondered what silent mechanisms could be at work, when big cats appear for a short period of time then slip back into non-existence. I wondered if the big cats seen around Bempton and Danes Dyke are the same animals seen at Staxton. As the crow flies, the distances are quite short - only ten to twelve miles, which would be nothing to such an animal in its natural habitat. There is enough wildlife between these locations to sustain a large feline. Rabbits, deer and hares are in abundance. Farmers from the village of Grindale, between Staxton and Danes Dyke, told me of a sighting of their own. The father and son who own and work the farm say they saw a light brown-coloured big cat run into a field of corn. They also said that its tail was at least as long as its body.

231

Sightings of these large cats from around East and North Yorkshire are as strange as they are diverse. They seem to appear for short periods then vanish just as quickly, but I find myself constantly asking how and why this could be happening. They must be real or else how can witnesses, who are independent of each other, report seeing the same thing ? Again, I have to say that I believe there is something interdimensional about the locations in which they are seen. Regular observation of specific locations has to be the starting point. I am sure that this approach has more chance of a positive result than any other.

Below is an article of yet another multi-witness sighting of a black panther-like animal, seen near Filey in 2004. The creature was seen moving towards the rear of a nearby farmhouse, but instead of informing the residents, the witnesses remained within the safety of their car.

Bridlington Free Press - October 21st 2004

Brid men spot wild 'panther'

TWO Bridlington men spotted what they believed to be a black panther crawling across a field near Filey.

Alex Ethington and Matthew Traves, both 25 years old, were on their way to work at Infotone in Eastfield when they saw the creature on farm land near to the A165, just outside Filey.

Mr Ethington of Grasmere Grove said:

By Jodie Beecroft

"We went past a roundabout and saw it crawling towards a load of hay bales in a field on the left-hand side of the road."

The pair pulled up and watched the animal crawl behind a farmhouse. They said they were going to tell the owner, but they did not want to get out of their car.

Mr Traves of Willow Drive said: "It was like one of those big black cats you see on wildlife programmes on the TV.

"It was really low to the ground like it was stalking.

"I know it wasn't a dog, it was a wild animal. I nearly crashed the car because I was so shocked."

Many people have spotted panther-like animals in the Scarborough area over the years. The most recent was in 2001 when a creature was believed to have attacked a lamb.

There are a number of theories about the sightings, but no-one knows for sure what these black cat creatures are and what they are doing roaming the countryside.

232

The Bempton Panther

A chance conversation with a local farmer from Flamborough on October 2nd 2015 revealed that the area had a large black panther-like cat stalking its fields. I had heard a few rumours that a large cat had been seen around Bempton and Flamborough that same month, but I wanted a first-hand account.

I stood beside the farmers truck and as we chatted about the local area, I asked him if he had heard or seen anything relating to the black cat sightings. His eyes instantly showed an interest and he jumped out of his truck and began to tell me what he knew.

He told me that he had a few log cabins on his land, used by holidaymakers throughout the summer season. He said that about six weeks earlier a lady, who had been staying in one of the cabins, told him she had seen a huge black cat early one morning. She told him that it was much larger than an average-sized dog and its movements were strange.

At the time he assumed she was mistaken and had probably seen a fox or even badger. He thought little more about it, until about four weeks later when another lady, who was holidaying on his land, came to speak with him in a concerned tone. She told him she had seen a huge black animal which she was unable to identify. Her account instantly added weight to the first report, especially when the lady told him that her father was a game keeper and she was familiar with all types of wildlife within the UK. This large black animal was something she had simply never seen before.

It appears that both sightings were in the early morning and down towards the nearby cliffs, so after our conversation I decided to check out the area and speak to local people. I began early morning visits walking up Hoddy Cows Lane, which leads to Bempton cliffs. Arriving before daybreak and heading up the lane, I thought that if this creature was real it would be active in the early morning and at dusk.

I saw nothing too unusual on those trips, but on my way back I did speak to several dog walkers who had heard the stories. One of them claimed to have seen a large black animal in the distance one morning and said that it was 'slinking along a hedgerow' about quarter of a mile away. Another lady I spoke to told me that it had been seen on more than one occasion close to the RSPB nature reserve.

Having no success in the early mornings, I decided to observe the land at dusk. My only clues were from the people I had spoken to, but it had to be worth a try. The Flamborough farmer did not want me to visit his land until all his holidaymakers had gone home and I had to respect his wishes. It is surprising how word spreads, even a subject as surreal as this creates interest. In many ways the reports do sound ridiculous, especially considering that people refuse to accept that the big cats are real. On the other hand witnesses want to keep quiet about them in case it causes fear.

By now I had spent many evenings observing the land around Bempton and Flamborough and thought I had exhausted all of my contacts. Then out of the blue I received a phone call from a lady named Mildred Penistone. She told me that she had seen the big cat on several occasions, while she was with her husband walking their dog. They both agreed to meet me a few days later and the three of us walked up Cliff Lane towards the RSPB nature reserve. They showed me where they had seen the cat and said in no uncertain terms, that it *was* a cat.

Her husband John suggested that it was a panther and not a lynx or anything smaller. He seemed to have good knowledge of wildlife, saying that he had looked at it through a pair of powerful binoculars.
"It had no feathers on the tips of its ears, so it was not a lynx. It was jet black, a huge black panther."

John was clearly convinced of what he had seen. They have a Golden Retriever and they agreed that the cat they saw was of a similar height to the dog. They said it was much longer in the body and had a long tail that curved in centre, touching the road. They pointed out the area of road where they had seen it cross on several occasions, saying that once, it was sitting by the roadside and a car passed right by it. This helped them to gauge its size, but they were surprised when the car simply drove by and they could only assume the animal was not seen.

During our conversation I learned that people had first reported seeing the same big black cat in early 2014. The couple later introduced me to three other locals who had also seen it. So now I had nine independent witnesses who all claimed to have seen the Bempton Panther.

I think the only way to provide more proof would be to actually film the cat and this is something I have been attempting to do, but without success so far. However, nine witnesses who all say they have seen the same thing, in such close proximity, is all the proof I need to continue looking for this elusive feline.

One final observation came from Mildred and John Penistone. They told me that whenever they had seen the cat, it was always traveling from Bempton's old RAF base over land known as The Leys or crossing Cliff Lane. Although the base is now sealed to stop people accessing the tunnels below ground, I do not think it is beyond the realms of possibility that a cat could have found a way below ground.

A FEW FINAL THOUGHTS

Conclusions to the puzzles reported in Truth-Proof are many and varied. They even seem to alter slightly with every witness account that is given. The only thing these mysteries have in common, is that they are all equally bizarre in strangeness and timing. Yet this tells us nothing. If we want answers, our starting point has to be the study and observation of the actual locations where these incidents of high strangeness occur. This would also provide us with a better opportunity to actually document any phenomena as it happens, due to the high concentration of unexplained incidents within these locations.

Early man gave us clues when he stamped the land with earthworks. These ancient markers should be our focus for future observations and research. East and North Yorkshire are not unique in this. There are locations throughout the world with similar concentrations of high strangeness and within them we find impressions on the land, left behind by past civilisations.

The lightforms are real; I cannot deny what my own eyes have seen, but I am not alone, because there are so many others who have seen them. Many witnesses feel confused after a lightform encounter. This is understandable, as there is no one who truly knows what they are and we have no official body to turn to for answers. The same can be said for all the mysteries covered in Truth-Proof.

People from all walks of life see and encounter the unknown. Denial of witness statements in mainstream media is a form of discrimination. If this were something more widely recognised, groups would form and protest. But this phenomenon runs silent and deep, often causing mental trauma for witnesses, which can retreat into the mind and refuse to resurface. So we are left with a gap. There is a 'knowing' that continues to be heard and is real, but is not acknowledged by the mainstream and the powers that control the masses. Yet other unexplainable phenomena, such as religion, serves to control the populace and is therefore accepted.

The only thing that stands in the way of acceptance is denial. This is due to a lack of understanding and the refusal to believe that human beings do not have all the answers. There is a void of nothingness between seeing and believing, which the human mind seems unable to cross at this present time. For decades, various government bodies have collected information on unusual phenomena, but keep tight-lipped about what they know. Their official line, in the case of UFOs at least, is that they have no real interest in the subject. Yet the number of documents released by Freedom of Information requests show this not to be the case. Would so much time, effort and money really be spent on investigating something that does not exist ?

We should accept that UFOs are real - and to those who still need proof, I suggest that they read the title of this book once more and stop presuming that science has all the answers. Can all of the accounts within Truth-Proof be put down to misidentification ? Step outside of the book and look worldwide, then say that these things are not real and happening.

The aircraft which have tragically crashed into the North Sea are no less difficult to explain. The information I have found adds to the creation of a mystery, but it is a mystery which was worth including in Truth-Proof. In 2014 when I called the RAF historical records office, to inquire about an aircraft that had crashed off the Flamborough coast, the man on the phone said the area was known as the Bermuda Triangle of the UK. Perhaps this was a 'tongue in cheek' comment, but it fell from his mouth without any prompting.

This alone does not make these aircraft incidents a mystery, but consider the story of RAF Lightning XS894. Much had been written about its encounter with a UFO off Flamborough Head long before my interest in the story. Yet the pieces of the jigsaw I have unearthed raise even more questions. Just what was happening below the sea and in the skies during September 1970 ?
Can three separate incidents in the same area of sea and in such a close timeframe, really be coincidence ? The recorded first-hand accounts from the trawlerman who found Tornado ZA610 cannot be denied. Tom Quinn had nothing to gain by recalling the events of 1985. Everything he told me, regarding the location and the names of the boats involved, was accurate, so I have no reason to believe his memory failed him when he related other parts of the story.

Tom did not come knocking on my door to tell a fantastic tale of the sea. I found him. In fact Tom was a man I had worked with years before, but he never mentioned ZA610 until I asked him about it in 2014. And what makes a Tornado ejector seat potentially radioactive ? Even more bizarre, why would the navigator's underwear be on the outside of his flight suit ? Tom and his crew mates were ordered to discard their catch, yet nothing about radioactivity was ever reported officially. How is it even possible to find a second body in the vastness of the North Sea, on the same day that the Tornado's navigator was found - and it not be the pilot they were searching for ? Could this really be possible ? The answer is yes; because this is what we are told happened. So if the facts exist, no matter how impossible the odds are, we can accept them.

The accounts of other fishermen, who talk of compass malfunctions and magnetic anomalies out to sea, all add to the high strangeness of the area. How this ties in with the other mysteries is not clear, but it indicates that a window of unexplainable phenomenon is active in this area. Then from time to time, we are faced with a mystery that does not fit with what we have learned so far – and everything we think we know and understand is thrown out of the window and it lands in a place that science has not yet even begun to accept.

Most people just do not have the time to stop and think about events of high strangeness. The web of modern living holds them and emphasises life in the material world. Perhaps this even suppresses acceptance, without them even needing to understanding mysterious phenomenon. Food is wrapped in plastic, news is fed into our eyes through TV screens and explanations given by the mainstream are accepted as fact. We are being dumbed down by science and the human connection has been lost in this age of technology.

If some of the mysteries documented within Truth-Proof occurred in ancient times, they would be seen as folklore by today's standards. Yet these things are being seen and experienced now, but they are regarded as little more than fantasy by academics. Even the inter-mind experience with the lightforms is being eroded - because science and the media fail to provide an answer. Instead they offer up unproven theories that are blindly accepted by the masses.

I hope that after reading Truth-Proof, your mind is opened up a little more to the genuine mysteries that are experienced by many people. We have to remember that just because we are told that something is impossible, does not mean that it is not happening. To admit that any phenomena is real but 'unknown', means that certain mysteries may be out of our control and beyond our understanding. We just have to accept that we do not have all the answers.

The lightforms are a real phenomena and they are active in North and East Yorkshire, as well as many more places around the world. Dedicated research and observation is required to learn more about them. The disappearances of males around Bempton and Flamborough are truly dark and unexplained events that cannot be denied. Reports of phantom big cats that appear from nowhere then disappear are much more than misidentification. Perhaps the most surreal of them all are the werewolf accounts, that reach far back into the past and are still surfacing today.

Accounts of 'incidents of high strangeness' do not end with Truth-Proof. I am continually being contacted by witnesses who wish to share their experiences of strange events in the area. Only a few weeks ago I learned of the sighting of a werewolf in Barmston, just south of Flamborough and I am currently investigating reports of a cattle mutilation nearby.

I truly believe that this part of the UK has a quality which overlaps into other realities and it allows us to see and experience the unimaginable from time to time. This is the truth that leaves no proof.

LIST OF AIRCRAFT LOST

The following is a list of known aircraft crashes and their locations, both over land and sea, covering an approximate sixty mile radius around Flamborough Head. The range is extended beyond my usual thirty mile radius of research, since the distance between two points when flying are substantially reduced.

It is not my intention to attach mysteries to any of these tragedies - unless information should surface to suggest otherwise. Each entry is for information only and contains the date of the accident, the registration and type of aircraft, the location it came down and, where known, the approximate distance from Flamborough Head.

* * *

June 16th 1954
XD716 Sabre - Collided with XD711 4 miles north-west of Hornsea, East Yorkshire. 14 miles from Flamborough Head.

June 16th 1954
XD711 Sabre - Collided with XD716 4 miles north-west of Hornsea, East Yorkshire. 14 miles from Flamborough Head.

March 16th 1955
XD755 Sabre F4 - Driffield. 15 miles from Flamborough Head

January 19th 1956
XD609 Vampire - 5 miles south-east of Leconfield. 21 miles from Flamborough Head

July 7th 1956
WV392 Hunter – North Sea 2 miles east of Filey. 10 miles off Flamborough Head

October 11th 1956
WR785 Venom – Driffield. 15 miles from Flamborough Head

December 22nd 1958
XG227 Hunter - North Sea 5 miles off Middlesborough. 50 miles off Flamborough Head

July 3rd 1959
WL481 Meteor - 6 miles south-east of Driffield. 15 miles from Flamborough Head

January 19th 1960
WV664 Provost T1 - near Pocklington, East Yorkshire. 29 miles from Flamborough Head

May 15th 1961
XG188 Hawker Hunter - Pocklington, East Yorkshire. 29 miles from Flamborough Head

May 7th 1963
XK991 Whirlwind Helicopter - North Sea off Bridlington. 3 miles off Flamborough Head

September 10th 1963
XJ428 Whirlwind Helicopter - 2 miles south of Bridlington. 3 miles from Flamborough Head

December 13th 1963
XM421 Jet Provost - 2 miles north-east of Church Fenton. 45 miles from Flamborough Head

April 16th 1964
XL594 Hunter - Carnaby disused airfield, Bridlington. 5 miles from Flamborough Head

April 27th 1964
XN785 Lightning - Hutton Cranswick disused airfield, south of Driffield. 17 miles from Flamborough Head

April 20th 1965
XM428 Jet Provost - Collided with XN631 over Northallerton, North Yorkshire. 50 miles from Flamborough Head

20/04/1965
XN631 Jet Provost - Collided with XM428 over Northallerton, North Yorkshire. 50 miles from Flamborough Head

September 14th 1966
XP616 Jet Provost - Newgate Bank near Helmsley, North Yorkshire. 40 miles from Flamborough Head

October 4th 1966
XR645 Jet Provost - Stilling Fleet six miles north-east of Church Fenton, North Yorkshire. 50 miles from Flamborough Head

December 30th 1966
XE646 V Hunter - near Leconfield. 21 miles from Flamborough Head

September 22nd 1969
XS926 Lightning - North Sea. 60 miles off Flamborough Head

June 17th 1970
WD355 Chipmunk – Rufforth near York. 46 miles from Flamborough Head

September 8th 1970
XS894 Lightning - North Sea. 5 to 10 miles off Flamborough Head.

September 17th 1970
XW297 Jet Provost - Kiplingcotes, East Yorkshire. 26 miles from Flamborough Head.

February 24th 1971
XN465 Jet Provost - Easingwold, 10 miles north of York. 45 miles from Flamborough Head.

March 2nd 1971
WP312 Percival Sea Prince - Collided with XW300 near Turnham Hall, Selby. 45 miles from Flamborough Head.

March 2nd 1971
XW300 Jet Provost- Collided with WP312 near Turnham Hall, Selby. 45 miles from Flamborough Head.

May 26th 1971
XS902 Lightning - North Sea 9 miles south-east of Spurn Point. 30 miles off Flamborough Head.

June 13th 1972
XV162 Buccaneer - North Sea off Bridlington, Yorkshire. 4 miles off Flamborough Head.

September 6th 1972
XS455 Lightning - North Sea off Spurn Point. 38 miles off Flamborough Head.

July 30th 1976
XS937 Lightning - North Sea, off Flamborough Head. Distance unknown.

January 23rd 1978
XW426 Jet Provost - Riggs Farm, Dalby Forest, North Yorkshire. 25 miles from Flamborough Head.

September 21st 1978
XX530 Bulldog – Bilsdale, North Yorkshire. 45 miles from Flamborough Head.

May 25th 1979
XS931 Lightning - North Sea off Hornsea. 15 miles off Flamborough Head.

July 23rd 1981
XR765 Lightning - North Sea. 30 miles east of Spurn Point.

July 30th 1981
XN643 Jet Provost - near Snaiton, North Yorkshire. 22 miles from Flamborough Head.

August 26th 1983
XP753 Lightning - North Sea, off Scarborough. 17 miles off Flamborough Head.

November 8th 1984
XR761 Lightning - North Sea, 10 miles off Spurn Point. 38 miles off Flamborough Head.

March 6th 1985
XR772 Lightning - North Sea. 20 miles north-east of Skegness.

September 19th 1985
XS921 Lightning - North Sea. 50 miles off Flamborough Head

December 12th 1985
ZA610 Tornado - North Sea. 16 miles off Flamborough Head.

June 6th 1986
XW407 Jet Provost - Collided with XW411 and crashed near Middle
Heads Farm, Helmsley. 40 miles from Flamborough Head.

June 6th 1986
XW411 Jet Provost - Collided with XW407 and crashed near High Leys
Farm, Helmsley. 40 miles from Flamborough Head.

July 15th 1986
XR760 Lightning - North Sea off Whitby coast. 30 miles off Flamborough
Head.

April 11th 1988
XR769 Lightning - North Sea. 33 miles off Flamborough Head.

March 8th 1989
XN547 Jet Provost - Near Malton, North Yorkshire. 27 miles from
Flamborough Head.

April 4th 1989
XT893 Phantom - North Sea. 45 miles east of Flamborough Head.

April 25th 1989
XX517 Bulldog - Great Langton, near Catterick. North-west of
Flamborough Head.

July 21st 1989
Tornado ZE833 - North Sea. 30 miles north-east of Newcastle

August 14th 1990
ZA464 Tornado – Collided with ZA454 10 miles east of Spurn Point. 38
miles off Flamborough Head.

August 14th 1990
ZA545 Tornado - Collided with ZA464 10 miles east of Spurn Point. 38
miles off Flamborough Head.

August 16th 1990
ZA561 Tornado - 10 miles north-east of Spurn Point. 30 miles off Flamborough Head.

September 25th 1991
XZ147 Harrier - Great Driffield. 16 miles from Flamborough Head.
June 7th 1994
ZE809 Tornado - North Sea. 45 miles north-east off Scarborough.

March 10th 1995
ZE789 Tornado - Eleven miles east of Spurn Point. 38 miles off Flamborough Head.

October 30th 1995
ZE733 Tornado - Collided with ZE210. 60 miles north-east of Berwick.

October 30th 1995
ZE210 Tornado - Collided with ZE733. 60 miles north-east of Berwick.

May 13th 1996
ZF270 Tucano - Wetwang, Great Driffield. 16 miles from Flamborough Head.

June 15th 1998
ZE732 Tornado - North Sea. 20 miles off Flamborough Head.

May 17th 2002
ZA599 Tornado - River Humber, near Brough, East Yorkshire. 32 miles from Flamborough Head.

July 23rd 2003
XX183 Hawk - Sinnington, North Yorkshire. 29 miles from Flamborough Head.

August 8th 2007
ZA934 SA33E Puma Helicopter - Near Catterick Garrison, North Yorkshire. 65 miles from Flamborough Head.

Paul Sinclair lives with his wife and family in
the UK seaside town of Bridlington,
on the east coast of Yorkshire.

He began his research for Truth-Proof in 2002
after creating the ILF-UFO sightings website.

Paul is also a talented artist who creates
huge surrealist artwork.
He enjoys countryside walks and
never leaves home without his camera !

Paul can be contacted via Facebook through the
Truth-Proof page. He also has a Truth-Proof
channel on Youtube.

Printed by Imprint.co.uk